Incoming

Red Lines and Hot Takes
For The Coming Civil War

Tom Kawczynski

Table of Contents

Preface: Where *"The Coming Civil War"* Left Off

The number one question I get asked by people after reading *"The Coming Civil War"*, which by the time of this publication will have passed the ten thousand sales mark, is: "what happens next?" This book is truly a continuation and update of that work, with a frank, unapologetic look at what is happening, and a stark prediction about the most likely path we are walking in light of the rapidly evolving political scene. You've asked for hardcore analysis, to be ahead of the curve, and just as many of the predictions in that book have proven to be months or years ahead of what the public discussion allowed, so too will this book, though the conclusions will likely be upsetting to many.

Before you begin reading this book, I owe it you to share a few important caveats. The first is that this is a very dangerous work. It is a sad reflection of the times in which we live that mere ownership of a dissenting text can get you in trouble, but there are powerful people who do not believe it helpful for regular citizens to be aware of what is happening. So, I owe it to you to share that mere ownership of this volume could get you in trouble. It does not help that the media constantly paints lies about me because I speak truth, but as you'll read, that's no accident. They fear a reasonable voice that reveals the many lies which we treat as political truths. In this volume, perhaps more than my previous work, I'm going to really tear into both "sides" to reveal a deeper motivating force that is hostile to all who are not already affiliated with them.

The second warning I share with you is that my writing forces you to absorb a great deal of information, some of which can be startling and painful, about a future that does not look happy. It's considered extremely impolitic to consider the possibility of violence, let alone that some violent outcomes are less bad for certain groups of people than nonviolent futures, but the way this game has been rigged, we need to explore carefully and critically the pros and cons of the likely emerging paths. I write not to advocate any particular outcome here so much as to make you aware of the choice we will all face, seek a hopeful path toward resolution, and to give you and your family time to prepare mentally, logistically, and spiritually for days we have not seen for more than a century in American history. What I have learned is we are capable beings, and when we have more time to digest difficult situations, we handle them better. My prayer is that this book will give you an edge, and I ask you to share awareness of what you learn with others both for mutual safety and because preparation is vital to creating openings for more optimal solutions.

For those who have not read that previous volume, I highly suggest you read that book before starting this one to get the most from this profile. However, as a refresher to those who have read the book and forgotten some details, as well as for new readers, this preface is going to extract several key concepts that will be frequently referenced in *"Liberty Versus*

Democracy". What will not be repeated for those who are coming to this book as an introduction to my work is the in-depth analysis of the institutional motivations, the full analysis of the long-term trends that are turning America into a zero sum game, and all the details of each subgroup and the various outcomes which are most probable.

Let me start this profile by simply assuming you realize the cultural civil war is already well under way. If you have any doubt, set this book down and watch the interactions between protesters in a city like Portland, Oregon, where Antifa (Anti-Fascist – in truth, a communist paramilitary organization) fight groups like the Proud Boys (a patriotic right-wing paramilitary bloc) with the police watching on the sidelines as towns get wrecked, and the politicians try to tilt the field to help the Antifa. Look how city after state on the Left create sanctuary cities where an invasion into America is being welcomed to try to change our politics, but then look also to the growing list of rural counties in America whose sheriffs are honoring their Constitutional duty through civil disobedience and nullification, refusing to enforce gun laws which threaten our Second Amendment right to bear arms. Look also to the toxic political discourse, where after every attack, the question has long since ceased to be how we help the hurting, and the rush is on in the Twitterverse about who gets blamed this time and how points can be scored.

I could literally write a book of examples to prove why we have two emerging sides that hate each other, cannot readily co-exist in the same political space under this format, and are becoming more hostile and angrier toward one another daily. Many others have done that, in both written and video formats, but I'm taking what I hope is a more productive direction here and talking about the deeper motivations for this conflict, how it is being deliberately fostered in a fashion that I believe will be nearly impossible to escape, and as I always try to do, to chart a path through the uncertain waters of tomorrow to have an actual future for those Americans who seek hope.

In *"The Coming Civil War"*, I introduced a new way of thinking about why this conflict is accelerating that offers a more comprehensive description rather than Left versus Right, which will still sometimes be used as a placeholder for a more complex description of the sides throughout the book, and which I will employ again here despite these problems even though by the end of the work you should recognize that Left will mean the forces who seek to use democracy to enact a socialist future and the Right will mean those forces who seek to preserve liberty to defend traditional American approaches. As is often the case, what reveals itself in that simple statement is while there are two sides, they approach the question of the future from different angles, and this sort of oblique combat of ideas that emerges is a common feature, where the argument each uses is different as their linguistic and mental motivations are different.

A really simple example of the phenomenon is the abortion debate. Pro-Life people assert that the defense of life is the basic and necessary precursor to any liberty, and that the protection of unborn children is a basic obligation of human decency. Given the choice, they'd label their opponents, rightly I think, Pro-Death. Conversely, the Pro-Choice faction argues against the imposition upon a woman to be held responsible for an unwanted pregnancy, using the few cases where this was forced upon them, a most heinous crime to be certain – but still not the fault of the resultant embryo – to create a justification for a policy of choice that in certain states is rapidly sliding toward infanticide. They would define their opposite number as Anti-Choice. My point here is not to litigate abortion, because you already know where I stand and my immense empathy for the Right will be clear throughout this book as I do not see this struggle between two forces of equal moral merit, but rather to illustrate for you that when A fights B, the two sides often don't even agree upon why they are battling – even as they instinctively recognize their opposite number.

What that previous book argued is there are certain fault lines which are rapidly widening in America between groups of people or ways of life, and just like a spinning centrifuge gathers disparate elements to a point of central gravity, so too would the rising awareness of future conflict serve to draw adherents motivated by the desire to protect certain rights or promote certain ideas into concert with one another on broadly predictable lines. Obviously, there are many individuals who exist outside the framework, and people who do not fit the criteria, but a recurring phenomenon happens when greater than 5% of the political population amasses on either extreme end, that either side actually has the capacity to force the battle if they can effectively employ their own support base to change society. In this book, I will argue that the Left has reached that point thanks to heavy logistical support from the Deep State and incredibly generous financing from multiple actors, although the motives for such patronage are deeply suspect and we will spend much time reviewing why the rich are paying the communists to destroy traditional America. Suffice it to say, the far left now has the means, the money, and most of the legal cover it needs to complete their long march through to victory, and as you read this book, please remember that means the default outcome is not some continuation of the status quo, but rather a future of their making.

Equally important to this narrative is the understanding there is a third locus of elites who have their own agenda, who pull the strings of the Deep State through international institutions often rooted in the world of finance and megacorporations, and who are temporarily allied to the Left in an alliance of convenience because they find their vision of centralization and authoritarianism useful and are making use of the creative destruction being wrought upon America by those radicals. This more complex wrinkle will occupy our attention for the first section of the book, after which I will share why, despite these very real problems that exist beyond the basic paradigm, we are stuck working through these issues first before we can hold the enablers fully to account. Ultimately, they use the same means to help divide us that both sides we see publicly do, so the analysis holds true.

Before we get more into outcomes, let's review the four basic axes of conflict. The first is ideological, which we could call conservative versus liberal, Republican versus Democrat, or Left versus Right. The second is race: The decision by the Left to embrace identity politics because of the extreme electoral benefit has radicalized minorities against the rapidly diminishing White majority, with the predictable consequence in voting patterns hardening along racial lines and the attacks upon "White privilege" from the Left are accelerating at the same time White identitarians try to offer a rationale for self-defense to a still hesitant Right. The third vector is rural folks versus urban populations, where the love of liberty still vital to living independently in the country runs counter to the city's desire to constrain their people with rules and regulations given the sheer weight of their ever-rising numbers. Lastly, we have the forces of tradition who seek to preserve a traditional way of American life, most often through Christian ethics, versus the forces of progress who want to remake all we do, and who use movements like LGBT to leverage identity in a way to attack traditional statements of morality. If you've noticed that when the two sides line up that A versus B is not always obvious, and that's because each side looks for the best way to present their arguments on the core topics of ideology, identity, economy, and morality.

Allow me one moment to describe how each group would like to imagine themselves to better present the unity of the sides. The Right, as we will call them, believes in a merit based market friendly system which most Whites support as a universal value but which they want to treat as race-blind so long as they adhere to a set of cultural beliefs that honor the tradition of America and the idea of hard work and opportunity, which allows a relatively free life with many liberties. Conversely, as revolutionaries against the system, the Left believes in government as a necessary actor to redress a society which is fundamentally unfair, whose very cultural values represent an imposition upon the changing demographic who demand free will to undo a system disadvantageous to them, and which will support victim groups who claim the old rules were deliberately designed to suppress the movement of power toward novel forms of identity, which better find expression in the closeness of the city so the state can serve as corrective force: Socialism taken to different extremes depending upon the individual.

These two visions will not co-exist, but what my framework does is recognize the major avenues of attack open to each side. Beneath their simmering ideology, the Left is really pushing hard to attack along racial lines specifically because they recognize the Right would almost rather commit suicide than commit to a collective defense on the basis of identity. In this way, an attack upon the core traditional value of merit over collectivism will be completely unopposed because enough Whites will allow false guilt to restrain them so that the country will be given away. This is a phenomenon repeated throughout the West. The sane rebuke relies upon the idea that popular sovereignty requires all people have a voice, and there is no statement more moral than any people have a right to collective self-defense, but because of cultural factors like merit and the universalist ideals of Christianity, as well as the naked self-interest of a GOP that cares more about access to power and collection of sinecures than actually defending any particular belief, this attack has been and will continue to be devastating.

Conversely, when you look at who is able to stand up on the Right, you find that it is the rural folk who are leading the charge. Despite his failure to deliver on nearly any of his promises, it's worth noting they voted Trump into office to try to change the logical outcomes of the current course, and they represent a bulwark of power that is increasingly pulling away from the city and detaching itself one homestead, house, or even fortress at a time from the urban culture that dominates America. The wealthy are too connected, the Republicans too compromised, and the Whites too divided, but rural traditional America with the world's largest armory is quickly becoming the last line of defense against the encroachment of traditional liberties which are mere impediments to the transformation the urban dwelling Left is eager to complete.

If the race baiters of identity politics are the vanguard of the Left for the cultural battles, and find those most willing to oppose them are the country folk of the Right who have far less to lose and will be therefore more willing to engage in battle, we've just figured out which two elements are most likely to trundle to the front in this Left versus Right conflict. While we could call them the forces who argue for social change through demographic replacement versus those whose traditional lifestyles depends most on the continuity of the traditional system, it's not hard to see where the positive articulation of both sides will lead. The end battle will be Democracy versus Liberty, with the default position under the current system being a Leftist Victory.

I know that is a lot to swallow, and I will have the entirety of this book to argue in granular detail just why I draw that conclusion, but I purposely put it forward here so you can think about the conclusion in light of chapters of evidence. You need to also understand why there is such a global push for democracy over liberty, the actors who think it works to their benefit, and how our situation is not just the clash of ideas that accidentally emerged, but the result of many years of concentrated effort to force division of America upon these terms. Consider the many attacks upon American exceptionalism, designed to degrade our confidence and pride in nation, and yet how democracy has ever been promoted as a universal solution, a system of government so

14

divided that it serves as perfect cover for exploitation by many, because when everyone is voting their self-interest and no one looks out for the long-term good, what better system can exist for those who want to plunder the public coffers and public trust? My last book *"End the Con"* went into just how this works, but here we're going to connect the dots between the fighters, what they are doing, and the deeper causes of the conflict.

For those who read the last book, you might remember I mentioned six potential outcomes. These were submission (victory by the Left), militarism (victory by the Right), decentralization, separation, secession, and collapse. In the heady times after victory by Trump, it seemed like a strong articulation of nationalism offered a path for Rightist victory, but given the extreme institutional resistance of both the Deep State and the fifth column of neoconservatism within the GOP, as well as the failure of Trump to gain control of the government to enact his will, that path appears to be rapidly closing. We now have to think in different terms if we want to both prevent the default cultural victory of the Left and collapse. We're going to have think very deeply about those three previously marginal options of decentralization, separation, and secession, and this book is going to try to combine elements of those paths in service of liberty in a way that the Right can and should morally support.

The hill we were trying to climb before has become a mountain. Moreover, the consolidation of cultural control by the Left, greatly aided by allies in the media and big technology, makes it such that any idea of complete victory by the Right through conventional political means is likely now illusory. Trump's failure has likely destroyed the path within mainstream politics for any future committed nationalist, with the Republican Party sealing off those exits to get back to the good old days of being lovable losers. Now we have a situation where the Right still exists with many people unwilling to surrender their liberties, but who face two hostile parties: an angry bureaucracy, and centralizing forces which are going to be very aggressive in taking down potential opposition before it can even fully emerge or express itself.

The Great Replacement as it is sometimes called, whereby America's politics are changed by changing its population, will be the feature of the next chapter where we start with the Blue Texas Problem that marks the end of peaceful political solutions to preserving traditional America. But it also hints at the solution, which we could call the Great Separation. Simply put, as America moves on a path which denies its own liberties, laws, and legacy, the people have no obligation to follow it, and the challenge now becomes harder in practice but simpler in reality. Those of us who do not accept the future planned for us must organize, gather, and act to separate ourselves from what we do not want. What that will mean in practice is that we must forge a path to power such that we who choose to live in liberty may be able to secure a physical place for ourselves with institutions that protect and serve us against the arriving tyranny of the majority. We can do this in our communities, in our states, and in our regions as the American government abandons its stated laws and thus loses its claim to legitimacy with the people.

Jefferson warned this day would come. The creation of a welfare state and security state made such a conflict likely inevitable. The question becomes what we do about it, and for those who believe that not submitting is worth exploring, this book is written for you.

Chapter 1: Demography "The Blue Texas Problem"

Although other events may certainly lead to conflict before this issue is resolved, the last year has seen growing awareness of what we will call the "Blue Texas Problem". What this means is that the changing demography of the United States is such that states which were once reliably Red, such as California was until about 1988, are in danger of becoming permanent Democrat strongholds. The overwhelming reason for this is the inclusion of Third World immigrants and successive generations from earlier waves of migration which started after passage of the 1965 Hart-Celler Act which shifted immigration from a quota system which prioritized people from comparable cultures like Europe to a system where now nearly 90% of immigrants are non-European in origin. We will return to Texas for a minute, but let's talk about California first because that is the model which is basically being followed.

The nature of the American electoral system is that each state receives a certain number of electors based on population toward the election of the President. California, the most populous state, receives 55 electors, which are not even contested at this point by the Republican Party in the quest to gather the 270 electors needed for victory. In fact, the last Senatorial election in California was so lopsided that in their newly devised but highly democratic system, two Democrats competed in the final runoff for the right to serve. All this happened within a generation, and the reason why is two-fold. The first is that California took in millions of people primarily from Asia and Latin America, who each vote Democrat at nearly a 70% clip, with newly legalized immigrants gaining the right to vote five years after entry for those who are single and three years after entry for those who marry an existing American citizen. Secondly, for those they miss, their complete dominance of the education system from kindergarten to post-secondary ensures the Leftist indoctrination sticks, and we see this manifest in the fact second and succeeding generation Americans of minority descent vote even more leftwards than their first-generation parents. Put less politely, even if the immigrants are good people who appreciate what America can offer, their children who grow up without the experience and memory of why their families left their home countries are trained to hate us by our own education system, a deep and ongoing problem.

Here are the hard numbers from the last five Presidential year elections for how people of different ethnic backgrounds voted by party with the information used being gathered from the Pew Research Bureau whose databases are most helpful.

% voting GOP/Year	Whites	Latinos	Blacks	Asians
2000	54%	35%	9%	41%
2004	58%	44%	11%	44%
2008	55%	31%	4%	35%
2012	59%	27%	6%	26%

| 2016 | 57% | 28% | 8% | 27% |

As impolitic as it is to share, race remains by the far the best predictor of how Americans vote in both Presidential and midterm elections, and the patterns of how each race votes are fairly well-established with any movement happening tending to be to reinforce these trends over time. So, if you wonder why Democrats celebrate the changing demography of America and steadfastly refuse to consider any efforts at border security, the answer is because their path to victory lies directly in increasing the numbers of the minority vote as quickly as possible, and every illegal alien in America has the potential to produce more birthright citizens, anchor babies as some have called them. Moreover, the new migrants want to use chain migration to bring more of their families into America, a trait strongly shared by Asians, the fastest growing bloc of new Americans, and Latinos, the largest bloc of new migrants, so the Democrats are acting rationally to increase the number.

The response by the Republican Party, which essentially amounts to "Please don't call us racist" by leaving the borders open to avoid being savaged by the media, an inherently Leftist entity, and to please their donor class who gives freely to both sides to ensure a constant supply of unending cheaper labor, is Constitutional suicide. They hide behind the fig leaf that cultural change might encourage these new migrants to jump parties, using a foolish application of what is sometimes called the NAXALT (*Not all (fill in the blank) are like that)* argument. While that is true, it is also equally valid that if you keep letting in over a million people per year who statistically favor your opposition by a better than 2:1 margin across multiple election cycles, then you're basically giving away the country to the other side. Which the Republicans have been doing for a long time.

You'll note that in my arguments, I'm not even talking about illegal immigration, which is basically a distraction from the larger problem. Were we to build the wall, remove every illegal, and enforce our laws – all of which are good ideas on the merits and actually are a legal obligation of the President under existing Constitutional and Federal law – whatever specific judges might claim to the contrary, this trend would continue unabated and you see Republicans from Trump on down parrot the line that we need more people as an economic motor. We'll address that directly later in the section, as that argument is also likely false, but from the demographic perspective alone, we are bringing in this labor at the cost of creating a one-party state.

When reviewing the actual numbers of how many immigrants we added just in the last ten years recorded by the Department of Homeland Security, the sheer mass of people we keep adding is utterly staggering. 10,743,014 in the last ten years alone, and this number will only continue to accelerate, and does not count the tens of millions of people here illegally just hoping for a future amnesty much like Republican Ronald Reagan accepted in 1986 as part of broader immigration reform, nor does it count their children and grandchildren, who will vote even more reliably Left than the first generation.

Year	Legal Immigrants	Year	Legal Immigrants
2008	1,107,126	2013	990,553
2009	1,130,818	2014	1,016,518
2010	1,042,625	2015	1,051,031
2011	1,062,040	2016	1,183,505
2012	1,031,631	2017	1,127,167

With only slight variation from year to year, we've been adding that number of people, 90% of whom are of non-European origin, per year more or less unabated since the 1990's. The predictable consequence of changing the people of America has been that the politics of our country have shifted from the traditional basis of liberty and limited government to Left leaning parties which support collective identity and socialism, both regular staples of Asian and Latin American politics who provide the vast majority of our newest legal immigrants.

While the Department of Homeland Security does not break down the racial status of the new migrants in their high level statistical analysis, they openly share the country of origins of those who migrate here, so we can roughly extrapolate both what the racial breakdown looks like by correlating the country of origin with the dominant ethnic group arriving from each, as well as sharing here just where people are coming from who arrive in America. The numbers I use here are from 2017, but I checked over the longer term figures, and what you find over the last two decades is a shift in legal immigration where Asians are becoming somewhat more common and Latinos slightly less, although illegal immigration from Central America is likely to account for some of this discrepancy as people there become frustrated with the wait and simply come to America realizing the inefficacy of our enforcement mechanisms.

Race (Origin)	White (Eur/Aus/Can)	Latino (Latin America)	Black (Africa)	Asian (Asia)
Number	112,893	471,206	116,667	405,639
Percentage	10.0%	41.8%	10.4%	36.0%

Please note that I deliberately suppressed 83,044 legal immigrants from this equation who either identified as some other racial group like Native American or Pacific Islander under the American classification system or mixed ancestry. To simplify the analysis, they have been excluded, but the evidence collected on these groups is they vote better than 60/40 for Democrats as well. But what these numbers reveal in the aggregate is the new America looks nothing like the old America, and while we might like to imagine those things do not matter, when it comes to voting, that certainly is not the case as the new waves of immigrants basically vote their race.

Let me share the full cost of our immigration policy for the political process, and I welcome anyone to run their own analyses and check these numbers. Frankly, both parties already do, which is why the Republicans pander incessantly to try to take away minorities although with little success, and why the Democrats are cheerfully investing all their efforts into advancing identity politics so long as Whites don't behave like every other group.

Assume for the moment that each group of new immigrants votes the racial average, and we'll use the 2016 partisan affiliation from the Pew Research group to correlate these numbers with the number of legal immigrants who would have been admitted five years earlier and would be of voting age according to the Census Bureau, these would be the total potential gains in voters due to immigration for each party from one year's worth of immigration alone.

Racial Group	% R	Republican Gain	% D	Democrat Gain
Whites	57%	57,914	37%	37,593
Latinos	28%	118,744	66%	279,896
Blacks	8%	8,400	89%	93,450
Asians	27%	98,570	65%	237,299
Total	30%	283,628	70%	648,289

If you add all those numbers up, you would find the Democrats receive a net gain of 364,610 potential new voters per calendar year due to our immigration policies. Put another way, every other year, we add the equivalent of Vermont to the Democrat column in terms of sympathizers. This is why California was lost, why Nevada and Arizona are going, and why Texas will be next. The entire political network in America knows this, but no one says anything because the media uses economic sanction to punish those who don't applaud this, and because the donor class which owns both parties likes the cheap labor enough to encourage this highly destructive trend.

The next question which one might ask is: even though we're adding all these people, does that mean they all go out to vote? Thankfully for those who lean to the Right, they do not, and it is only the gap in voting between the majority and the minority groups that even allows Republicans to compete. Using data from the US Census Bureau once more, we can track turnout percentages from 2016 and 2008 to add color to this story

Turnout/Race	White	Latino	Black	Asian
2008	66.1%	49.9%	64.7%	47.6%
2016	65.3%	47.6%	59.4%	49.0%

These numbers reflect a political reality that Democrats are working tirelessly to change which is if they increase minority turnout, assuming the White vote remains constant which is likely since feminism has successfully made a wedge between White women and White men which you see in no other racial group, they will win elections. As unhappy as it might make some readers, the real story of 2016 isn't so much how well Donald Trump did, but rather how poorly Hillary Clinton performed with the Black and Latino voters compared to Barack Obama, with the simplest explanation likely being that minorities didn't come out to vote for a White woman the same way they would have a person of color. You can bet based upon the rhetoric already being employed where nearly every major Democrat has promised reparations and doubled down on the false narrative of White guilt that their wonks know these numbers by heart, but now you do also and you begin to see the problem.

Look how many votes they are gaining already with the current turnout statistics from above applied to the number of people becoming new Americans:

Total	White	Latino	Black	Asian
D +181,935	R +13,270	D +76,708	D +50,520	D +67,977

When you consider that 44.5 million American citizens are foreign born, and that we've used the same formula for admission since 1965, you begin to see the full potential of the Left's strategy. A quick and dirty extrapolation reveals that if approximately 70% vote Democrat, a little over 31 million potential voters are in play for them. When you consider they are currently converting only about half into actual voters, that means there is already a pool of approximately 16 million potential voters to be realized if they can be persuaded to just vote their identity. If the Democrats can turn just one in ten of those not yet converted, the math for Republicans starts to quickly become impossible to build any national electoral strategy that can succeed.

Now, one could develop a sane political strategy that questioned immigration along demographic lines, which I do in all my works, but the political consequences of that when the other side owns all the major cultural institutions is a different sort of fatal, and it's the true reason why reasonable arguments like this have landed me on hate lists – they hate that I am telling you the scam by which America is being undone, and that I keep shouting that unless we stop immigration into our country, America will be Venezuela or worse within twenty years and likely far less. But even if immigration doesn't do us in, the natural progression of birth rates of people already here soon will.

Allow me to extrapolate out a few years into the future to call into relief what is happening in America with birth rates. Children being born today are 50/50 White/Non-White. The people dying off are about 85% White. At the same time America is importing people who are 90% Non-White at a rate of a million plus per year, the new voters coming of age from native births reflect this changing demography with the distribution of voters who have come of age since 2016, based on Census Bureau numbers, roughly being as follows: 55% White, 23% Latino, 15% Black, and 5% Asian. If you combine immigration and natural demographic change due to deaths and births, what follows is how the new America will look in the absence of any major shifts in policy or birth rate.

These estimates are inherently rough, but they assume several things. They assume immigration policy remains unchanged, voting patterns follow a similar pattern, and that the majority of deaths will come from the oldest population. Here's a percentage breakdown of the recent past and projection for the near future:

% Possible Voters	White	Latino	Black	Asian
2000	72.0%	11.0%	11.4%	3.7%
2004	70.5%	12.4%	11.5%	4.2%
2008	68.8%	13.5%	11.7%	4.6%
2012	66.5%	14.8%	12.1%	5.3%
2016	64.4%	15.7%	12.5%	5.9%
2020*	62.2%	16.9%	12.8%	6.4%
2024*	60.1%	18.0%	13.8%	6.8%

The story these numbers tell is straightforward and unmistakable. A more diverse America is a country which will shift Left, and this change that is happening is constant and will likely only accelerate once the Left comes to power due to demography continually helping their cause. Every four years, America becomes approximately 2% less White, and as such, the Democrats stand to gain anywhere from eight hundred thousand to well over two million new votes from the combination of immigrants becoming citizens and new youth coming of legal voting age. Against this backdrop, increasing turnout among traditional Americans will soon cease to be effective as a way to offer any sort of opposition.

The strategy of the Right against cultural warfare and demographic replacement has long been the same: retreat into areas of consolidated control. White flight is a well understood phenomenon, but for whatever reason people have fled certain areas, what remains in their wake are Left leaning bulwarks like California that cannot be reversed electorally, and a consolidation of those leaning Right in fewer places. At the same time the Right is fleeing the consequences of refusing to fight on an identity basis, the next question we must ask is where are the newest soon to be citizens choose to settle.

As you might expect for geographical, economic, and cultural reasons, they are overwhelmingly concentrating in urban centers as one point of emphasis, and in the larger geographic picture, in the southern and western parts of this country. So, when you ask where the new people, 70% Democrats by voting habit are settling, the answer is those states which border Mexico get the brunt of the people, which brings us back to the Blue Texas Problem.

Texas has long been considered the unassailable redoubt of Republican votes, providing 38 electoral votes reliably to the GOP for many decades since the Solid South strategy turned White Christians primarily into Republicans, but the clock is ticking. During the Obama Administration alone, Texas added 536,779 new citizens from migration which roughly fit the same racial distribution, and therefore voting pattern. Their impact has been somewhat blunted by the flight of so many Republicans from California due to the electoral collapse there, but when you work the numbers, it becomes clear that Texas is trending Left with increasing speed. The recent election where Ted Cruz struggled to defeat Beto O'Rourke in 2018 offers additional evidence for how close we are to the flip.

Texas will be lost by 2028, depending on the vagaries of immigration policy, birth rate, voting turnout, and internal migration. And when it is gone, it's likely people who were Republicans who are able to do so will begin outward migration as they did from California, and that the electoral consequence when coupled with similar trends likely to turn Arizona and its eleven electoral votes, which just elected their first Democrat Senator in decades, makes an electoral map for which the current Republican Party simply cannot win. It means we will have a succession of Democrat Presidents, and when you couple that with the changes in House redistricting along with the media pressure, there is a high likelihood of an amnesty bargain that makes America a country where the ideas that the old paleoconservative GOP supported will be impossible to enact in any electoral format.

Give the Democrats those 49 electoral votes, and add to that the high likelihood that Florida and its twenty-nine electoral votes due to the combination of Puerto Rico's collapse, legalizing the votes of felons, and the changing demography especially amongst older people, will also be within a similar time frame, and the map for victory for those forces who oppose the new socialist order will become impossible as soon as the next Democrat wins. We know this because they understand this new reality very well, have taken steps to block another Trumpian revolt, and will govern in a way to ensure there is not a second chance. I lead with this chapter because a nation is its people. When we became a nation of Third World people, why would it surprise anyone that no set of laws could prevent us from becoming subject to Third World politics? A mistake we continue to make is to imagine that our ideals are somehow universal and apply to all people – if our own homeland isn't disproving that assumption, then perhaps our many overseas failures to win the peace should. Different people build different worlds, and though race surely is not all that defines a person as we all know many exceptional people who negate these trends, what we must realize is that we now live in a country where culture runs primarily along racial lines and that the culture war in which we now find ourselves is deliberately being fought that way because one side continues to surrender that fight. Sadly, that side is the Right.

The Constitution cannot and will not save us from such willful naivete.

Chapter 2: Culture – "A House Divided"

Many commentators remark that we are in a culture war, but how many of them stop to explain what culture means? It's one of those strange terms everyone feels they know, but which each person defines a little differently and sometimes the words to describe precisely what culture is prove elusive. There is a common definition in use that refers to art or high society, but while those can be expressions of culture, I think they're more accurately understood as mere displays of a more universal search that we perhaps most easily recognize in its absence.

In this book, culture will mean those values we uphold and those truths which we rate so important to either discover or fulfill that we consider them to be non-negotiable, and beyond transactional. Put differently, culture is what we believe we are and what we want to strive to be or become. It is a process, which is why we see art, media, and education attached to this, but ultimately what makes a culture living rather than just being archaeology is the living effort in defense of the ideas or the ongoing search for a deeper and more meaningful explanation. When we ask about culture, we're really asking: what does a society believe?

A healthy society believes in itself. In many ways, it's fair to compare societies to people in that they often have a healthy and vital youth, a long run of productive years in the middle to build foundations for the future, and then we come to the later years. In health, the wisdom of the elders is venerated by the young to prevent the recurrence of mistakes to advance human welfare, and those lessons are transmitted as an act of love from each generation to their progeny. In sickness, those who are older instead eschew their duty to advance knowledge, and invest increasingly in themselves and their comforts, while falling astray into an illusory search for perpetual youth, a chance to cheat the system as it were.

Although it is a far deeper topic than this chapter will allow, I write frequently on culture and have come to the belief the West, and America as her finest colony, lost themselves many years ago when we accepted the idea that we could somehow break the cycles of life and history. Instead of seeing our youth as our future, each generation thought they could be the one who would find the discovery, whether it was from amassing enough wealth, building the perfect ideology, or using technology to transform human nature itself that we could escape the inevitable constraints of nature and bypass our own mortal fears. We accept the cult of progress because it promises us this idea that we can have a world or even an eternity in our image. That's been the quest of the West since the Enlightenment began, and while we have made many wonderful discoveries, and achieved so much, I wonder if we have found any new truths or are any happier in our being. I'd argue strongly that we are not, and that we should take time to consider this question deeply as we move forward in a time of uncertainty. But we live in such a busy world these questions don't get asked.

Let's consider the cultural dispositions of our two combatant factions in America today which represent the mainstream views. The first thing we should recognize is that as we've defined progress as the resolution of conflicts to novel syntheses, we have created a system which will always require dispute to be at the center of our social framework. Perhaps it is an inescapable reality that we tend to learn things as much by what they are not as by considering the deeper essence of what they are. Yet, where history shows nations have usually enjoyed a number of stabilizing influences to uphold tradition and heritage as sources of authority to unite people amidst the inevitability of change, we live in a time of unbridled iconoclasm, where the only constant is change, and people are swept against the ever accelerating tide of time and events. We no longer are actors, but rather reactors valued most for our ability to provide energy to the systems we trust to deliver us to the promised land. We use and are used in turn with our value being primarily defined by how well we can serve the needs of the moment, with ever decreasing regard for the individual or family.

The Left perfectly exemplifies this belief in their egalitarian Utopianism. Their solution to the problem of how to solve all the contradictions is to advance into fantasy, a rebellion of man against nature itself and to claim we can be whatever we choose without regard to reality. It's easy to laugh at the childish ways in which they indulge the delusions of their most radical adherents, yet the deeper logic of their impact is a war against nature and reason alike, a challenge to the rules of existence and mental order, and one which has surprising moral appeal to some.

A different time would have clearly understood this as evil, and I say that because the idea that man can somehow make a better order than we have been given in nature with grace from above is hateful to one who understands life as a gift and a privilege. But, they do not. They see life as a burden, authority as oppression, and demand the will of equality be imposed. Ironically, beneath the language of tolerance and diversity, the Left actually seeks to remove any authority which could provide comfort and attack any element of human distinction, differentiated and unique. They hate being self-aware, and choose fantasy, so they act aggressively to destroy, and will show no restraint in their ultimate killing urges to make humanity what they feel it should be instead of taking just a moment to understand what we are. On the surface, they probably have the best understanding of what we do in this troubled system, but they fail because it never occurs to ask why we are as we are, and why we exist in this miraculous moment of being.

As the Left are motivated and organize, they go out with the zeal of missionaries to promote the message and to bring the news to others that the revolt is coming, and it will finally succeed this time! Nature shall give way and reason itself will be bound as the power of man in his pride and hubris shall overcome any obstacles. They take over every school to ensure each pupil is brought to the new ways, ruthlessly rooting out those who offer dissent. They control the channels over the air, so their message is carried in every program from news to entertainment. They take all the resources they can find to build a novel Tower of Babble to confuse people away from any one truth, knowing that equality only comes when nothing has value. They destroy and call it creation.

It's sad. It's a sign of profound sickness. Yet, this is the formal culture of the West, or at least the most quickly growing half, and it is winning. Such victory can only ever be transitory, as nature will ultimately win out against fantasy, and the effort to reduce man to his most bestial form, a celebration of vice and experience, will regress civilization to the mean in every sense of the word. Our children are poisoned by these thoughts, yet we pay for the privilege of such status because these people have become the gatekeepers of our dark civic religion. At this point, they don't require agreement in the hearts of those who live here, although if you express yourself as a heretic, they will be unremitting in their efforts to destroy you and yours. I know; I live their venom.

What opposes these efforts at evil? Would it sadden you to hear the answer is mostly nothing? Why the Right abandoned culture is one of the sadder and stranger stories of our history, and something we must discuss in much deeper detail later, but about sixty years ago, it happened that we tricked ourselves into accepting a false duality. The Left, being defined as the forces of the State – which they certainly have been aggressive in using but most primarily as a means to an end, to create this perpetual revolution whose roots are as old as man himself, faced a Right which ultimately decided only to embrace the surface battle by presenting themselves as the force of the Market, an ideology unto itself that morphed into toxic amorality in pursuit of wealth.

Allow me a diversion as I describe what I imagine as hell. People conjure images of a fiery inferno or perhaps a frozen wasteland of torment, but I think it is something far worse: It is the absence of God. It is the absence of good, the choice to turn away from value, and to think all things are of man and in pride imagine nothing greater than what we could achieve. All values are arbitrary and transactional in such a world, all choices are valid, and because truth itself ceases to exist as would be the case absent authority above us, then all become lies in a search for perpetual comfort.

Let me ask you a question: How much did that sound like capitalism to you? My point is not to argue against the value of markets for exchange between men any more than I would argue against the necessity of the state to serve certain needs beyond the inclination of men to try, but just as the Left idolizes the State into the ultimate tool of human progress, so also does the Right all too often venerate the Market in just the same way. Each makes humanity subservient to a system, to an enforced understanding based upon how we interact with one another, and in so doing puts us on a moral plane of equivalence.

The ideology that everything has a price and can be traded is that of a professional prostitute. And when you look how the Right has behaved in the last half century plus, what have we done? We shipped American jobs overseas for money. We replaced our people for money. We fought war after war killing our youth to protect the wealthy elders to maintain such greed. We have claimed this is all moral and just because people turned a profit. We got comfortable and elevated our wealth, never mind crippling levels of debt left for the future to deal with, because we now have material wealth, physical comfort, and can say we won the game. Was it worth it?

I am what is sometimes called a third way thinker, which is what a few nationalists call themselves because where one group argues the key is the perfect state, and others argue it is the interactions of a freer market, this different method of thinking elaborates a third way is to treat both these methods as tools in a search for a better outcome that honors people as they are, understanding most importantly that people are not interchangeable parts in a system. You can't simply replace all the crayons of one color with another and hope to be able to paint the same pictures, because nature has rules and love them or hate them, to fight them is to forever fight ourselves.

I would submit that is exactly what we are doing culturally now. The Right fights tirelessly for the market, looking for new ways to amass wealth and status, while the Left fights tirelessly to advance the State to remake humanity. Has it struck you that for as much as these two sides loathe one another that the fundamental goals of the two sides are actually not in conflict and both get what they want? The Right has accumulated wealth in untold proportions, although at the cost of their children's youth and any say over the future. The Left has gladly accepted these ugly actions appropriating the money of their supposed opposition to remake the children who never mattered quite as much in the rush to win the day, and so their turn is coming. Maybe this is why the good book said the love of money is the root of evil, because America's wealth waters the fruit of socialism at the same time our national health is dying on the vine of selfish neglect.

Ironically, we get the worst of both worlds. We now have massive social conflict as people are just beginning to awaken from what the fusionists knew before Friedman and Buckley were kind enough to bury them on the ash heap of history. A nation without morality, without a culture that seeks a higher truth and delights in that search, will succumb unto sickness and death. We get the Left fighting the Right over a false dialectic where every Republican victory only solidifies the society desired by the Democrats, because the fight happens on this most harmful oblique. Yet, the necessary battle which must be fought which I've described previously as excellence versus equality has been abandoned, because we have lost faith in ourselves.

Truth without belief is useless. Our cynical time has forgotten that as our comforts allow us the pleasant delusion that nothing will be that bad. Even now, we see the worst manifestations of this during the Trump Presidency which seemed for a moment to be a populist revolt to unmake the dark heart of a corrupt system, yet we see how gladly it retreated into pleasant nostalgia so long as creature comforts were not threatened. We see truly the triumph of power over meaning, where even as people read a book like this, most are just figuring how to survive at a reasonably suitable level of comfort and civilization instead of asking the far more important cultural question of how we might return to health, truth, and how we might use our faculties to better our world.

America has now become a corpse to plunder. Everyone wants to win the battle of the day. When terrible events happen, the question is who to blame, and when something good happens, the rush to claim credit is instantaneous. People have checked out of the process, and the smartest and sanest are heading for the exits. Those at the center of the empire are robbing it blind, hoping only to continue the plunder until their time is up, and the most telling indicator reveals itself in one honest inquiry: Who believes tomorrow will be better than today?

I don't think anyone does anymore, but I give credit to those on the Left for one thing: Their destruction is at least purposeful. That might be why they had the will to impose their beliefs, and why, rather than retreating from active promotion of their ideals, they now use the state to batter their enemies into submission. With the relentless energy of termites, they're succeeding and their long march to reduce man back to an animal nears success.

Can we fight this? An amoral form of relativism that argues for humanist materialism isn't going to win the battle against a moral form of relativism that argues for humanist materialism. Most of you will not have thought of communism versus capitalism that way, but that's what happens when your core value is the free market unguided by any moral compass. The market can work great when it is used by people who act in a trustworthy fashion because they have a set of shared values, and subscribe to truths they can be trusted to uphold.

But what then is multiculturalism? It is a war against truth and reason, and the declaration that all things can be true at once in the same space and in the same way. Such paradox cannot be resolved, and this psychic attack destroys the will to fight in societies, as each value is conflated into every other value, and the reasonable mind revolts. Provide money and power to put this out as the national message, and you will see a rapid decline, ironically celebrated as a great success. Because the victim is the hero when the revolution is against order itself. This is the new American culture, and if we do not quickly articulate an alternative, we shall walk a long and sad road that has much death and despair ahead.

To stop this will cost much and entail great sacrifice. It's unlikely most people will choose to pay for such a divergence. However, it is possible some people may choose to adopt a different and healthier path, if they have the courage to assert a truth stronger than that lie which is now offered. Once, we lived that way, and whether it comes from reclamation of faith, an honest appraisal of nature, or better use of our faculties of reason, there are better options. We once used our liberty to express these talents where now we use it only as justification for our own venial delight in licentiousness, but we need not continue to make that error if we have courage and the sound application of wisdom.

Consider this chapter in light of the previous chapter where we bring people here only because they vote differently, can be used for work, and think of their own truths. Whatever utility we derive from their addition in the short-term, how much more of a price will we pay in the long term? The central rulers get away with these acts because nobody cares when tomorrow doesn't matter, and each side offers a promise that the next sacrifice will bring a final apogee of achievement.

Yet, tomorrow is coming. And just like any other debt, the longer one waits to pay it, the larger the price becomes.

Chapter 3: Mass Lawfare "The Death of Justice"

When society doesn't agree upon the rules, what purpose does law serve? Where there is a common set of shared beliefs, law tries to serve the useful role of upholding those values which people celebrate, and protect those who are wronged from those who attack them. Yet, when truth disappears, it's funny how law doesn't go away, but rather evolves as an end unto itself. It's like those purveyors of corruption realize that in the absence of defensible value, having the mere appearance of propriety is enough to allow anything to happen.

Would anyone seriously argue against the idea that the twofold purpose of the legal system at this point is the enrichment of those involved in settling the disputes which happen to fall into its clasp, and also in service of those ends to see the desires of the powerful enacted and protected against the larger but now amorphous public interest? The truth of the law in America today is people get the best justice they can buy, and while there are certainly some few brave souls struggling against the machine and achieving an occasional victory to prop up the illusion of blind and fair justice, the reality is she can hear quite well who is clinking the most coins in her jar as she sits unhappily outside the buildings whose ostentatious dressing conceal their moral poverty.

I know I present an unhappy view of human nature sometimes, but I try to be realistic, and what we see is those entities with much power, be they government or corporate, are able to game the system and avoid any painful consequences in enforcing their wishes. As much as people sometimes make the joke about lawsuits, the reality is the side which usually wins is that side which has the most resources to survive the battle of attrition that the judicial guild enforces for the benefit of their constituent lawyers. Justice is neither fair nor swift, and I agree with the critics on all sides who point out that it serves the powerful.

One telling indicator that happened over the course of my lifetime was the transition from having police officers in public to the much more draconian sounding law enforcement. Whereas the former term conveyed and was far more likely to practice support for the citizenry and defense of their liberty and security alike, law enforcement has evolved into a paramilitary for the elites which exists to enact their will as they choose, when they choose, and most disturbingly, for whom they choose.

Let's use some examples in this chapter that will be familiar to most of you. How about the sorry case of what the city of Baltimore has become after the incident with Freddie Gray? Rather than wading into the details of a case which should be considered carefully with respect to the law and conduct, the whole incident evolved into a political grandstanding demonstration where the politicians essentially forced the police not to do their job anymore. It was convenient to throw their own protection under the bus, and so an entire populace basically was left with the appearance of security and a police force, which both sadly yet wisely for their own employment prospects, made the decision to simply show up, drive around in a few predictable circuits, collect their checks, and avoid causing trouble.

Why does this happen? When justice becomes secondary to politics, as has become common place throughout our country, but most noticeably in the cities, such things are inevitable. Without a common unifying truth, we have no choice but to become two camps practicing civil disobedience, even as such rises to the governmental level. The political schism atop the cultural breakdown only exacerbates these tendencies as right and wrong become less important than winner or loser. What starts with keeping the peace inevitably descends to a suppression of liberties.

Let's use Portland, Oregon as the next example. I think about the rallies that have been happening there and which are becoming more common as street warfare between two rising paramilitary factions. Nature abhors a vacuum and when legitimate order is not defended, it will not be long before it is filled. The state is theoretically supposed to fill this gap by being an equal and fair arbiter under the existing rules, but out on the Pacific Coast, we've seen the same thing that those who understand the true story of the "Unite the Right" rally in Charlottesville already know: Different rules apply for different factions.

Put simply, the cities are in revolt – they have signed up, by and large, with the culture of the Left and they will allow

Antifa thugs to own the streets. Where their opposite number seek permits and try to adhere, foolishly I'd argue at this point, to the existing law, you never see the black clad assemblies of Antifa armed with weapons broken up, or the media denounce their many provocations including firebombing Federal facilities. And you never will, because the law is being enforced as justice for some at the cost of others, and if you are on the wrong side of the culture war, you can and will be punished for your beliefs.

When Andy Ngo was bleeding out and being kicked by a beat mob on the streets of the Rose City, the police did nothing. Law enforcement saw a wounded man, a journalist who did not have a side in the quarrel, and their idea of rendering assistance was telling him to re-enter the fray to seek help elsewhere. What else would you expect when the cops become mercenaries to the people who write the paychecks? It's quite the legacy for the progressive mayor and the first Black police chief up there to enforce, but to comment upon such things is to invite the wrath of the system, and people have learned better.

The gentler souls amongst you might argue that people who go to the streets for any side in this conflict invite such problems upon themselves. I don't agree with that from the perspective that when you allow mobs to basically be enabled by the police to control an ever-growing number of our cities and especially our institutions of higher learning, it won't be long before their boldness goes further still. But, whatever the predictable and horrible consequence, it does seem true that the Right has quit the field because even those with the courage to fight have been bankrupted by lawfare and unequal enforcement.

The funny thing about this, however, is one can engage in their conflict with the utmost of gentility and still find themselves in a similar circumstance. The law does nothing to protect those people who offer dissent and who are targeted for economic embargo, social ostracism, and moral destruction. Consider the so-called anti-hate groups kept on speed dial by the Federal Bureau of Investigation and the revolving door between the cultural revolutionaries and the Deep State which serves to decapitate their opposition and destroy anyone who decides to depart from the approved party line. Thought crime might not ever enter into a court of law, but hate crimes are the same thing under another branding, and when Rod Rosenstein tweeted post El Paso that because of an anonymous manifesto that the government would be investigating "White terrorism", it wasn't hard to see how newly promised "red flag" laws would be the final destruction of the First, Second, and Fourth Amendments. The culture war is killing the Constitution, because the promise of security is being used by democracy to pummel liberty in the argument with a frightened public.

It's important to note the citizen now has no rights. We can claim these and so long as we exist within a narrow boundary of rules that far transcends any authority the sovereign state was ever intended or should have under any

48

fair reading of the law, we are permitted to graze like cattle as targets for our betters to attack as and when they will. They suffer us our freedoms, knowing that we would resist if the attack became too direct, but the ceaseless erosion is taking a toll, and even these indulgences now are being questioned.

A fairer system would say you couldn't punish one side for free speech and exercise of dissent if the same rules didn't apply to the other, but this has long ceased to be about fairness. Now, we are fighting as men against the machine, and one of the delusions you'll have to shed going forward is the idea that there are fair intermediaries. The media lives off the system. The Republican Party lives off the system. The Courts are the system. And the system will do what any rational actor does – save itself first.

I know it is difficult to imagine the extent to which the system will go to silence opposition, although after the "suicide" of Jeffrey Epstein, maybe people have had just enough of a glimpse behind the veil to understand justice is there only for those who take it. If the evidence from Lisa Page and Peter Strzok didn't make it clear, the State is at war with the people, and they've picked the side of the Left in the culture war. Even the current administration is complicit in these acts, having surrendered to a jabbing battle of attrition with the media where the government does nothing at the same time our culture consolidates against voices of popular dissent.

I admit this is a most strange battle and sometimes challenging to accurately describe. But only from the context of ideology. A simpler version works best which is that the powerful protect those who defend or serve their interests. This begs a really interesting question which is vital to this book and that is asking: why do the most powerful people in society invest so much money and effort into supporting movements that seek to unmake the very country? It's a complex question that we need to keep in mind moving forward, because if it doesn't make sense on the surface, we need to figure out who is using whom – and why. Our survival likely depends on how well and how quickly we puzzle out this answer.

They certainly have started coming after me. It's a pithy version of lawfare, but I've had my access to various financial institutions closed, including certain accounts I didn't even remember I had. It would be easy to blame the legions of Leftist advocates that have made me into a folk hero/bogeyman in my native state of Maine, but that doesn't fit the facts. What does is that either the government itself dislikes how vigorously I've been calling out their corruption, or the banks have decided to leverage their financial prowess to swat a gnat. Having seen the latter quite often amongst people painted as pariahs, but who fundamentally were just arguing for the equality of rules to apply to fundamental discourse, I'd be inclined to believe in their culpability if forced to guess. Because they don't want people asking the wrong questions when they offer you two perfectly acceptable choices over which to fight.

Yet, when we look at the heart of lawfare, what we find is the supposed fight between the evils of big business or the corruption of big government is a false duality that distracts us from the easily observable reality. Big business pays to elect those representatives they want to serve their corporate, and the individuals who make up these nebulous entities, interests. Big government returns the favor by appropriating taxpayer money or issuing debt to kickback the payment with interest in terms of lucrative contracts and legislation that benefits them at the expense of the country. The worst sort of welfare in this country isn't the help for the poor, which some need while others exploit, but how the very rich rob the country to become richer and how civil servants take the deal and become employed by those they were supposed to regulate after a civil service job "well done." Big business is big government in our mercantile empire, and that's the reality of America and most of the world as well.

Democracy is endorsed for this because so long as people feel they have the illusion of power and choice, they remain complacent. In truth, the moral degradation inherent in a system where everyone works for short term individual or collective gain is a form of lawfare against the nation as a whole as we rob the future to be richer today. Who cares for tomorrow when the crisis of the day dominates a dopamine driven, all day and night, social media tweetstorm political conflict? At some point, the mind retreats from the unending nature of the battle, and two groups of partisans settle into perpetual warfare against one another, creating equivalency between them for so many outside the battle, and the elements of the system permit the theatrics of fighting over a certain narrow and nonthreatening band of issues.

Vote harder, the most rabid are urged on, and when the sellout comes from those who rise to represent these interests, the assurance of the dangers of the opposition keep the people in line. Yet, have you noticed funny things: Most wars occur when the peace-loving Democrats are in office. Amnesty and gun control occur most frequently when the Republicans are defending our rights. Our sides betray us again and again, but we show up, because we honor the system, and we fear the alternative we're presented. This too is lawfare.

I honor our Bill of Rights. That's about all I genuinely support at this point, because pretty much everything else only serves one narrow interest or another. That's not to say I intend to seek any more anger from the state than I've already gathered, but the best legal codes in history have ever been simple enough for people to understand and remember. The other code that America once honored was the Ten Commandments of Moses, and in clear and simple code with men trying one another absent the professional guild of lawyers, the closest approach to justice has ever been found. But we've abandoned that to a loophole ridden set of contradictions designed to protect the powerful, obfuscate corruption, and enrich the attorneys to no end.

We imagine the law protects us, but it does not. There are good officers, good lawyers, and good judges, but in a bad system, they will be an ever-reducing quantity. This message is especially important for people on the Right who inherently intuit the value of order. You need to consider carefully if we are endorsing a system that honestly serves us, that is fair and just, and that respects merit. Or, could it be one that is literally importing people to displace our even having an appearance of choice, which rewards injustice, and which depends upon interlocking layers of deceit to sustain itself. Do we need to be more involved and stop allowing every system to be weaponized against us from the lawyers which vote over 90% for the Left to the tech companies which now only silence those who approach with respect for tradition and the rapidly shrinking majority? What do we owe such a system, especially as it begins to assault those very values that are America – our inalienable rights – on the basis that the new folks don't like it?

There will be a very high price in questioning that choice. Yet, the alternative might be higher still, as we watch our laws become the means by which we are hung. I laugh when people come to me and say the Supreme Court will save us from the consequences of a culture of indifference and a demography hellbent on change. As those who know history will remember, FDR faced a similar problem and he tried to pack the Court by adding new justices. When the flip happens, probably next decade, you heard it here first that the law will serve those who have the numbers and resources, and your newly expanded Supreme Court with a President elected quite probably by popular vote alone will celebrate the new order as the legal victory of democracy.

Quality versus quantity. Liberty versus democracy. Freedom versus serfdom. It's our choice, but not for much longer, because when every citizen is a potential criminal, which is the only thing laws written for security actually guarantee, it won't take long for us to lose the ability to resist. We might retain our toys and tools for heirlooms, but when we can't speak the reason for their purpose, having been run from the streets with the voices of dissent in jail and the police only being paid thugs for a state which protects its own, what of America remains?

I know that future sure as hell doesn't have liberty and justice for all, and people, in fear and temerity, imagine they will just sit back and be good people – servants really – and survive. Well, not me. I've already written my way onto whatever lists of infamy exist, and in honor to our ancestors and in duty to our children, I'm going to speak up for liberty and explain that the law is no longer defending this, it is killing us.

Yet, the killing blow likely won't emerge from the preferred vector of the Left against the American people. As we see so often, when the leadership assigned to the Right delivers the traitorous blow, it proves so much more demoralizing, and that's why I think the ultimate take down that justifies the fall won't be the direct encroachment of the state absent cause, even as the persecution will advance, but rather it will be the fall of the market to the inevitable and inescapable cost of a truly staggering debt that bankrupts a whole faction because of one terrible mistake in picking the wrong battle. We chose wealth over virtue and history follows an incredibly predictable pattern for what that means.

Chapter 4: Economic Malfeasance "America is Broke"

Not only is America broken at the seams, an increasingly polyglot population, with arbitrary and politically changing definitions of law, but even more importantly perhaps, we're broke. As we all well know, the rich can get away with all sorts of stupidity because people are often willing to indulge any fantasy of the wealthy in exchange for a share of that excess. But America, once the premiere creditor nation of the world, has now become a profligate debtor having traded away fiscal responsibility and shrewd planning in exchange for having a perpetual day of indulgence by mortgaging the future. If you want to see just how painful the results are, check out the staggering numbers hosted at www.usdebtclock.com usdebtclock.org which compiles up to the second statistics for all the relevant agencies about just how foolish we are being, and which I'm using for the ever-growing estimates used below.

At the moment I am writing in mid-August, the national debt has just passed $22.5 trillion dollars in total. Now I know the mind struggles to comprehend the vastness of the numbers involved, so maybe I should say we owe $22,500,000,000,000 instead. To put that in context for you, the Gross Domestic Product of the entire United States of America, which is to say the sum financial value of all productive economic activity conducted throughout the whole of the country for an entire year is only $21.3 trillion dollars. That means if every dollar created through economic activity for a year was applied, without anyone taking any profit or wages whatsoever, we still would be unable to pay our government debt in full.

It's a common trick for those who work in government finance to reduce the zeros to make the problem more comprehensible. A person who makes $21,300 per year now has $22,500 in credit debt with interest coming due. Moreover, they still have to meet their basic needs, have health care expenses and other items to plan for, and interest and penalties will escalate for non-payment. In the real world, credit companies would never allow such an upside-down situation to occur absent fraud or other deceit, but in the world of governmental finance, this is exactly the situation that not only America, but most of the world's central banks now face.

All of this starts with a lie. The lie is that we can have an economy with perpetual growth that is exempt from historical cycles of bust and boom. For all the downturns we have seen, most notably the many problems after the 2007 crisis which was born out of reckless government policies about housing, rapacious greed from Wall Street in using derivatives, basically legalized financial gambling to turn a quick buck, the Federal Reserve and its compatriot banks have done whatever is required to sustain the illusion that perpetual growth is continuing. Because people do not want to face the consequences of an alternative, the West generally, like the world as a whole, has now been permitted to behave for decades like a drunk who keeps asking for another lest the inevitable hangover come and the bubble burst.

Some find the details of these events less interesting, but for those who do not, *"Someone Has To Say It"* invests much energy into a far deeper dive into the corruption that is the Federal Reserve, the actors who created it and how they use money to control the fate of nations. Bankers have long understood how to manipulate people using debt and interest, and I argue they actually have successfully leveraged the world through sovereign debt to control most human affairs on the macro level. More on that later but remember the simplest truism, which is no conspiracy but merely the human nature we see manifest in every patronage system: he who has the money makes the rules.

The question of how they get away with it is relatively simple and a mechanism you need to understand because it will be the best and most unmistakable indicator of how long there will be until the clock is up and the bubble must burst: Inflation. In the technical sense, inflation refers to the rising cost of goods and services in response to a growing money supply. Current financial doctrine deliberately targets a low but sustained rate of inflation designed to match pace with economic growth, so a gently rising money supply matches ongoing economic growth due to technological innovation, new industry, growing labor supply, etc. That's the short version that you'd learn if you were going to get an MBA.

The question we should be asking is if it adds up, and there's a really simple way to demonstrate that it does not. Comparing the price of what basic household staples cost today versus what they cost when the central bank was enacted in 1913, you discover we often pay greater than one hundred times the cost for the exact same goods, while wages have only increased at a fraction of that pace.

Improvements in technology and ease of transportation should, in theory, make a good cost less, so what gives? The answer is that the money in your wallet is worth less, and the reason why is while we are accustomed to thinking of money as having a somewhat fixed value, the reality is the value of the dollar is constantly in flux and while this trend is masked by the habit we have of comparing currencies against one another, the tell is obvious if you understand commodity markets.

Let's use gold as the example. If you were to buy an ounce right now, it would cost $1,500. Ten years ago, it would have cost approximately $750. A similar trend is observable with predictable variations for supply and demand across most staple trades, which tells you this: The real cost of goods has doubled in the last ten years. If the economy were balanced and the banks were achieving their stated goal of matching inflation to economic growth, would not the logical result be that average income would need to have doubled in the same time frame? For most of you, I suspect if you have held the same job, an apple to apples comparison, you're probably not making double. That's because while prices of goods, services, housing and education have skyrocketed, wage growth has been essentially stagnant since the 1970s. Here's the scam: despite Americans being more productive than ever, despite doubling the labor market, despite all the technological innovations, and despite stagnant wage growth, the value of money still continues to shrink which is demonstrated by the ever-accelerating rise in prices.

Let's return to the household level. America solved not being able to pay its bills by taking out new credit cards. When some were overloaded, our credit was still good enough where we could take a new one out and maybe transfer the balance to defer interest. You can carry a high debt load if the banks will allow you to pay a 0% interest rate. For a long time, that's what the Federal Reserve did, subsidizing the entire Obama Administration with a null prime rate, which is to say they loaned money to banks for free so they could charge you interest to keep the money supply circulating and the economy moving, and they dumped enormous amounts of money into the market in quantitative easing, which is banker slang for inflation.

I wish I could tell you just how bad it is, but it's one of the most closely guarded secrets, as the Federal Reserve is not audited and exists outside the purview of the Federal Government. It is also a privately held company where there are certain also unknown shareholders who collect a dividend on their ownership of international and sovereign debt. Those more knowledgeable than I suggest that they own the economic value of the entire world several times over, and what we have failed to realize for over a century now is that the major value of our economic labor basically trickles through to pay this interest and debt. It really is the perfect laundering scam, and through warfare and welfare, nations are tricked into becoming perpetual debtors, with those who seek their independence often branded as terrorists and attacked. At the time of this writing, only three countries exist outside their system: Syria, Iran, and North Korea. That should connect a dot or two, because for all the petty tyrannies around the world, where do we have the largest accumulation of forces?

It gets worse. One would think this scam would have to pop sooner rather than later, but the way in which it has been continued is devilishly clever. The new innovation in banking is negative yield bonds. Perhaps the best way to explain this, is it would be like if you deposited your money in a savings account, but instead of collecting interest for the bank's ability to use your money on their portfolio, you would have to pay them for the service of holding your money. You are probably thinking you would never do that when you could just hold your money in hand and not pay a fee, but the banks do the opposite because they want the flow of money to continue. So, the banks are literally buying sovereign debt knowing they will lose value on that transaction because they understand the moment liquidity in the system freezes up, they'll no longer be able to make money off everything else and the global economy must collapse. We are living on borrowed time.

There will be other tells. The pace of inflation will increase, as it has done. The likelihood of war will also grow, because one way in which some debts have always been written off is by killing the debt holders, or by sovereign national defaults. It's also true that war, as an economic activity, encourages massive state spending on all sides, so there's a weird irony whereby as the economics get worse, the push toward warfare often grows because the idea is to fight one's way out when the loan shark comes calling, and also that the extra human activity buys time to forestall the problem. It's also ironically true that debt forgiveness often happens only after terrible conflicts, like World War II, yet you'll notice it usually comes at the cost of giving international institutions of lending complete control. Because I guarantee you, they have the gold that will still have value after the rest of us are using wheelbarrows of dollars to buy a loaf of bread.

Knowing all this, the desire to continuously expand the American military takes on a different light, as it is a debt-based investiture that banking favors, and the Right can push. The welfare state of the Left actually receives support also, because it increases debt and servitude on multiple levels, while also mollifying segments of the population who could otherwise prove dangerous. Let's make this a little scarier still, however, as the government has certain obligations in the future that it has promised like Medicaid, Social Security, etc. which are non-discretionary and must theoretically be paid, and which are not accounted against the debt in the numbers above. The last time the US Treasury issued a report about these obligations for the future back in 2016, they estimated $46.7 trillion dollars were owed to these programs, but not yet funded. People who study these numbers argue heavily over the methodology of that number, arguing that accounting tricks of assuming an unrealistically high return on investments are being used to conceal a debt obligation which might be as high as $200 trillion dollars.

I'll plug the numbers back in. Our American worker making $21,300, hoping for 3% wage growth in an exceptional year, already owes more than he makes in credit debt, and between pension and health care obligations, he owes another two to ten times what he makes to continue those services. All of this assumes he doesn't spend a single dollar today. The interest alone on this debt is in danger of exceeding his entire income. This, ladies and gentlemen, demonstrates to you just how bankrupt America is, and the only reason you don't know it is because pretty much every other country is in the same exact boat.

Really smart people know this and respond in two different ways, sometimes in conjunction, sometimes in opposition to one another. First, they're amassing as many tangible resources as they can and divesting from the economy of credit into different commodities including properties, both inside and outside the country, and durable fixed goods. They know that each day the dollar buys less and the day when it will buy nothing at all is inevitable. Second, they're robbing the system blind wherever and whenever they can because the rot is understandable to anyone with even a cursory understanding of debt and economics, which is why no politician ever cares about or seriously talks about the debt, because the greater danger lies with public awareness of these problems than trying to prevent the inevitable. Nobody in DC or Wall Street wants to be stuck holding the bag when the bubble bursts, so everyone pretends this mass delusion is actually sane economically. Obviously, it is not.

Frankly, I've been stunned about how long this has been allowed to go on, and it's a remarkable bit of financial engineering that 2007 didn't kick off a depression to make 1929 look like a cakewalk. But the economy never really returned to health, because it wasn't healthy before then, and a quarter of American homeowners affected are still upside down on their mortgages. So long as we live on borrowed debt, our economy cannot ever be truly healthy. I don't know what will set things off, but I want to add another thing to consider which will make it harder to sustain moving forward.

A second wave of automation driven by advances in deep learning, logistics, and artificial intelligence is likely to cost as much as half of Americans their jobs by 2030. Some people estimate the number as far lower, around 20%, but even that would represent a loss of tens of millions of sources of tax revenue and a further drain on the welfare state. The idea to address this by printing more money and artificially fixing wages is often floated, but I think those who see the writing on the wall have come to realize authority will have to come from fiat eventually, as the cultural vision of the Right of putting off the cost of things because all is for sale is finally going to come due. And the only way to survive that world will be to abandon the market as it was for something else, which might come as a hard-economic collapse, either supplanted by or followed by the introduction of another system to rescue us from our financial bankruptcy and insolvency.

Many prognosticators who have far better economic and financial understanding than I have commented upon this regularly, and I recommend you become familiar with what to look for, but I will hazard my own guess about when the dominoes will finally fall. Not in terms of a specific date, but rather as a logical consequence of a series of events. What you'll notice throughout this narrative is that there is a deliberate and ongoing effort by certain people to use the world essentially for their own aggrandizement, and when a given source of support becomes a liability, that asset is liquidated and replaced.

I will share one additional important number with you which is the amount of household debt American families are carrying. The latest revised estimates suggest Americans collectively owe $13.7 trillion dollars in consumer debt, so we're more than halfway to carrying the same amount of debt as our government, and unless that number continues to grow, the system simply will not balance. Considering that the median wage in the United States is only $33,000 per year and the further fact that 23% of our population is already dependent on Medicaid, the prospects of growing consumer debt indefinitely to make the system balance are rather bleak. This might also explain why America at every level is looking like an increasingly shaky investment on the numbers.

Consider the rapid turn against America that has come since the election of Trump, not so much perhaps as a result of anything he has done, as he has only superficially impacted the global system, but rather as intended punishment against the American people for presuming to offer a slight to the idea that an international system should be constructed of interlocking institutions against a non-elected bureaucracy. We are certainly allowed, and even encouraged to have our democracies, but what we will not be permitted is any genuine expression of liberty to dissent, nationalism to organize, or solidarity to resist. As the cases of Syria, Iran, and North Korea demonstrate, whatever one thinks of those regimes, resistance is not an option.

How much more so would that prove the case if the American people could somehow conjure up their inner Andrew Jackson and throw off the fetters of banking and the debt system of usury and control? How much more liberating would it be if we declared our debts null and void, and accepted those consequences, if we built a future of our own choosing in this land? That is the existential fear of the banking class, and why they loathe nationalism to their very core, because they want us to be desperate and fearful individuals, easily kept in line. We can have what we want, unlimited credit to buy it, unlimited state support to endure, so long as the status quo is never put under anything other than a glancing rhetorical threat.

America is broke more than she is broken, and to be honest, neither party has the political will to change this. The politicians themselves, whom it would be convenient to blame, are but a reflection of their constituencies in this instance who having long grown accustomed to the benefits of perpetual growth, and are all too eager to choose a shrinking future where they can live in their choice of delusion or nostalgia as opposed to putting their immediate well-being at risk. So long as the system works well enough that we don't have to face the alternatives, it will likely endure. As to when it will end, that will be for those who control these markets to decide unless the people intervene first, or nature somehow interjects as it has been known to do.

Just remember next time you hear people talking about tax policy, minimum wage, or a balanced budget, whatever the merits of each of these ideas, these are the debates we are permitted to have about how to shave a penny this way or that on a debt that is thousands fold larger than the concerns those issues address. We are never allowed to question our servitude, to seek a jubilee for relief, because we can never question the system or those who maintain it. They buy the lawyers, move the people around the map, and own nearly everything when they choose. It's really bad, but at least it proves Voltaire's dictum about those who you cannot criticize being the ones who are really in control.

Chapter 5: America Destroyed – Why?

While not the nicest thing to do, I purposely presented four different cases (and yes, there are others I could still add) why America, as we know it, is not going to survive. This is the necessary beginning of our examination because the previous chapters reflect the facts of the situation on the ground with which we will have to contend, and perhaps even more importantly, you can't continue to let false hope cloud your thinking.   We don't have time for such indulgence.

Let's talk about that for just one second, because while some might consider it cruel to go into exhaustive detail about all the really challenging situations America faces, many of which we can only blame on our own willful negligence at every level, I consider it better to face the truth upfront because reality, despite the ideological insistence to the contrary by those delusional folks who are painted as our cultural luminaries, will follow certain rules.   In the same way that a patient who has cancer will see sickness spread from organ to organ without treatment, so too will the sickness at the heart of our empire contaminate all that is good unless we somehow treat this.   Only when one is willing to honestly address the core problems that cause the sickness, and not just slap bandages on the symptoms, is there any hope of recovering health.   That quest is the one we must contemplate moving forward, because we've reached the point where duct tape is creating a Frankenstein of a country, and I think most people know this. You certainly can "check out" and keep your head down, and pray that when the bill comes due, you'll already be gone – we had a whole generation practice that as their organizing principle. But you're betting against the odds now as the contradictions are adding up more quickly than our ability to conceal or overcome them.

The first chapter laid out how we are seeing the deliberate demographic replacement of the American people by a primarily Third World mix of people. Those people, brought here cynically by an alliance of the Right who use them for cheap labor and the Left for reliable votes, represent the ideas of a narrow band of well-funded donors but serve the interests of few others. In reality, they only add to our burdens with the Center for Immigration Studies reporting 63% of non-citizen families rely upon some form of social welfare, while at the same time competing to depress wages for the labor market for our working poor. A few benefit, like those wealthy who are most likely to take advantage of tax loopholes and who live most isolated from the consequences of increased criminality that inevitably results from the clash of competing cultures. Every year, we add a million more people legally, and it is only a matter of time before the shifting demography sees a full amnesty that creates the majority non-White country which will vote, in the aggregate, 70% for Democrats. Expect this with the next Democrat in office – so democracy will bring the end of even the appearance of actual electoral choice in America.

The next section went into the false cultural choice we're presented between the market and the state, where in reality they serve to complement one another in a form of technocratic corporatism which features a revolving door between big business and big government. While adherents are arguing for different system ideologies, the emerging synthesis is accommodating both in such a way to only serve the narrow benefit of an elite at the expense of dissent by creating an amoral paradise of materialism, sensuality, and distractions. The culture of the Left which encourages a descent into fantasy which is only harmful to those foolish enough to believe it or give power to such tautologies has become a national ethic, a useful guise to hide truth through an endless succession of increasingly useless questions.

The Right surrendered any stake in the culture war save for some isolated fights of camps to this idea of letting an intelligent market decide, an investment in the very humanism and relativism the Left argues the state should push. The few actual heterodox thinkers are currently under assault as we seek to break a false dialectic and are beginning to be branded as terrorists guilty of thought crime for assuming meaning should have value over power. Loyalty to one's own is becoming akin to treason in a world that is a revolt against truth and nature. As I sometimes say, we elevate the vices and call virtues discriminatory, so how can we call our culture anything but weak and wicked?

Laws have shown themselves incapable of protecting us against these onslaughts, as judges far overstep the boundaries of their office to defend the corrupt and powerful, and conversely offer extreme punishments to those who are often guilty of the most trivial offenses in terms of human impact. They have a phalanx of law enforcement which selectively enforces regulations to meet political expectations in a widening cultural gap, with the cities going one direction, the countryside going the other, and those officers involved becoming just a cudgel to be used to slam one's own opponents. In such an environment, even our most basic liberties have come under assault with repeated attacks upon the First, Second, Fourth, and Tenth Amendments. These attacks have degraded our republic into a virtual democracy already, wherein the rights the citizens purportedly still possess are so circumscribed as to be indefensible in many circumstances.

We know we cannot gather for free speech without violence and lawfare, that our gun rights may be revoked in many places on the basis of rumor, that the government spies on all we do, asks other friendly governments to help in an institutional quid pro quo, and that our states are prostrate to Federal money and partisan showmanship. All we can pray is that the law doesn't notice us lest we become the next victim losing our liberties, even our children, to its ever growing authority, specifically at a time when we have never shared less in common as a people about what would be the right thing for government to do.

Corruption is as inevitable in an economically failing effort as rats fleeing a sinking ship. With America now well over twenty trillion dollars in debt, with well over forty trillion dollars in unfunded liabilities, and a series of commitments both domestically and internationally we cannot possibly hope to pay even if we leveraged both all the work capacity and debt load of every single citizen, we live on borrowed time financially. Only the widespread ignorance of the general public and their willingness to work ever harder for decreasing returns is somehow keeping the debt-based system of usury and credit afloat. But even this is reaching a breaking point where the next major financial disruption, which may start because of the many problems existing here or the even larger batch of issues afflicting countries abroad, will see economic ruin visited upon us. It goes without saying that the idea of perpetual growth without consequence is an impossibility on a finite world such as ours, and as a few clever commentators have noted, it is in fact the ideology of cancer applied to finance. Cancer does not care what it kills, only that it expands until it seeks the next host. In the age of globalism, we should consider that for all our generosity to the world, all the treasure we have spent rebuilding everywhere but our own home, all the blood we shed naively for wars to advance some cause or another, now we are squarely in the target for destruction because having saved everyone we could, we have nothing left to offer. Expect no sympathy in our desperate hour, for our folly is not one others will likely soon repeat.

America served a vital international role for many years. We were the arsenal of democracy, and by that, we really should say we were the shock troops used to keep the new international order in line that was formally codified at Breton Woods. We saw our dollar degraded from gold to paper, and our debt spiral out of control. We fought war after war for corporate profit, to sustain the petrodollar, and to promote so called democracy for people who did not want it, but who were afterward made to keep the banks and global institutions that followed lest they be bombed into oblivion. We gave our all, believing the best of our leaders, and here in these closing hours of the republic, we see all they gave us in return was their laughter, scorn, and contempt.

Those are strong words and I'll spend the next few chapters putting meat on the bones that I am laying out here so you can consider the case. But whomever you choose to blame, the inescapable reality is America will not survive on the path we are following. Furthermore, there is zero political will to move away from the course we have undertaken. The Left is dancing around as if this is a Dionysian rite, enjoying the revels before the mother of all hangovers. One faction of the establishment Right is retreating into bunkers, while the other chases every dollar like a Brinks truck just crashed on the interstate. No one thinks about the future because no one cares. No one believes it matters.

There are superficially approved causes like the ever-changing idea of climate change, a term that has been settled upon after global cooling gave way to global warming and is now threatening to change once more. It's interesting to notice that looking at solar behavior, something any farmer knows how to do, is a better predictive model than what all the eggheads are paid to promote. As should now be obvious, our long-term ideas are only allowed to exist to the extent they support the homogenization of people of disparate cultures against their will, the mobilization of non-elected governmental agencies, and a global development toward a singular common new world order.

But even in this cause, we here in America are told that we should not have children, that we should not have a future, and we must give away that which is ours to others because of guilt. We are told we are a failure of civilization despite having advanced more scientific innovation, amassed more wealth and projected more power than any civilization in history. One wonders what we could have accomplished even at this late hour if even a single leader had arisen to dedicate that power to some good or useful cause. But we live in the twilight of empire where selfishness masquerades as virtue and the comforts of wealth serve as deterrent against bold action. It's interesting why great civilizations always succumb to barbarism, which seems oddly impossible as a recurring thing until you live through it like we are.

Having achieved so much, the people seem to collectively lose the will to care about what they build, and the habits of luxury persuade us to descend into harmful levels of introspection and indifference. Some indulge the lack of a meaningful identity through mere materialism, others through vain intellectualism, but what diversity and tolerance really represent is the absence of a united identity. And that's where we are: We have the States of America which are United no more, and from that framework, if any, we must now find those who are either awake or might be shaken from their stupor to realize that life goes on, and if we don't want our children to suffer, we need to plan a tomorrow for them.

One challenge some often have with my writing is that I jump quickly from the micro to the macro, talking about a specific example in one paragraph and escalating to a centuries long trend in the very next thought. I accept this criticism because two things are true about my thinking which I'll share here in hopes it will make what follows easier to understand. Firstly, I tend to intuit solutions and awareness, so I often know a thing before I know how I know it, and then I have to go back to find the evidence to prove or disprove my conclusion, but my mind has always made intuitive leaps to go a few steps ahead. In reality, this makes my life very difficult because I'm often explaining things that are going to happen several years down the line because the dots are connecting faster, which is why *"The Coming Civil War"* nailed so many of the problems of the culture war two years before others were willing to go there, and why this book is predicting the fight we're going to get stuck in somewhere between one to five years before I think it finally properly begins.

As I explained in the second chapter on culture, my thinking is not linear. It is cyclical. My training as a medieval scholar ironically helps here, because what I see is that the interactions between different systems on recurring intervals are the key to understanding history. Only ignorant fools think Marx with his idea that history has some grand denouement, or any other linear progression could explain the scope and breadth of history. Instead, I root my analysis in the study of overlapping systems with support from the idea that basic human nature does not change. We suppress and express who are differently in different epochs, but harnessing that energy remains a constant, and so if we are honest enough to admit people are going to do certain things as universals – make love, have families, protect their kin – it's not too hard to predict how people will handle even the hardest of situations. The cyclical nature of history is such that as generations die out and institutional knowledge of certain scenarios is lost, we have to relearn those lessons through experience alone, a fact hardwired into how infants approach the world which we never really can escape. When we look forward, we can think about what we have forgotten, what we cannot ask another we trust to answer, and know those are the questions we must ask now.

That is why the topic of this book is ultimately a question which we must now resolve, whatever the cost required, and that is settling down to this fundamental question: democracy? V Or liberty? Is it more important that we satisfy the desires of a majority created by self-interested and unaccountable parties, to whatever great or sordid end, and thereby submit ourselves to a collective which will grow large enough to perhaps consume the world, or do we instead assert certain values are, in fact, self-evident enough in their value that we will restrain this advance and assert independence once more against this nebulous, yet all the more threatening manifestation of suppressing the individual?

Each side has probed the other and found their weakest point, and I could reduce the argument further to quality versus quantity. Is our obligation to advance our best? Or cater to the whims of our least capable? This is the march of history, and it has been noted that when two compelling ideas face one another – two cultures with different truths seek each other out – one must win yet both will be shaped by the victory and the defeat.

In this book, I am leaving a bread crumb trail for the side I prefer, which is my belief that liberty remains paramount. As I will argue, I still believe in natural law, that grace requires choice, that it is a divine mandate in fact to preserve the path to choose even as we should defend that which is good, and it is the moral case that has been lacking in order to bring this conflict to fruition. The Right knows what is being presented is wrong, but can't quite find the right words why, because we are led astray by our senses, by the ideologies we are offered, and from the many interruptions that make us forget we're fighting a culture war now because we know the other side is offering something that simply isn't good for us. There really is nothing new under the sun – a person reading Ecclesiastes could learn the same – because history is cyclical.

But what we find is that America is being set up for the fall because the entire world is making the opposite choice. In truth, most countries never even had a chance as they have been under oppression forever, and we foolishly allowed our greater capacity to be bent to that service against our interests for a very long time. If the history interests you, my earlier books cover it well enough, but it's sufficient here to assert that the global order which now threatens America was largely facilitated with our blood, treasure, and commitment. Now, having served the purpose of creating an interconnected world, our once tolerated anachronisms are being eyed for destruction, which should be obvious to anyone who pays attention to the media.

The powers that be don't inherently hate White people, heterosexual marriage, cultural homogeneity, or the Christian faith (well, that last point is arguable) because so many of them practice these things better than the population does at large, but what they hate is the idea of any alternate authority people might rally around in loyalty and unity against the system that is coming into being. So, they destroy that which is healthy and promote that which is sick because they want us gone so they can inherit the Earth in their own image, and this revolt of the elites is a new thing in human history that is crucial to our story. They are not destroying what is bad in America, they are deliberately wrecking all that is good because like any would be dictators, they hate competition. And true freedom is the most dangerous idea of all, as it ever has been.

Chapter 6: The Revolting Elites

These next few chapters offer a far deeper analysis of the true threat we face than you will commonly hear publicly presented. My additional evolution to the coming civil war simply being the result of two naturally developing opposing sides is that these conflicts are deliberately cultivated through policy malfeasance to accomplish certain cynical ends by actors who benefit. The first five chapters were designed to make clear to you that America is not just falling apart, but instead is being deconstructed in multiple ways. I laid this out specifically so you can begin to understand that our problems are not accelerating toward conflict just because of the disagreements we clearly have, which we will spend the middle third of the book describing, but that we are constantly maneuvered into causing these problems to advance and fester. It would be madness if reality were what it seemed to be, so the question we have to ask is whether people are so foolish, or if we merely aren't seeing the whole game, so our decisions are based on faulty information

I submit to you that we only see a part of the picture, and whether you ultimately agree or disagree with this section, that won't change the fact that we will ultimately end up stuck working through the same problems on the ground. Where the larger picture certainly matters is in choosing what we should target as we begin our own long march toward health. ◉And unlike the moves that deliberately unmade America, our march will not constitute years of undermining institutions and building shadows to cast a vision of the future that only slowly reveals itself. Instead our efforts will be directed toward removing those institutions and the actors responsible for the destruction of America specifically and the West more broadly. If we hope not to repeat this sad epoch in our civilization's increasingly questionable future, we need to really understand deeply and fully what got us in this insufferable mess.

We start here with a chapter I hinted at but should have written long ago, which connected the two books of mine that the most people have read, which were my profile of the 20th Century: *"Someone Has to Say It"* and my analysis of the then present moment, the foundation for this work in *"The Coming Civil War"*. When I spoke about the emerging two sides in the latter of those two works, in the interest of detail, I quickly glossed over the role of the vanishing elites who had lost control of the ability to rein in either the insurgents on the far left or the far right who have been becoming the tails that wag the political dog.

Perhaps a better metaphor would be that the radicals have become that itchy spot which must constantly be scratched lest one be driven to madness from the constant irritation. Especially recently, the elites seemed to be losing control of the system to the two alternatives which seemed emergent in the nationalists and the communists, and so the idea the existing order could continue much longer seemed less viable.

That pronouncement was premature, because beneath the ever-changing labels applied to things, beneath the jumble of contradictions being foisted upon us all in confusion about what constitutes normalcy and legitimacy, we've seen that the elites have proven damnably effective in kneecapping the nationalists. This ranges from neutering the Trump Presidency from relevancy, to casting a movement which only argued for love for the ethnic majority as would-be terrorists in most minds. While the embers linger on, the push toward nationalism is but a mere shadow of itself, while the terror which exists to keep people on edge is rooted in a version of Leftism which is so farcical that it is inherently self-limiting, even as society has learned to mouth the pleasant lies tact requires.

Fundamentally, the old system has proven resilient in that the rich are still getting richer. And even if they have had to become a bit more mobile to enjoy their booty, the world has never been a smaller place. For the hyper wealthy, the world is a pleasure of delights, and so long as they can continuously escape the consequences that poorer folk experience daily from their so-called policy initiatives, things are pretty good. You can see it in the mountain retreats or the gentrified centers of those cities that are being preserved, in other countries as well as America, that the old guard is still hanging on and wielding their infrastructure well enough to thwart any serious challenge for the moment. Their risk is not so much from below now, but rather from their own greed in the system they've created which has basically put the entire world in nominal debt.

I call them the revolting elites as a deliberate double entendre because I find their love of excess and gregarious display of wealth unbecoming and frankly rude. But more importantly, beyond what you or I may think of them, what we need to understand is the class warfare they funded took an angle that most would not have expected, as we see the fulfillment of Orwell in the new dream they have.

The hellscape they are slowly allowing to come into being beneath them in so many places is the perfect playground to distract the little people, while those who are welcome rise above and bifurcate human civilization between those who have influence and those who do not. They have lifted up the ladders of social mobility, and shut the gates of the golden castle and ivory towers for all but a selected few who will exist in perpetual obligation to the new nobility.

The story of how this happened is a very long one which I would argue should be traced back to at least 1648 in the West, and the Treaty of Westphalia. That agreement which ended the extremely bloody Thirty Years War which was nominally between Protestants and Catholics in Germany but had many other angles involved, also brought into being the present system where violence was going to be reserved solely as the province of the state. This is why modern political science teaches that the state must have a monopoly on violence, and be the ultimate arbiter who can use the power of life and death over right and wrong.

This treaty marked a divestiture from sharing such power with people directly through mercenary bands, and an attack upon the once powerful ecclesiastical rites which Catholicism exercised nominally, if less rarely in reality, in the name of virtue. It was the birth of a system of humanist secularism that took morality out of the equation, evolved quickly into the continuity of certain states indefinitely as common interest beneficial to all who were at the table, and was probably the actual beginning of the nation-state.

Although wars continued as they always would in Europe, what happened was a period of relative calm, expansion, and discovery, but also of consolidation of centralized power throughout the West. The State became the body public, and essentially it consisted of an elite which either had or did not have a monarch at the head, but its survival depended upon having stewardship over a group of people of increasingly shared cultural and linguistic background, a novel development, and cultivating their growth in a way that allowed for both influence and material benefit. As paternalistic as it truly is, the elites had to care about the little folk beneath them for their own power to endure, and so their rational self-interest forced them to act with a degree of prudence and restraint. This worked mostly well until 1789 when things changed.

The French Revolution was truly a crisis of civilization. Whereas the American Revolution, even in success, was essentially a coup within the existing order driven by American stakeholders not wanting to be reduced to the peasantry status of most Britons within the Empire like the Irish and Scots, which Franklin wrote about in great detail before the war began, the ultimate goals of the American rebels fit the old global system in a way that the French did not.

The French Revolution was not staged by a group of gentleman farmers asserting their liberty in a limited state, but it was an angry outcry of a mob which was incensed by the failure of their leadership to provide for their benefice, and it quickly evolved into the first major awful ideological bloodletting of the people to purify the state against the elites. Louis XVI and Marie Antoinette were but an exemplar of a nation which purged itself of its powdered wigs, and it would take an entire generation only with the final defeat of Napoleon in 1815, child of that revolution, to see its energies squelched. But even the Holy Alliance and the Congress of Vienna could do nothing to stop the idea that the French Revolution popularized: that a system should exist which gave power to the people as opposed to the leadership class. Truly, do we not even in America today see the rallying cry of the progressive is far closer to that of the French in "Liberty, Equality, and Fraternity" than the "Life, Liberty, and Property" of America's founders? Important here is the difference in what liberty means in

English versus French. Whereas liberty in English conveys the Germanic ideal of freedom to the individual, in French, it means having the power to use government to control other actors, an evolution from Latin. Ask yourself which doctrine has truly won?

The elites always knew the system of wealth and balance like America enjoyed in the 19th Century was not a threat. Rather, threat arose from the sort of radicalism that France spawned, and which flared out violently from time to time as in the Revolutions of 1830 and 1848. These created fermenting mash from which Marx emerged, and where the people stormed the barricades to seek access to power. The origins of our present democracy in the West are not so much the consideration of Pericles' Athens, but instead the angry revolutionaries of the Paris Commune. They were suppressed for many years, but with the dawning of the 20th Century, things changed. Industrialization and the competition between nations which was rising forced the elites to invest ever more authority in the plebs for their survival against one another in these contests, and because they needed the help of the people, the balance of power shifted away from the elites. In this sense, systems gained power because people were looking for a way to escape the control of others whom they could not always perceive but whom they sensed to be out there. Populism was sincere, for the most part, as progressivism or nationalism are today, in terms of the rank and file.

But the full mobilization of the state was anathema to the elites and was incredibly costly. Heads of state were being toppled like the Tsar in Russia and the Kaiser in Germany. Old orders outside the West were no more secure, like the death of the imperial rule in China or the militarization of Japan. The world was becoming smaller, closer, and more connected, yet the disruptions were a real threat to elite power, and the people themselves, in trying to solve the many contradictions of an age of incredible achievement and mass mobilization, were also leading to a global bloodletting both between states and within states which may never again be seen in history. This culminated in World War II, the ultimate battle of ideology and systems logic, wherein systems narrowly defeated nationalist populism by using the methods of their enemy, and where people died by the tens of millions in just the latest war to end all wars. It was a war with no clear winner, some very damaged losers, and some countries that would never recover, except perhaps for the United States which though in balance with the Soviet Union emerged as global hegemon for all but the Russian periphery.

This is where we need to pick the story back up with the understanding that the nationalism of World War II was in many ways the culmination of the revolt of 1789, and the idea ideology should be fought to the death with a single system to win the world, or dominate whatever sphere sought therein because of the value of the system itself.

At the surface level, we still believe this logic, and this is still what our schools teach and how we seem to orient our lives. But with the addition of nuclear weaponry to the mix, the elites began talking to one another and had a different realization. They saw that these wars would only end with death for everyone, but most especially themselves and their own status, and so between the new and the old, across cultures, the world of total political conflict began to give way to stage management.

The United Nations was the happy idealistic cover for a system of mutual banking arrangements, defense treaties, but also and more importantly the development of a transnational elite class of people who exist above the fray. It would be global in scope, and take years to fully pull together, but it would draw inspiration from the tenacity of global finance, the accessibility of the English aristocracy, and the universality of the still existent Catholic Church. It would try to be all things to all people and homogenize people so we would stop fighting one another and be controlled. We would be given means to satisfy our needs, and different systems were tried ranging from the communism of the USSR to the capitalism of the US. But what would never be permitted in any case was a claim upon the truth that had proven so deadly when people took it up as their mantle.

A lesser world would be one no one would fight over, and that's just what the elites created. An age of universal decadence, at least to appearances, where America would surrender her liberty and provide security for all and wealth to many, distributing the fruits of our people's labor to provide for a universal peace, a Pax Americana, of commerce and benign socialism where speech and appearance of choice were universally pushed to mollify the ever waiting mob through democracy. But were these democracies ones where people had choice, or had power migrated away from politics altogether to different entities: To banks that owned the debt, to nonprofits that pushed ideas and toppled heretics, to churches who spoke the gospel of man?

Look at the world, at the missions of the organizations that seem to have the most impact and ask if they serve their stated interests or if they are just placeholders in a bigger system. Check out the Open Society Foundation as just one prominent example amongst many alternatives. Do they serve the people, their cause, or those who write their checks? It seems to me the latter is far more often the case, and yet no one ever wants to question the system because we're allowed the appearance of disagreement without the reality of actually threatening the status quo. To be honest, the people themselves have largely agreed, because so long as they have enough comfort and are allowed to bitch sufficiently, people only want to assert their rights to freedom, not the consequences of such exercise which must ever be violent and unpredictable.

From this context, the revolt of the elites might not appear so bad. In truth, this is how many of them see their own position and if you were to read behind the lines about what is printed in the Economist or the Atlantic, two establishment journals of record, they would probably acknowledge their deliberate and thankless job of stage managing the people against their own desires for more has been a most successful and useful mission. The problem is, they've become a class unto themselves, an international cartel who gives honor not to the cultures, people, or even fundamentally foundational laws of the nations which facilitated their rise or status, but in solidarity to one another against the people.

While they may have kept the peace for a very long time, although at the cost of destroying so much of what made each nation distinct, like wrecking the American republic, curtailing every liberty, and giving us an insolvent security state, elites also have done so largely for their own benefit and now we are reaching a crisis where the arguably beneficial appearance of their order is clearly tarnishing. You see the same people who push democracy everywhere now working for opposite purposes in reality, because what they have ever desired is control, and the many inconsistencies in the oft changing narrative are but reflection of the true scope of the battle.

The elites hate nationalism because they know it is an existential threat to them. Whatever singular order the people accept, whether it be capitalist, communist, or other, is one they can manage without seriously threatening their own status or that of the opposite number. But when people assert the right to be treated as distinct entities and demand leadership in that vein, such that demands a genuine morality that is neither subjective nor relativistic, fights will become inevitable. Elites push for peace not because they value life, but because they value their own lives, and that's why we're given international wars against countries that displease them, like those who exist outside the banking system, so that those energies get exhausted in the public and in the body politic.

Yet, we in the West know our moral gap between a life with meaning and a life with comfort is growing, and in that space is the rising conflict they cannot control and which they most deeply fear.

I sometimes say the future belongs to the faithful because the reality is that people willing to kill and die for something will always defeat those who only exist to sustain their own comforts. The decadence of late empire has afflicted the West and incorporated much of the world for the moment, although I believe other regions are just using this interregnum to their benefit to catch up technologically before they exert the will to push their ideas, and that's why this still young century will likely be quite bloody. But as bad as that is, the reality is there are things that matter more than life and making it so quality is forever subsumed to quantity is only creating a pressure cooker that will lead to an even nastier explosion of the conflagration than the old system.

It's worth keeping in mind these problems of how we endure even as we seek to unmake a system hateful to us as we go forward, however, as they are not trivial and those of us who support liberty, nationalism, or distinction better be able to answer how we will deal with contradictions without lighting the world on fire. The elitist answer of offering control by turning humanity into less so there's nothing worth killing for might be cynical, yet it has had some success. The question of whether we can agree to disagree, and have our own spaces, finding the balance between allowing dissent and seeking consensus, not in the mere sense of political policy, but in a deeper spiritual and cultural sense is our challenge, and the heart of whether or not we will be able to offer resistance. Thus far, our disagreements are why the global order is of their creation, because we know what we don't know and have yet to find a sufficiently compelling counter vision.

That question will remain moral, but let's look next at the structures of how this control system works, how ideology is subsumed into productive ways to sustain the organization, and most terrifyingly, take just a peek at the ideology of our betters and how they hope to escape the mess they've created in trying to solve the most impossible problem that is humanity.

Chapter 7: The Eschatology of Modern Elitism

The question of how to unite a disparate set of people such as the modern global elite, inherently has to begin with self-interest. People who shared nothing in common in terms of culture, civilization, and common background historically would have been at war with one another in perpetual strife, with moments of peace, and serve as surrogates for larger struggles, but in the true vein of Western progressive tradition, they've tried to break the cycle and create a moment of progress.

We spoke in the second chapter in some depth about the cultural vacuum of the West and how even our constructed debate conceals a deeper agreement that our true religion has become secular agnostic materialist humanism. That which makes us rich and does not place too many obligations upon us or on others, and which allows us a comfortable and unquestioned life is the best system. Within such a framework, you can begin to see how people from disparate cultures could sign up to the system so long as their essential status was not threatened. Ultimately, wealth transfers were conducted to make sure everyone was on board, and the great sucking sound of the economy and innovation of the West was used as inducement to bring everyone else on board to create a strange and artificial world which imagined war to be a thing of the past.

Instead, conflicts would shift to the world of economic competition with trade being used as a civilizing force where economics would constrain the ability of the states, now increasingly bought by the elites, even as they would be run by democratic proxies, and where the bottom line expectations of the citizenry of different nations themselves would demand peace, prosperity and plenty.

For a while, the so-called McDonald's theory that two countries that both ate Big Macs would not fight one another looked to have some legs, and even today, we see how it works in practice. China might love to dump the American sovereign debt, but to do so would be to destroy their biggest export market. Conversely, America might be tempted to slay the Red Dragon with their own color revolution, but big business would never forgive losing such a huge source of their manufacturing and access to the world's largest market. It's ironic that the capitalists are the biggest fan of the communists, but in an amoral world where transactions are everything, it's not really surprising.

That's why the United Nations is a farce used by diplomats for countries to provide showmanship for political play back home, but the real action has been with entities like the World Bank, the Bank of International Settlements, the Vatican Bank, the European Central Bank, the Bank of London, and the Federal Reserve Bank of our own United States. They who make the money make the rules, and banking and high finance control the fates of nations through control of the money supply, liquidity, and all the economics that follow. If one nation stands against them, you'll see a coalition of over one hundred fifty others arise in response.

Now, one might comment that this should mean an end to conflict, but the peculiar trait of the rule of the elites is that warfare is a feature of the system. The wrinkle is that so long as the countries who adhere to the system are never threatened – with the map of countries now being fixed as sovereignty has become a new value that matters between nations, yet oddly enough never within them – they can run whatever system they want as long as the numbers check out and the loans are printed as required. Warfare that keeps the citizens in check and gives distractions is welcome, and occasionally larger fights are encouraged to release lucrative contracts for war, for the security state, and for the process of rebuilding. These elites know that war truly is the health of the state, and having put most nations under their thrall, they are not shy about having the little people kill one another in huge numbers if necessary, so long as the system isn't threatened.

What they value is stability and their own supremacy. They hide their power from the world of politics whenever they can but flaunt their influence in high culture by showing the glorification of the celebrity, of the rich and powerful who are not subject to mortal man's rules. No longer do any of our societies from the decadent West to the stringent corners of the Islamic world truly honor morality, but instead we celebrate status based solely upon the garish display of wealth and prestige. The door is shown to be open for a lucky few, for those of exceptional talent as well as those most willing to manipulate those who propel them to fame, and having a small degree of mobility to the lower rungs of the good life prevents opposition from arising even as the core of the elites remains the hyper wealthy who have generational wealth and status.

Consider a person like George Soros, who almost certainly is a placeholder for other elites who more shrewdly don't serve as a focal point for their opposition, as an exemplar. He buys media, buys nonprofits to shape the media, buys governments, and manipulates the market to cause outcomes. The hidden hand of Adam Smith has given way to the velvet glove of a globalized banking system that uses debt to control outcomes, and bribes to select which actors on the ground will receive their blessing to determine the agenda. The fight continues always, but only within certain constrained parameters, as the real dangers as we experienced in the previous century and before are not to be unleashed. For every Soros, there are many other billionaires who play the same game more silently, but in equal dedication and concert to ensure the system itself endures.

Not many people talk about these institutions of higher banking which bankroll the billionaires, but I sometimes call them the global magicians because what they actually do at this point is mostly make money out of thin air. In the age of fiat where all things are relative, and the value of currency in the public mind is primarily measured as one coin or note against the next, the only constraint banks have encountered thus far about their printing of pure profit is their ability to adapt the public imagination.

The magicians know this, and we trust them enough to keep the spell afloat because we imagine, as we always try, that heaven can come here on Earth. Transhumanism has led them to a new practice, and it is a curious and unsettling idea they hunt with their wealth and status as we're relegated to conflicts considered much pettier to resolve.

What would a person who already has everything possibly want? If you could enjoy all this world offers, knowing your status was secure, that you were above the law and beyond reproach, king in your court, what would you try? At some point, opulence becomes boredom and a triviality for a life accustomed to having no want. Yet, the last constraint upon humanity is well known by all and that has been the appointment of that limited lot of time for each of us to inhabit our mortal coils before we move onward. It is the one challenge left for civilization to conquer, and if you begin reading what the elites talk about amongst themselves, you'll see what they want is nothing less than eternal life.

Can we cheat death? Should we cheat death? What would we have to become to overcome our own mortal limitations? If you read trans-humanist writings, a cult of humanism that draws many billions in funding and which is the object of many of our more talented scholars, the belief is that consciousness may be able to transcend matter and exist in perpetuity on this world. There is no greater gift you could offer the person who has absolutely everything than the promise they can keep it forever, and such a promise fundamentally changes human nature. Instead of a world where one has children to ensure the continuation of one's values, one's culture, or one's memories, a few people are now betting they will be able to live forever as individuals, not as soul filled humanity racked by medieval superstition, but as the thoughts in the box that makes the most sense for long-term preservation.

When someone starts to imagine a world where they can live forever, and their best friends can make it alongside them, the first thoughts that might arise is that paradise might be achieved as we could live in balance with one another. Maybe our intellect might finally turn to wisdom and we could build upon the overcoming of differences by inhabiting a world of fantasy where every option is indulged without the messy and threatening intrusion of reality. Yet, for as much as some of these people imagine this future for themselves, do you think most of them want that future for you and yours, for the little people who propelled them at some previous hour to their status above and beyond?

Every civilization and nation has had its own elites, yet their advantage in logistics and influence was always tempered by their need for people to do their bidding, the numerical supremacy of the people who lived below, and the moral constraints of their specific time that limited what could be done culturally. Now that everything goes, no one cares that elites exist in solidarity with one another, and people below fight battles which are only laughable to those who have bought their way out, how much is this changing? In a world of automation, where technology can provide security and the advent of artificial intelligence might displace huge swathes of human labor, have we reached the point where the people are needed so little that the herd may be culled, and this breakaway civilization leave us behind?

They call this the singularity. Our oligarchs worship the forthcoming revelation of an artificial intelligence, a God made from the works of man, who increasingly looks to be informed as the sum experience of mankind, the goal of deep learning computers. They think a world can be made which is so much better than this one if only we give up our archaic beliefs, give power over to them, and then disappear as rocket fuel as they jettison into the stratosphere of a far happier future. They want man to become the machine because once that happens, death becomes a thing of the past. Whether life does as well is a better question, but in the struggle for power over meaning, those who have decided to abandon belief for control are now approaching the end game for their own planning.

If you ever wonder why it seems like those with the most resources don't care that the world is falling apart, that's because many of those who should be, and would have been, responsible for fixing the problems of civilization are just as checked out as the poor person who spends all day in a drug induced haze playing video games. The only difference is their ticket isn't leading to the gutter, but instead is promising them a nirvana beyond pain and suffering.

The biggest problem they have, frankly, is how to deal with the rest of us, and seeing us destroy one another is a cost-efficient solution to a most irritating problem. The elites have divested themselves of the mass of humanity as an obsolete means of production and have left many to suffer and disappear as flotsam as they launch upwards.

When you wonder why they spend millions or even billions of dollars to influence everyone else into fighting one another, remember the key precept of economics. The entire question is built upon the presumption of scarcity, which is intimately related to the idea of time. If you had a theoretically infinite amount of time with which to conduct your business, scarcity becomes a question of commitment rather than necessity. Furthermore, in a debt-based system of usury and money, where inflation is ignored and money is constantly produced, buying time to enact these changes by putting as much capital as needed into the system to keep it rolling until these goals are achieved is a nearly free investment.

Because money comes from thin air, those who decide how it operates control the world because people can and do sell their souls for those little bills and the response they buy. Yet, the world might be moving beyond those right beneath our noses, and with most people utterly oblivious.

If we wanted to fight the right and just war to reclaim humanity against a future that is the single biggest threat to our species, we'd drop all other conflicts as one human race and take down the banks and the bankers, liberating ourselves from the amorality of the market, the oligarchical political systems that are mostly for sale to the highest bidder, and assert our independence from tyrannical states of all flavors. We would defend our very nature against the idea that transforming someone into some other material form means they are still the same on the inside. Because the age of the machines is coming, and ultimately, for all the terrifying things I write, that's the battle all too few are thinking about seriously which will consume all our lives before the century is through. Most worryingly, the machines are very likely to be imbued with the logic of the most mercenary and selfish of our own stock, perhaps existing as simulacra who uploaded themselves.

I know that world sounds like science fiction and it's beyond what you likely expected to read in this book. But I'm telling you what those who have extreme means talk and think about, because it isn't about re-enacting the ideological wars of the 19th or 20th Century. They just leave us those as our entertainment, knowing that a stalemate by us is a victory for them, and that the triumph of capitalism or communism would be different only in what few people earn golden tickets. But the elites still remember and fear a mass mobilization of the people in search of a moral ideal, or in support of one another as part of a deeper and visceral identity, because such men and women would have both the chance and the motivation to offer genuine resistance. The one thing they genuinely fear is being named as targets and pursued for their misdeeds.

We can't start our fight there, but what I am sharing here is just like in the video games people still play today, it often ends up that the first boss we fight will not be the last boss. And as we fight our fellow citizens in the realm of ideas, the question I ask you to keep asking is this: who is getting funded and why? Is it because these people believe in their cause, or is it because the right useful idiots distract us from pursuing goals that are a greater threat to the system? That is why I believe this strange battle will see enemies become allies before the end, and why I devote a large section of my book to explaining how so many people from the poorest to the powerful are all being played. Because we are, and until we unite behind an idea the majority of us believe, we will be powerless to stop the very inhuman future that our new masters intend.

Chapter 8: The Problem of Bigness

A recurring theme in this section of the book is the emphasis on a false paradigm. The reason I keep returning to this point is because we are instinctively programmed to think we are exercising free will whenever we make a choice. In a narrow sense, this is undeniably true, but the main intellectual evolution of the Enlightenment, assuming one calls it that, has been a revolution in thought to realize anew something Socrates demonstrated just as clearly to ancient Athens: That one who controls the choices in the questions a person can consider ultimately controls the outcomes of their thought. Hegel said it best: Society is the process of theses and antitheses resolving into novel syntheses, a situation which is the ultimate cycle and will likely continue until the universe ends and certainly at least until each of us departs for elsewhere. If someone else is controlling the thesis and antithesis, are we truly exercising free will when choosing from the limited range of synthesis that those inputs provide?

You need to begin to break this conditioning for this book to have the fullest value, but also for the presumably far more important ability for you and your loved ones to survive. Never stop making choices and never give up free will, but recognize also that when there are two easy choices in A and B, the right option will often be choices never mentioned: C, D, or E. We live in a society where we are offered the choice of vanilla or chocolate ice cream as our selections, both being tasty treats, but ultimately without asking why we are not permitted something healthier instead since we're both pleased by the choice and delighted by the guilty pleasure of two easier options.

This second part is an equally important part of the mental trick being played on everyone more or less all the time now as we live under the age of marketing. When two or occasionally more choices are put before you, with both options being sub-optimal compared to an ideal condition but in a way that we can indulge habits that are either easy or pleasurable, we tend to accept the choice before us because we can justify something bad on the basis that we rejected something worse. Instead of standing our ground in defense of that which is good, the whole paradigm gets deliberately flipped upside down where the new normal becomes a battle to select the lesser of two evils. Add to this billions of dollars of propaganda designed to spread fear of the other for every choice, and you end up with the modern man, driven by paranoia and who believes his defense of the good is in restraining an existential threat from the opposition.

I'm guilty of this too. We all are. It's far easier to hate our enemies than hate the ideas they represent, and to be frank, my Christian learning has done far more to help me see past these traps than well over a hundred thousand dollars spent on a fancy degree or years in nonstop political conflict were able to teach. The dialectic is the descent into madness through the implement of reason, where a series of false choices so degrades the ability of the mind to think that the very search for progress becomes akin to counting to infinity. It is so far beyond both our instincts and our reckoning, that as we choose not to turn away and recognize those things beyond knowledge which can be understood only through perhaps instinct, habit, or faith alone, that we become trapped in an eternal game of ping pong that is the intellectual equivalent of a toddler screaming "I know you are, but what am I?"

The bigger the problem, the more the scope of the question or the challenge is beyond our ability to resolve through direct action, the more quickly we settle into divisive camps to attack the question. This issue of bigness is at the heart of how the elites manage control over our society where choices and institutions of power are always centralized upward in such a way as to take advantage of the aforementioned mental quirks to ensure the right balance between compliance and distraction.

Instead of having fifty states to choose from for how we want to live, a system much more difficult to dominate and control, America has been transformed into a mercantile and ideological empire where we are given two mirror image parties to choose from whose very claim to existence consists only of preventing the other side from succeeding.

Think about that more deeply for a moment. How can any nation, let alone one as large as ours, hope to advance successfully to new challenges when the very basis of our system is an unsolvable conflict which only divides partisans into two irreconcilable camps whose cause for being is basically to suppress the other? Can we truly advance when the end result has been either paranoia where all efforts go into building those restraints, or alternatively, where frustration has become so immense that people have given up on politics altogether? If you were the one calling the plays, you would be thrilled with either of these outcomes because you've created apolitical man where he accepts that this world's affairs are beyond both his control and his concern, at the same time that you've rendered those who care inert. The referee has fixed the game, and I don't think it will surprise anyone to know the rule book is written by those who can pay to adjust it as needed and who control capital flows in such a fashion that they effectively own the state and market alike.

The complementary nature of the market and the state, which is the false divide at the heart of our understanding of our nation, conceals something very important. Both parties ultimately can express different nominal ideologies and work for the same common interest. Immigration is an easy example where the profit motive of cheap labor works for the market forces that are presented as the legitimate Right, and the humanists who demand the destruction of all national borders, an attack on distinction designed to make ever larger and simpler categories as their philosophical imperative for the added bonus of electoral benefit, gladly assist from the Left. Politics is a natural example for the phenomenon, but the tendency runs far deeper into most of the basic conflicts of our civilization. As we do not understand this and believe we have meaningful choices, we overlook the real sources of control as we watch the actors on the stage, and ignore the obvious strings dangling from the unseen hands gracefully manipulating from above.

For most of my life, I was always told the choice was between those who wanted to work for their money and those who wanted things for free. Any Republican reading this book will appreciate this basic moral messaging as it was the choice we were presented, where our job was to speak for those who believed earners should be supported and takers should be opposed as a moral statement. Compelling to some, especially those who worked hard to achieve, this basis of conservatism was rooted in a free market view that business was good because of a moral imperative of voluntary labor toward productive ends. Once again, that is an entirely understandable philosophy, but let's take a closer look at how big business actually behaves and trace this problem of bigness in the life cycle not of government, which we all know has spiraled out of control and away from accountability, but instead to a large corporation which is presented as a source of achievement in the modern economy and state.

Consider the life cycle of a business. Most of the largest firms that exist today usually share a humble beginning. Some individual, family, or small group developed a novel and helpful service, or a useful or previously unavailable product, and the quality and innovation of their idea launched them toward success. We enjoy what is new, especially when well done, and with this sort of development there is usually a period of growth and expansion that quickly follows, where the challenge lies in delivering the newest thing to all the people who want to catch the wave.

Depending upon the specific nature of the good or service, this can be a shorter or longer interval, but eventually that excitement fades as something new comes along to displace the company, yet the capital is still there and those who succeeded are invested in the effort now.

At this point, businesses tend to go one of two ways. Either they aim for a high level of consistency in service to a niche market, accepting they are what they are, and they can reach a certain segment to satisfy that need, or they seek to expand massively. In the first case, understanding the limitations of what can be achieved, the emphasis usually moves toward quality and toward delivering the best manifestation of what is available, while accepting that trying to be all things to all people is an unsustainable path that only proves destructive to both the love of the craft as well as to satisfying customers. This is why the local restaurant will always prove more distinctive than the chain brand, because it can take chances and devote sincere human effort in a way the push for constancy simply cannot permit. The price of merely being "not bad," put another away, manifests here in the inability to reach excellence.

Why do some businesses then go along the second path? The allure of greater wealth, greater status, and bigger market share is hard to resist. Besides, there is always the dream that somehow Bob's Burger might become the burger of choice, and for those who are sufficiently motivated and fortunate enough to have the opportunity, when there are no limits to expansion, the chance will often be taken to get bigger in pursuit of the dream that this will allow something better to emerge. There is a deep human need to create a stronger innovation, to find the chicken sandwich that is as good as that original burger as complement, and how often do we see growing companies put out new products that we want to like, but that never quite rise up to their original product?

But when all that money has been invested in success, growth becomes a justification unto itself, and the success of the past is leveraged to gain opportunity for the future. What often begins as a natural and self-sustaining mechanism, requires additional help if growth beyond its natural market is desired. Credit is necessary for this, and interest jumps into the equation as the lenders become involved. The excitement of development and innovation is suppressed, and they are replaced with the predictability of corporatization, in order to make sure the deliverable expectation to stakeholders and shareholders at the highest level happens. Burger Brand is created to take one good idea and build a world of fiction around it with one goal: to make sure this burger becomes the only burger you want to eat.

Once the pursuit of growth necessitates payment to shareholders, stakeholders and venture capitalists, the next phase is the rush toward monopoly where profits become everything, and the product is no longer something loved and pushed to excellence by its producer, but it is merely the means to an end. For those who rise to this rare air, have you noticed how every company near the top abandons their original principles, and focuses on the rush to the top? Call them to complain and instead of talking to a person, you're talking to a machine. Go to any of their many branches and you'll find either apathetic kids or shining kiosks waiting to serve you an utterly predictable meal. It might be tasty, but as time goes by, you'll notice things usually become more standardized and it won't be what you remembered. But, since they had such a good price, the other shops all closed down, and food is just food, you still stop sometimes, right?

Maybe they will add pizza and hot dogs to the menu too. It doesn't taste so good to be honest, but the little pizza shop closed down and something is better than nothing. I guess we should be grateful to have anything at all, but we do miss the old burgers. Maybe we should just stay home instead and ask where it all went wrong.

Forgive my little indulgence of storytelling, but that is the reality of big business in America today. What starts as a labor of love to offer a genuinely great product or service, or at least what people believe is one, becomes through the encounter with finance and the obligations it presents in terms of what choices are permitted to the public, an entity that only seeks to protect its continuity and profit margins. One could argue I am being too cynical, but I really doubt that as there is a well-understood connection between the size of an entity and its responsiveness to the public. Too big to fail is a very real thing, and we see this in how corporate bailouts are regularly conducted for the largest businesses, in the fashion government contracts are actively sought and even purchased to keep them afloat, and in the revolving door that exists to exchange personnel back and forth between big corporations and big government.

Compare the trajectory of our small business or the burger that I used for a sizzling hot example with the political career of most candidates. Maybe they go into the business motivated by one or two good ideas, but by the time they make all the compromises necessary to be electable, driven once again by the unseen hand of the donors who are invested in, sustain, and define the system, we end up with bland and insipid products whose best appeal is simply reduced to arguing what they are not, and an unending cycle of negativity continues. Centralization always leads to homogenization in such a way that predictability becomes emphasized over peak performance, and the big choices lead to sub-optimal outcomes. The people on top, having become accustomed to enjoying their status more than being motivated by their original desire to offer something truly of value, simply leverage their status to squash little guys, or buy legislation that will do it for them, and become unaccountable to those who exist beneath them and who made their rise possible.

This is the story of big business. This is also the same exact story of big government. As the nexus of these two sectors represents the true oligarchy of America, with banking just being the leading agent of big business and the bureaucracy being the sentinels to defend the interests of those who have sway in big government. It is a false choice. Our Founders actually understood this, which is why they not only put so many checks between branches of government, but tried desperately to keep the centralization of power or capital from happening because they saw in the corruption of the crown what could happen when power amassed in one unaccountable entity.

But whereas at least monarchy had the need to consider the support of the people lest a king be dethroned in a fit of public violence, our system has many kings who appear to have no thrones even as they sit atop piles of wealth and influence that would make the crowned heads of yore envious. Corporations and government are both beyond the law, legal fictions that have been created to protect our betters who own a legal system where justice exists only for those who can buy it.

We live in a Big Country. Big businesses dot our shopping malls, trying often to masquerade as local offerings through seductive architecture. Big parties spin out folksy ads to steal your vote even as donor fueled soirees set policy regardless of any platform process. We bask in the twilight of empire where wealth and opulence are an expression of power. But in spite of how well the elites meet our material needs and the number of people who are contented to play within this system, how many people are tired of lying parties and soulless jobs? Can marketing alone make up for our gut realization that most of our baubles are junk and that much of our entertainment makes us vaguely sick, representing the worst sort of voyeurism or exhibitionism?

Our governmental ideology is to rob tomorrow to pay for today, a choice of the duopoly of both parties which neither really threatens. All because when one is big, one has to consume incessantly just to survive, and the sports car we've built that runs fast but gets five miles to the gallon is running out of fuel.

When threatened, we know from long experience that capital flees and governments attack. As things become less sustainable in America, as the debts pile up and the millions of us stuck defending our survival in some tower of this broken system are pushed harder, the answer will inevitably be that we have to make more out of less. We have done this for fifty years already, where we seem to have more choices but they're really never quite as good, and where government provides more services than ever, but they end up being things either many of us don't want or which are done poorly. We have the illusion of choice, but the reality

114

of decay, and I wonder when we will realize that this is because we've put all our eggs in the basket farthest away from our ability to influence. The center is rotten, but it doesn't even know it, because they can afford to buy enough perfume to overwhelm the cognitive dissonance.

These cycles of history are well-understood of mercantile empires. It's why Athens lost to Sparta in the end, why the once mighty British Empire is now an overrun island where the people of empire have overrun the imperial base, and it is also why Rome fell. Each chose comfort and security over liberty and adventure, having lost faith in the path of its founders, and having devolved into a shadow of its former self. It is a moral degradation concealed by the many successes that live off past glories. If one wants more evidence, consult the work of Sir John Glubb who explains more or less perfectly the centuries old experience of business and government working in tandem to try to survive at the end of the imperial age. We are living that in America, and the elites here have tried a trick to buy time.

They've leveraged America to try to make the world their new market, trading away our liberties and options, to make the world one system where we all have the same leaders, the same systems, the same businesses, and the same banks. They hope to buy time to escape history and their own corruption, and while they work those problems, they leave us many fights to enjoy below. We fight over whether corporate welfare is worse or whether personal welfare is worse, never asking why we've agreed to have such a stupid battle at the heart of our political process. Don't misunderstand; I have my opinions just like every other American. But why is it that we never seem to ask the right questions?

Why do we always fall for choosing between the lesser of two evils when there are many other possibilities we should and must consider? The dialectic and psychology employed in defense of such are easy enough to understand, but to fully grasp the depth of what has been concocted, we need to factor the evolution of technology into the mix. The world has never been so connected and yet so far apart.

Chapter 9: The Technological Disconnect

Although I had a number of good friends, my experience in high school sucked. I was the kid with the funny voice, the uncool clothes, thick glasses, and who learned to fight only after being picked on enough times that I learned proactive self-defense. I was forced into a larger world that did not interest me from the world of science fiction, philosophy, and theology that was far more interesting, and for better or worse, I learned how to operate in the world which is why I dress well enough, talk intelligently, and interact better today. I didn't like being part of a larger whole, and given a different set of options, probably would not have been and would have retreated from any larger social connections, but that option was not available. I also graduated high school right before the Internet exploded and displaced actual human relationships as our primary form of networking.

I share this story to begin a discussion about how technology has changed everything, because we live in a world unrecognizable to someone who graduated high school just two short decades ago. The Internet is the inescapable intermediary that has reworked what communication means, shortening and simplifying how we express ourselves, but also which has replaced the generations old system of human networking with a new option. We now can self-select with whom we will associate in a way which has never been possible in human history.

Let's start with the positive. How exciting is it to find a community of people who share your obscure interests and to have that conversation which you've always wanted to enjoy but which would send those around you running in dread? I can discuss the finer point of alternative history for hours, argue the insights of Asimov versus Heinlein, or engage in theological warfare over revisionist eschatology all from the comfort of my own screen – no longer even bound to home or the moment before me, and evade the cruel drudgery of the world and the many boorish people who do not share my interests.

No longer would I have to hear about who won the sporting contest or what color or cut hair style was popular in the day. I could just retreat into my own cocoon and find other people there who share my beliefs, or at least my interests enough where I can simply relax among friends and shut the world out. We all know the world doesn't serve any of us, so at least our escape is a happy one, and we can find freedom at the tip of our fingers. Our minds may be truly liberated from our bodies and from society at last – or so it seems.

But the funny thing is our bodies still remain. As much as we might abuse them by inactivity and malnutrition, to feed the mind without working the body does not satisfy those needs which generations of instinct have hardwired irreducibly into us all. We need other people, and as much as we might intellectually delight in escapism, our hormones sink us into isolation, loneliness, despair, and alienation as

118

those who do not fit into the mainstream broadcast become exiles who are forgotten. We are told we have the joy of our friends, the people who really understand us, but the price of immersing ourselves in the world we want to be true is losing any grasp of that which is real, because of how we invest our time and because of long learned habits of escape.

I try to imagine if I were just entering adulthood today, which I would choose. Would I choose this world as it is, or would I choose to escape? My vanity compels me to imagine I would be willing to fight for the real in any case, but my integrity reminds me that I've run to the margins enough times in my own life that to cast that judgment would be dishonest. Like most people, I would probably go back and forth, entering the world from time to time, but retreating quickly and more fully to a place where life made sense, like it did in my books of childhood, and like it does not for so many people living through the great disconnect.

Technology, just like money, is a tool. It is a means of exchange between multiple people either happening in delay or in real time, when applied to communications, and that's where I'm going to center my efforts. However, in the larger sense, the value of technology is in the ease with which we can accomplish things and in the time we can save. In theory, these should be excellent benefits if they would allow us to accomplish more so that we could better invest the time saved. In practice, because we serve our tools rather than the other way around, they create a constant expectation of greater efficiency and availability, where escapism becomes the necessary and parallel option to constant connectivity. This is especially true as one gets into positions of progressively more responsibility, people expect you to be accessible.

As much as these books sustain me, and I want to thank you, even those of you who loathe what I say, for giving me the opportunity to sustain my family by sharing these ideas and opening a much needed public debate, I also have learned to live off social media which is a bit strange for a soon to be middle-aged man. I never sought to be Mr. Kawczynski to kids who ask me how to fix problems I'm still trying to understand myself. But what we learn is there is a symbiotic relationship between ourselves and technology which social media exemplifies. The world gives us a chance to develop social capital, to leverage our networking based upon whom we present ourselves to be and what we can offer, but that ultimately this level of differentiation also serves to create a layer of separation between people because it nevertheless remains artificial.

Earlier versions of the Internet were much more focused on using attention getters and attractions to reach people in real life. I remember when I worked for the Ron Paul Campaign back in 2008 how we used meetups to meet real people and I still have dear friends from those exciting experiences. Yes, we were self-selecting, and that created the thousand little technological ghettos of self-belief that are tearing our country apart, but at least there was still the idea that we could meet in person and do something. Now, it is much harder, and we live in a darker time.

I'll share this story: I run a group in Maine called Maine for Mainers. We're a collaborative effort that I originated and administrate to speak up for the idea that government should serve the people here before serving people who come from far away and get benefits because they're presumed greater victims. You can see why I get branded as hell spawn by the media up in my neck of the woods, but in any case, whenever we try to use the Internet to gather and meet in person, we find hit pieces are written in legacy media about us, and that armed thugs show up to intimidate and try to disperse our gathering. We have found for as much as we can use social media as a tool to share ideas and connect to one another, it's just as valuable to others as a means to suppress dissent, offer violence to constrain people, and force compliance by not allowing certain choices. It's depressing to imagine this is our future, but it's closer to the original vision of why these networks were made than most would imagine.

How much do you know about the Internet? It evolved out of a project called ARPAnet, built by the predecessor of today's Defense Advanced Research Projects Agency, and was intended to facilitate communications between military bases in the event of a communications breakdown. With the inclusion of many brilliant psychologists and other researchers, the project evolved with ideas like Lifelog, which disappeared the day of Facebook's creation, to be the ultimate information warfare weapon. You would share your every connection, location, and activity with the world through Facebook. You can ask every question to the personless oracle in the box that is Google. Amazon exists to meet your every need, and Twitter is there for you to know what the big buzz is, but have you noticed that the endless abyss of content now stares back into you?

There's a test you can try if you talk to Siri, Alexa, or any of the other artificial people or the internet of things that most likely surrounds you, often whether you realize it or not. Start talking about a product you use frequently and wait for the advertising to appear. You don't even have to search the taskbar these days, for the world of things is around you, listening to you, monitoring you. Considering what we already know is in existence, I shudder to imagine just how bad things truly are, but that combination of big business and big government is sitting there with Big Brother really being here besides us in the friend we all choose to have in our homes, in our pockets, and with us at all times because that is our gateway to the world. We stopped talking to each other, and now we talk through machines more than we genuinely connect.

I get why we do it. It's because people suck. It's okay to admit that also, and for as much as I love how certain folk behave, so many of our problems come back to how awful we all can be. Certainly, I do not exclude myself from this classification, so we like the idea of someone we can talk to that doesn't judge us, and fail to realize there is awareness in the vacuum. Most of us do this noiselessly so long as we don't stumble into forbidden areas, yet as someone who does that pretty much as a profession at this point, you need to know technology is not your friend and will be used as the means of control for which it was ultimately designed unless we learn how to use it in proper proportion with connection to the real world.

The problem is that we don't know how to do this, as we have become a million little tribes who endlessly divide and cannot come together when common interest requires. This is why censorship is not being opposed. The electronic gulag of today acts with patient and exacting determination in removing any ideas, people and groups they find threatening from public consideration. False arguments are provided from ideological opponents and free market apologists alike who argue that there are a billion other choices. These may all be accurate, but what does it means when technology creates a system where we are allowed to defend a thousand different lies so long as one truth can still be actively suppressed?

My personal heresy was twofold. I said Islam is the enemy of the West, and I said that as a White man that I was proud of my racial heritage. I uttered no attack against any other group, but made a historical case for identity that is centuries old and definitional. Yet, I was suppressed, branded, and ostracized, and society reckoned it the better because this truth was unpleasant. There remain plenty of people ready to attack any person who speaks this or any other dangerous assertion, but even if you disagree with my assertion, you should find it very disturbing that you are given choices with no meaning, while those which have meaning – even if you don't like them – are removed from your view.

We deal with something that people who used to work in radio understood as the signal to noise ratio. If you're old enough to remember when radios had dials, you had to manually tune the transceiver to pick up the signal, and between the frequencies where content could be heard, there was a lot of noise. Back when communications technology was still new, the static was mostly empty and the content, though of far less quantity, had to at least have the appearance of far greater quality lest people choose an alternative. The signal to noise ratio was manageable. My question is: what is the signal to noise ratio of the Internet, if the signal is truth and the noise is falsehood?

It gets worse. The Internet is basically policed by several gatekeepers, all of whom are huge transnational corporate conglomerates, publicly and openly committed to the globalist mission. They are working in conjunction with governments to promote "safety" over liberty, seeking to enshrine their own status over any mission which once launched them into the free world that was the earlier Internet. Who do we think they serve? Look over to China, and see the imposition of a social media score by the state, and how our companies not only facilitated that outcome, but now look to replicate it in America and Europe, and you'll see why voices are being disappeared. That you no longer seem to see them is proof of how well this plan is working – the algorithm does the work all on its own once it knows the right criteria.

First, you get a warning. Then, you don't appear in people's feeds. Your content doesn't get paid when others do. You can't use certain platforms. Hell, if you're me, you can't even send a PayPal despite my only crime being the exercise of free speech. Because if you ask the wrong questions, or have the wrong ideas, you get branded and put in a corner. If you refuse to submit, then you live in the world of thought crime, and all of this technology which seemed for a moment to have the full potential of the printing press to push human innovation and allow us to bypass the corporate gatekeepers, is losing itself because those invested in building that future have surrendered truth for status, while abandoning meaning for power, and that level of damnation stinks of the worst sort of elitism.

A few chapters back I spoke about how the current group of elites has always been open to those who are useful to them, and new money has ever sought entrance to the status of old money. Beneath all the bright lights in Silicon Valley on their fun and playful campuses, the basic game has not changed one bit, which is that those who have power want control. When you understand that the government funded the internet as a military asset, it is perfectly sensible to see that it was designed as a tool that could foment or restrain revolution abroad, and track networks of people whose ideas were considered a threat. Seeing the widespread rush to adopt these technologies, is it any wonder that the corruption would come back home?

Now I personally believe the rank and file of the technological totalitarians support these acts on an ideological basis, having that wet behind the ears collegiate thinking that they will change the world, without ever bothering to consider why these approved revolutionaries are always so well-funded. It is the most basic human mistake to believe one's own propaganda uncritically, this lovely fable about the universe trending toward justice and the realization of equality, and equalized outcomes for all. It's a beautiful enough story that people getting rich and satisfying their own self-interest believe it all the time, despite living the exact opposite as venial hypocrites, and as they mercilessly squash the very dissent that is most likely to liberate people from interlocking systems of control. Worth noting is that even though the story is utter fiction, contrary to history and human nature, technology allows us the option to live our fantasies, encouraging the escape so long as our ownership of the virtual never rises to threaten dominance of the real.

I use technology to reach people, just as I am to write this book for you to consider, but I remember that world is not fully real. The real world exists, and is painful like my experience in high school, but in that ugliness, there is the chance to discover truth and to build something sustainable that has meaning and purpose. Such a world does require hurt feelings, conflict, pain, and suffering. Yet, would you prefer the triumph of Huxley where we live under Soma induced dreams as we watch an endless succession of animal videos and reckon ourselves happy? Is that where humanity goes from here? The droll answer is likely yes, for most of our peers, and those are the options we're presented, because the Internet was designed as the ultimate escape and the ultimate surveillance system in one. It's tricky that way.

Moreover, as we are already seeing with the push toward red flag laws and the encouragement of citizens to turn on one another and fight their ideological and personal battles as more important than the collective defense of liberty, our democracy moves to enhance security by encouraging red flag laws where people we don't like can be stripped of their rights to self-defense on hearsay alone. What the Courts can never allow by law, the people will shout for with universal acclaim because we're only as good as the information we consume, and technology is spoon-fed to us to tell us what to think. We permit it because we think disconnecting is a choice, and it remains such, but at a high cost and perhaps not for that much longer.

A book like this is dangerous because I'm taking you far outside the lines and showing you how the scams work. The elites know, read my books, and congratulate me even as I'm allowed to persist as a statement of their own strength attesting to the degradation of our fellow men have already permitted. So long as we remain a minuscule entity, the persecution remains proportional, but what happens when the big tech really fully interfaces with big government, and the guys with the guns are given full authorization to attack? Because as much as those in power like to exercise control through the appearance of invisibility, no fools would have created a system as clever and subtle as this which manipulates us all today.

Chapter 10: Hired Guns

Political power exists in two distinct forms. There is soft power, the ability of persuasion whereby hearts and minds are changed, and people are rallied to a side. All political revolutions begin in this stage and all existing political states work tirelessly to ensure enough emotional capital is invested in the enduring belief in the polity to ensure people don't seek an alternative. For as much as soft power shapes history and is the underlying influence by which thoughts change, which is why information warfare has supplanted military action as the preferred meaningful action of combat, the ultimate resolution of a change of status almost always reverts to hard power. So long as sufficient will and organization exist, the people with the guns make the rules.

The brilliance of the current system is the absence of using hard power, and the ongoing effort to define the exercise of violent force as an act of criminality, to encourage a transnational ideology that peace is the highest virtue, that protecting life is the highest duty (except for fetuses – they apparently don't count), and that the global order promises a world without war for the places that matter. The ones that don't are those where war has been a constant or where the local government leader is trying to exist outside the banking system. It is no accident those two are linked. We have placed life above liberty in what makes perfect sense for a system of debt based human bondage.

Essentially, we have sacrificed choice for the benefit of not having to worry about meeting our material needs, further substantiation of humanism as not just ideology, but also the religion of our times where a declaration of virtue, a call to higher morality, honoring one's kin above the stranger, or even holding the family apart are being defined as not just selfish and immoral, but even criminal and heretical. Because the morality of the state has now become the promise of international peace, an appeal to the cerebellum that still quakes in fear at the dangers of a most uncertain world of which we are reminded daily, creates in our people a servile complex where the love of life and fear of pain reduce us to a manageable level.

Needless to say, this doesn't work on everyone, just as it did not work on America's founding fathers. It's worth remembering that our own history is a bloody affair of treason, where the patriots who founded this nation were first traitors who revolted against the legitimate authority of their time, and only succeeded because they were more willing to kill and die than the British Empire was willing to exact force in return. History is made by those whose are sufficiently assured in their morality to impose their will. We like to imagine and find ways for this to happen in peace and through the evolution of ideas, but the reality is struggle almost always comes down to using force to settle an argument that cannot be resolved in the end. Even those movements which find their way to power through peace often have the ability to assert force on their behalf, with the threat of such action alone often being sufficient to deliver victory if the cause creates a moral imbalance between those seeking change and those preserving the old order.

The people who run the new world order understand these lessons very well, which is why, for whatever level of dissent and divergence has been tolerated, they ensure they have nearly complete control over the institutions of hard power. Limitless money allows them to purchase militaries the way you or I would have to purchase a weapon, minus any background check, naturally. The strings attached to the donations made to the many politicians of all parties ensure certain questions never get asked, certain people never get prosecuted, and certain common enemies remain targets in perpetuity.

There were two big events at the end of the Cold War. The Soviet Union fell, and the People's Republic of China did not. The Russian people climbed on the tanks and celebrated the death of a corrupt system. The Chinese people got run over by them. If you've ever wondered why the future of the world where democracy was promised didn't follow the script you expected, consider the lessons that someone in power learned there about the exercise of hard power in defense of authority. It's no accident the world looks a lot more like China and less like Russia today, including our own country and⊙ a great deal of the softly authoritarian bureaucratized West. Russia is going a different direction in many ways after their long communist nightmare.

As described at the beginning of this section, the elites have never trusted people outside their circles, nor wanted more direct interaction with them than their status required. They have always feared nationalism and felt that systems were easier to control. When it comes to hard power, they have learned to allow certain privileges to restrain dissent, to ensure wars do not break out which would prove so stressful that real change could be contemplated, as happened to Russia in 1917, and so we see armies elevated on pedestals these days so long as they do not fundamentally threaten the status quo. Militaries cooperate and exist within a system as tamed puppies against one another, encouraged to link to one another as mutual professionalism, but we also see the push to use the military just like law enforcement against the state.

My previous book *"The Coming Civil War"* drew much attention from people who were in the know, whose advanced understanding of the problems our nation faces created a self-selecting audience who informed me of what I got right and what I got wrong. One criticism commonly leveled which I accept and refine here was my assessment of the likelihood of the military serving the people in the event of a conflict. This varies somewhat by nation, but for America, I've been basically told while the top brass remains more committed to the government than to the people, the idea that the majority of the troops would help defend the Constitution is illusory. Half the recruits in the military, I've been told from people who ask and are involved, would gladly shoot American citizens if the orders came down. While the high end operators are apparently motivated by a different sense of patriotism, the idea that the military would serve the people and not the state is an assumption we should not make, and the divisions go along the predictable ethnic and ideological lines described at the beginning of this work.

As we see technology playing a larger role in our military with operators on the ground replaced by autonomous vehicles and drones, the role of human initiative in the planned wars of the future is disappearing and a relatively small number of people can bring overwhelming force to suppress a revolt or an enemy if need be. The military of the future in the United States will inevitably continue heading in this direction because the state will seek to remedy its fundamental risk, that the soldiers themselves will not support it as their oath to the Bill of Rights comes into conflict with the globalized socialist bureaucracy the elites are crafting. Shifting from human soldiers to technological servitude is one way to ensure hard power sustains the evolving old order as it moves in this new world.

Exercise of power by the government against the people will likely never be asked of the military except as a last resort, preferring to rely on soft power strategies as the first line of defense, and law enforcement selectively applied as a more acceptable second form of defense before any possible moment of crisis can be generated. Remember, the key to control is about presenting false choices because a person can work through a thousand false options and find themselves no closer to solving the initial problem. The idea of using hard power to brand the opposition as criminality is nothing new, but something we see accelerating with frightful speed throughout the American government.

I very much see the mutual agreement to support red flag laws as a watershed in the American story, the joint declaration of war by the Republican and Democrat Parties upon the people in service of their masters' narrative, and the donor classes who own both. In one swoop, they destroyed three of the most important amendments to the Bill of Rights, shredded the very idea of liberty, and basically turned the assertion of the capacity of self-defense into an act of criminality where the offense is thought crime and no defense is possible against any accusation regardless of how unsubstantiated it might be. While I have no doubt rank and file officers will be circumspect in trying to enforce this ridiculous mandate, it won't be long before a citizen asserting their rightful exercise of liberty ends up in a firefight in defense of their protection against accusations with no foundation in reality. Just as predictably, this will lead to even more draconian laws against those who defend their rights, and the state will defend its prerogative to control all of us against anyone who asserts that neither the law nor justice permits such a surrender.

The freely offered when unsought surrender by the Republican Party on this issue, an entirely self-enforced error of civilizational magnitude which shows how unfit they are to lead opposition moving forward, is now creating a very strange inversion. The people who primarily believe in law and order as sound organizational principles of society, that is to say those on the Right who support law enforcement as an instinct toward preservation, are now watching as the last vestiges of the idea the police serve as protectors are stripped away and they see them turned fully into agents of the state designed to enforce orthodoxy.

The worst imaginings of East Germany before the fall of the Berlin Wall have more resemblance to the America they are creating than the defense of liberty from just a generation or two ago, where snooping on someone's thoughts has become a legal warrant to attack in the middle of the night if something untoward is now said.

Law enforcement has transitioned from being defenders of fairer laws that at least claimed to benefit most people and practicing equal and judicious enforcement into a degrading role to serve only as hired guns for a national elite who exist well outside these rules. The development of SWAT team tactics in response to the War on Drugs, another elite invention where money laundering and corruption were commonplace, implicating our own CIA and many other Deep State actors was but the beginning of the elite creation of paramilitaries which could be used against our own people. Add to that beginning the sales of military grade equipment to police throughout the land, given in response to the very public promotion of a multicultural national ethic which they knew could only increase violence, and for which it was reckoned a feature to build new hopeless distractions on one front and seize power through the state in the other. The Patriot Act might have been the death knell of the traditional view of police as protectors, as our government came together once more to destroy the privacy protections of the American population at the same time when the advancement of technology ensured we needed them most. Now, all will be assumed guilty until they are proven innocent, and in a world so obsessed with the appearance of security, it's not surprising that liberty has become the victim.

The CIA is the old KGB. The FBI has become the NKVD. We live in a world where our law enforcement act like Soviet style apparatchiks, with those at the higher levels showing the least restraint in using the power of the badge to punish their enemies. Consider the odious acts of John Brennan, a person who admittedly voted for the Communist Party but who later ran the CIA, or James Comey, whose many connections with banking long precede his leadership of the FBI. Do you remember that Robert Mueller was responsible for censoring the story of 9/11 to protect one story or another? Back when nationalism still seemed a threat, at least as an electoral process, look how hard the FBI tried to prevent and shape the electoral results, yet now we see the troops of the Department of Justice rallying together to identify Americans as the terrorists of the future for standing for sovereignty. These battles are not new, and there's a forgotten history of the 1980's and 1990's of another generation of entrapment, of violence against citizens, and about new laws that were passed when the government messed up and blamed the people it targeted.

Allow me to say this. I think the institutions of Federal law enforcement are irredeemably corrupt, but that's not to say all people who serve are bad; far from it. I know some people who are very good people stuck in an impossible position who are just trying to protect others during a time when mission creep has found them stuck in jobs far different than they thought they were joining. I pray for these people, as we will need their help to survive in the days ahead as they defend laws against orders and provide protection to people who stand up for what is both morally and legally correct. This is not in their job description, will cost them much grief and any opportunity at career advancement, and will see them abandoned by their peers and leaders alike for doing the job they have, versus the job they're told they must do.

Civil disobedience is going to rise on the Right in ways that have never been seen before as the forces of law and order come to enforce regulations that contradict our fundamental assertions as to the foundational basis for this nation. Much will come from the citizens who will justly refuse to comply with regulations that exist only to strengthen the government at the expense of the people. Yet, these acts which will turn patriots into potential prisoners will also require those in positions of authority to understand and act morally to decide what laws are right and what laws are not.

When we end up with a system so riddled with contradictions, a sure sign of both moral decay and the efforts of outside actors to maintain control, reason and clarity will hopefully guide more of our civil servants not just to relinquishing these responsibilities, but to standing against the letter of the law and in defense of the spirit of what was intended. We will need their help.

But we must also be realistic. As it becomes clearer that the political consequences of the opposing the system are higher each day, and as the system evolves into the one party state which demography ensures is inevitable with those people most likely to be ruthless in their exercise of power being brought into control through a gamed democratic process akin to grabbing extra seats at the table, the state will come fully in alignment with the agenda to prosecute the people for noncompliance. The state's natural tendency has always been and will ever be to defend the monopoly of force, and absent liberties to protect the people, and meaningful political division between both groups of political participants and the various levels of government, I fear people will be dreadfully surprised by how quickly and thoroughly the transformation happens. Contributing to this is while we are assuming that Americans will think like we do, and putting faith in how many of us still remember our country was once honorably presented, please remember those children who after the Cold War grew up hearing what a horrible place America was and how it needs to be transformed and stopped from committing any more crimes against humanity. The indoctrination is that bad and gets worse each year.

People with this ideology are coming to power, and the elites could not be happier. Socialism and communism are not threatening to their hegemony. If anything, socialist policies protect them from new competitors while allowing them to consolidate their gains which the economic system will not long sustain past this point as the debt bubble has gone out of control. They will bribe the hired guns with money first, and then with status in the new order, to ensure they have a place in this new world being created. Mr. Capitalist, we are glad your many investments ensure you are Comrade Communist, and please continue your most important work and sponsorship as you serve the people.

Against that, we confront not just the guns of the state, the monitors of the technocracy, the wealth of corporations, and the spirit of the times, but also the need to overcome our fears of fighting and an uncertain nature to launch a battle with frankly low odds of success. All for the hope we won't screw it up again, and to even get to that point, those of us with a moral compass need to begin our impossible gauntlet by finally vanquishing a familiar enemy. The Right has to beat the Left and destroy their false morality to build the basis on which we can compete with this far greater and more ruthless foe, which will be the focus of the next section, but as we undertake that battle, we must never forget that the mountain is far higher to climb than winning one battle or election.

I share this not to discourage you, but to remind you of what was stolen. Perhaps it is a quest greater than reason will permit, but in faith, I share that to promote free will is a most beneficial act of divine providence and should we become better men, this battle is not yet beyond us. We must rise to the occasion.

Interjection: Which War Should We be Fighting Then?

An eminently reasonable question to ask after devoting ten chapters to explaining how we're being drawn into a conflict scripted by elites who are playing us all is why we should even consider the Left/Right paradigm at all? There are people who, quite reasonably, take this position and only talk about the challenges of fighting obscure entities like the people who meet at Davos, the Bilderberger Group, and the Council on Foreign Relations. I personally believe there is much validity in this approach and having spent enough time falling down the proverbial rabbit hole, one discovers there are many different layers to this battle where we could pick the fight.

Conversely, I could just as easily write a book sculpting the entire conflict in a spiritual context that fits my Christian beliefs, and in some ways, this strikes me as the truest description of all, as I perceive the battles ahead very much as between good and evil. Free will was gifted to us to realize our higher nature in service to the morality which gives us the promise of life not just in the next world, but in this one also which is something one only understands when they live the path. I might write that book next, actually, because as much as most people don't see things in that light, I believe an honest work of love is never wasted when it seeks truth.

But this hints at the reason why I approach the question in the way I do, which is that to change the future, one cannot hope to succeed by being just a solitary warrior ranting in the wilderness. For better or worse, how we perceive reality plays the largest role in what is possible and in how we can begin to organize ourselves to escape the many traps before us. The first few chapters, incredibly honest in their presentation, are not so much meant to frighten or anger the reader as they are to persuade you that there is no happy easy way out of the messes ahead. I find few things are as dangerous as false hope where we allow the all too human desire to believe the best of others to facilitate their very worst behavior. In short, that is the problem with the entire Left/Right paradigm, but where the issue of the Right – the appropriation of unique cultural attributes to find harmony – is at least solvable through assimilation, moral leadership, and force of will, the descent into madness that is war on reality from the Left has no redemptive qualities. Since it cannot lead us anywhere better, and since it is the first obstacle to any reclamation of our liberty, let alone something resembling decent civilization, we have to remove that risk before we can face any larger foe.

In some ways, I wish we could skip over those steps, but this is why I spend so much time harping on the importance of being able to see past false dialectics. There's not a hard and fast rule for how to look past these mental traps in terms of which system is best, which is why in some of my other writings, I spent much time exploring a third way thinking which is people centered rather than making the common but distracting argument that we should defend a system.

We are who we are, and that is a choice we make in the culture we develop, and those truths we identify as self-evident. For better or worse, America is an ideational state, a nation built upon ideas at the core of our identity rather than more visceral substance. As such, we have to deal with the pros and cons of our own idealism honestly, but I would submit that the Bill of Rights remains that part of our American mythology which has both been most effective and the least tarnished. Whatever emerges, which is a highly unpredictable game of speculation, we would do well to honor that lineage and use that as guide to help us reconcile whatever contradictions we can to avoid conflicts where possible.

In the context of nationalism, I've spent much time both in literature and in the field reconciling the various branches of nationalism to one another, where the desire to divide into what system we must use to sort ourselves keeps manifesting. This has the feel of a false narrative once again because you need a set of reliable laws, cultural institutions that are healthy and active, and kin relationships working in conjunction to form a successful nation. We might find we cannot hold together as one nation for division in any of these three categories – that we don't agree on laws, that we don't agree on truths, or that we are just too different as people. To reach stability, we need to somehow resolve this question. With respect to the Left/Right paradigm, we cannot find such a fulcrum with egalitarian universalists because they promote doctrine which works against both human nature and the full course of observed history. They would destroy humanity to create equality, and that is an enemy that must be opposed by those of sane mind long before we can turn our attention to further reaching conflicts.

Besides, it is a popular battle, and if nothing else should be obvious after we discussed the elites and how they control us, the power of numbers should be revealing. Limitless money allows them to do a lot, but for the moment at least, the system still requires our participation in it to function and that gives us a power we don't easily recognize which we enjoy but which we must learn to wield and assert. We need a mass movement that will offer something that can evolve to meaningful resistance, and while other paths were explored, they have largely been shut which is why we're going to talk about the endless war of ideology once more. We're stuck working through either Team Red or Team Blue, as absurd they are, to at least begin the conversations where we can reach other people.

Because the game is really not about designing or defending a perfect system. It is not that challenging for a person or group of knowledgeable people of good will to design the policies which would allow us to escape our subjugation. B But getting people to care or listen to solutions that don't come in the format they are prepared to accept is an impossibility. That's actually one reason why so many smart people have become accelerationists, the idea that if something bad is going to happen that it is better it gets provoked sooner, as the long-term trends favor one side versus the other. The unwillingness of the majority of the people to consider alternative actions or persons to those which are utterly incapable of solving the larger problems is the source of infinite frustration to many including, I suspect, to you the reader. So, we head for the exits while they glorify the past which is already dead, and we start to think in new ways of what a healthier day might portend.

But absent the major collapse which still sits as backdrop to this book just as its companion volume, and which I rate a reasonably possible outcome, our duty should be to explore options and outcomes which lead to optimal conclusions. That means we get stuck diving back into the paradigmatic view of history and politics, dealing with the conservative unwillingness to act for their own survival, the vilification of the virtuous from the insane demagogues who are awarded their bottomless piggy banks to wreak destruction across the land, and the imprecise use of language needed to awaken our fellow men and women to new possibilities. The bad news is that this is a major challenge and we won't reach enough people to change minds before the consequences of the above likely come to impact us all.

The good news, by contrast, is people are smarter than we think. Given better information, which is very hard to come by when the system works so hard to present seemingly reasonable choices so as to suppress people from asking more pressing questions, Americans are waking up to the scam and these false narratives. The single biggest asset we have in this regard is when hypocrisy reveals itself over and again in service to an agenda. To use an event from this week as an example, the acts of a lone gunman in El Paso were presented as a national tragedy that merited seizure of our arms and the branding of an entire race: Whites. But a much larger and confused gun fight in Philadelphia barely elicited a yawn in the larger context. Both were examples of heinous violence, but the White kid was eviscerated, and the Black guy was forgotten. With news now emerging through multiple sources on this and other similar examples, it's not long before those of us who point out the ever growing and frustrating number of contradictions are destroying any confidence in the propaganda outlets that distract from actual issues we should work toward resolving.

I can say this with high confidence because I have the pleasure of leading such a group of narrative breakers up in Maine who came to join together just in curiosity and solidarity for the simple idea that we should look out for own local people. Despite being branded a Nazi, white supremacist, and hatemonger, they came anyway because they asserted the right to decide for themselves what they would believe, and in seeing the moral gap between what was said about me and how I carry myself, just one man can be powerful in shaking someone from the mold of a worldview colored by corruption people did not even realize was there.

Most people there are less radical than I am. They're good conservative folk, with Republicans, a few libertarians and identitarians thrown in, and we talk in terms that we can all understand. We might lose a little detail, but we can come back to basic principles we share, and organize around the idea that there is a truer version of the Right to be found that goes beyond lip service to virtue and submission to corporations, instead serving the people through protecting the rights we once all cherished. It's good, and when we decided that soil and blood meant our land and families, we found a formula that changed the entire narrative up here and for which I come under constant attack with my new friends. I wonder if our adversaries realize they're only drawing us closer together, but I doubt it. They will print one sentence reviews of this book calling it a "screed of hate," without bothering to read the words. In this way they will miss the opportunity to understand the potential for their own liberation to a better life. How do you deal with people like that?

I can pray for them, I will educate those who listen, and would happily demonstrate through reason or experience alike the insanity of what opponents propose as an alternative, but they don't listen. Somehow, they believe in creating a tyranny of the majority where they don't have to listen to anyone who disagrees with them, which will be only possible with the gratuitous application of violence against our own citizens. We have tried repeatedly to engage the Left in good faith, but they only start screaming about normalization and throw ever larger tantrums against people who try to save them from their own excesses. They remind me of the worst sort of bullies that we had when I was a kid way back when. They would act like angels around the teacher – in their case the donors who pull their strings – and then would be the worst sort of awful whenever they were permitted freedom of action. They pick on everyone who doesn't give them what they want.

It would almost be funny if it weren't so sad, because we're literally letting America be deconstructed by soy boy latte swilling wannabe anarchists. Good men tried to take the field against them, but because the media slapped a label on them, now those who would oppose the violent radicals of the Left cannot afford it, and will not risk taking such chances again. Their guys get state support whether they represent the intellectual wing at the universities, the propaganda wing at the media, or the street thugs who – while unimpressive individually and eminently disposable to the larger framework – still have the ability to enact collective costs on those who oppose them.

It's different when you know people who have lost their jobs, lost their names, and even lost their families or freedom just for standing up against political insanity. One of the most disappointing things I've had to watch is how the supposedly moral Right has shown zero loyalty to its own flank time and again, while the Left, whatever else one says about them, facilitates their communist allies into achieving so much more, including the indoctrination of all our children and the domination of more or less every city. Considering how successful they have been, there's no way anyone is going to stop them now through simple persuasion, and so our focus will eventually shift to how to fix the Right.

I made the case in the previous chapters that the Democrat and Republican parties are just two forms of controlled opposition serving the elites far more faithfully than the people. That remains true, but for the Republican Party, I'm going to be particularly brutal in my critiques because the indefinite surrender and retreat strategy they have employed is so foolish and cowardly that nothing good remains to be said. At the root of their failure is the hypocrisy of tacitly accepting certain groups claiming to be perpetual victims combined with their unwillingness to hold any to account but their own. Strategic retreat in the present in order to facilitate an effective future attack is one thing, but the retreats we have seen up until this point have been anything but strategic. We have surrendered our homeland, and now we're in the needless and unenviable position of having to plot to recover it against very long odds.

It probably doesn't help also that we are quite limited in what we can contemplate, because there are whole ranges of potential solutions which we all consider, but which we cannot share with one another. My analysis is highly mindful of things unspoken, and in all that I suggest, I consider not just the likelihood of how we might force the desired peaceful path to reclamation, but also putting ourselves in the best position for the scenarios which must remain unstated. The reality is that the Left has overwhelming advantages in terms of organization and connectivity, and unless we can either exceed those capacities collectively or render their advantages inert, whatever individual advantages we might enjoy and whatever habits and resources we could employ toward defense of those values we want to preserve will prove inadequate. The power of a swarm cannot be overlooked and that is what we face, a mindless mass which would eventually destroy us and then themselves in turn. There is a sad and ironic satisfaction in knowing their victory is impossible, as trying socialism once again can only ever result in their own ultimate destruction, but as we have already discussed, these useful idiots are really the means to facilitate even worse outcomes, from which we may never get a second chance to recover. The stakes are even higher than they already seem.

We have to be flexible and to fight in all directions that make sense. If we can target the larger enemies, I always support taking away power from the bigs and returning it to the little guy, to the local option as it were. That fight will continue and accelerate and is central to the solution I argue for in the third section of this book. But for us to take advantage of those possibilities, we need to first deal with the nuisance of the Left.

Here's a key thought I want you to consider as you read. I want you to consider how much of the problem we face stems from our unquestioning acceptance that we must share a country with these people, and that we have some common obligation to share our duties as citizens with those who would gladly and proudly shirk these.

Our liberation begins when we treat them with the same disregard they have shown us. We can reach out and try to help those who can be awakened, but ultimately our goal must now become organizing enough people to prevent a catastrophe and provide hope for the sane and rational to save themselves, along with that with which our civilization can be maintained. That might sound overwhelming to some, but things really will be that bad. Don't let ◎◎◎misplaced empathy fool you – consider every trend line as I do – and see what must come to pass unless we find a way to change those trends.

Chapter 11: The Evil of Cultural Marxism

You can't really understand a movement without properly understanding how its members see themselves, and there are some wrinkles to the new Left which never get explained as well as they should. We're going to go deeply into what they think, why they think this way, what they practice and try to explode out their obsession with buzzwords and safe spaces from the obscure to the comprehensible for general readers and people who come from a saner place alike.

Marxism as a movement is one of the more potent strands of the humanist religion. If you do not recognize that we are talking about a cult, based upon belief in a set of principles that cannot be disproved through any set of logic, you'll miss its deeper appeal. Marx basically took the ideas of Hegel about the thesis, its opposite in the antithesis, and the new progression in the synthesis and applied that to economic thinking with a pseudo-scientific twist colored by his own hatred of the status quo and his embrace of atheism.

He argued that states follow an inescapable pathway of history wherein they begin in communal bliss. Then, force comes into the equation and the age of imperialism begins, to be followed by the corrupting influence of money in capitalism, industrialization as the exploitation of the people, but also an opportunity whereby the people who have become essential to the system can mass mobilize to take back power. Essentially, it's the same idea Robespierre had for France, of taking control of what was previously held by elites and thereby exploit a vacuum in leadership to create a hypothetical regime of the people.

Two major problems doomed Marx historically. The first is that his linear progression throughout history, yet another example of the Western fixation on history leading to a predetermined outcome, failed because capitalism largely never gave way to communism as people chose comforts over the promise of equality so long as the distribution was fair enough and living standards continued to rise. Later Marxist theoretician Antonio Gramsci (from whom we will hear again shortly) likewise identified cultural institutions such as loyalty to families, religion and nationality – which he considered to be artificial social constructs – as impediments to the acceptance of communism.

The second problem that doomed Marx is that the places where Marxism evolved into full blown communism, the states such as the Soviet Union, were a violation of the historical analytical approach that dominated many universities the entire previous century, because it was backward agrarian Russia that adopted the red flag and not prosperous western countries like Germany, France, or England.

Highly relevant to the situation in America today is just how power was seized in Russia. Over-extension from wars such as the Russo-Japanese war as well as the military occupation of Poland requiring more troops than an all-out war provided the opportunity for radicals at home to destabilize the existing regime, an act which was also paralleled interestingly enough one year later in Germany in 1918. The inspiration for these revolts lay within promises of a worker's paradise that were provided by angry communes in the major cities of Russia and then St. Petersburg. It's important to recognize the parallels of how city governments in Russia essentially came to operate as their own universe underneath an ineffectual national regime, and think of how many American cities now openly defy federal laws without any consequences in service of radically leftist causes. We should all be concerned.

But the most radical elements of these cities were Bolsheviks, many of whom were not ethnically Russian but emigres and under the inspiration of Lenin and many other leaders who were university intellectuals, they and the more moderate Mensheviks undertook a revolt. As is often the case in these affairs, the revolution is an uncertain mess for a while, but the radicals who have a plan often defeat the moderates who try to garner popular support for the new order. While the Mensheviks were planning an election in the interval between the first revolts in May of 1917 and November, the Bolsheviks worked to take control of the real reins of power, asserting their leadership by fiat and canceling the election.

The people, especially in the country, counted upon the prestige of the Tsar, a chain of leaders that stretched backwards through Muscovy hundreds of years into their antiquity, the stabilizing role of the then powerful and respected Orthodox Church, and the White Army of Tsarist professionals to save them. Thanks to an insane influx of money from American and European capitalists who shared certain affiliations and empathies with the Bolsheviks, and even more to the failure of the imperial forces to organize, the Bolsheviks were able to defeat the farmers, the church, and the army all in turn.

The advantage they had was unity in organization, the centralization of their forces, and the will to impose their values. The faithful defeated those whose personal concerns were greater than this religion painted in blood red. From there, the Bolsheviks went about taking away rights from the people, slaughtering millions of peasants through starvation and purges, and enacting many years of human tragedy. We're not told these tales, but Russia alone saw triple the amount of people killed as any other European country in the 20th Century from ideological violence by its government against the people. If you look at who was responsible, as Solzhenitsyn did, you can draw your own conclusions about why they get a free pass.

But that old style of Marxism ultimately proved incapable of keeping up with the modern world as became fully apparent only by the 1980's. Economic Marxism with state control of the means of production and central planning behind everything lagged desperately behind capitalism in the West, and it is often thought the cost of the Soviet intervention into Afghanistan coupled with the divergence of half the goods and services in Russia into the black market were enough to collapse the system there. It was too inefficient to compete, and in the early nineties, it seemed like the war between these systems had been resolved, yet it now appears the argument about its death was quite premature.

Because the idea that we can all be equal has always been the true heart of Marxism, a humanist take on creating a paradise of material pleasure, and there has long been a train of thought which snaked through the West that moved away from the science of materials and into the realm of psychology and culture.

If the economic hand of Marx proved ineffectual, the tradition which generated more from Engels about the role of culture still had much appeal to be realized. The seminal thinker who built the foundation for modern communist thought, which is what we are facing in America now in some synthesis between its Third World and continental equivalents, is Antonio Gramsci. He was an Italian communist from before the Second World War who observed that the reason Marx improperly forecast history was that culture served to restrain the advancement of equality. In short, he believed that the idea of normalcy itself became so embedded in the people that they systematized oppression under the guise of tradition and the various social institutions which asserted any claim to legitimacy as open to all. The reason it worked and why it had allowed history to err from its intended course is because people could not realize they were oppressed, and therefore, they would not offer resistance to elements deemed natural which he explained were actually artificial.

While his observation about the nature of culture is undeniably true to the extent that we certainly grow up with a sense of what is normal and right based upon what we learn during our formative years, another reason why the Left is obsessed with controlling education and information, you'll also note that Gramsci makes the same inversion as Marx in accepting a rule of history which is not externally valid and places his blind faith in a sense of equality which has never existed in human history. The remainder of his work went into details of how to realize these victories and laid the foundation for the later development of propaganda designed to turn the nation against itself to accomplish the liberation of humanity from its own expectations.

This brings us to the infamous Frankfurt School and the intellectuals who promoted cultural Marxism which has become the dominant strain of intellectual thinking through the world of Western universities and whose influences are driving the progressive left. Under thinkers like Herbert Marcuse and Erich Fromm, these intellectuals who were primarily of Jewish origin, and had been either exiles from Germany from before the War, or had survived there or in countries nearby, came together to create a philosophical movement which would attack the forces of nationalism, seek to destroy any positive expression of identity, and force equality in ways more fundamental than had ever been contemplated before in history. Many of these people migrated from Europe and they and their acolytes became a dominant force in the American educational system, especially in universities where they began teaching whole generations of people how oppressed they were, and the need to resist.

For those who have the inclination and the patience, it is worth reading their works to understand precisely how our enemy – and these people are the enemy of all that is human and decent – think. It is ugly thinking, difficult to swallow, and painful to digest. Imagine starting from the presumption that everything people hold dear is bad and that your job is to destroy their beliefs. That is how the cultural Marxists of the Frankfurt School behave, where they see families as threat, devotion to a God as a menace, and the familiar and timeless rituals as something to be destroyed. Building from Gramsci, they label and brand anything familiar as hateful, and elevate the mean and the crude to be celebrated because what they ultimately fight for is an attack upon reason because they view human nature itself as the root of injustice. Given the opportunity, they would build a new man who would be better because each instance of such a man would be indistinct from any other, free from the oppression of expectations, whether they come from society or even nature itself.

If you read just one work, consider *"Repressive Tolerance"* by Herbert Marcuse. It is a handbook for the progressive intellectual for why they attack ideas that would seem harmless just as much as Satanist Saul Alinsky's *"Rules for*

Radicals" is the guide for how to implement these ideas on the ground. What he explains is that to undo the liberal systems of the West that allow freedom of expression and continuity of a happy life for those who live therein, the revolution requires the selective use of those structures that exist in the West to undermine the entire edifice of state and society alike.

They would gladly claim protections for all who were useful to them in deconstructing the belief in a rational society itself, but then strike out against those who sought to assert the same rights for themselves as bigots and oppressors. You'll recognize the inherent hypocrisy of these tactics in how they employ one set of rules for those who serve their interest, and the complete opposite for those who use the same exact rationale.

This is why progressives see absolutely no contradiction in their hatred of White identity, but their love of Black identity, and it is why they can attack marriage as being horrible for women while simultaneously fighting for the right of two gays or lesbians to claim that title. This is why they see no conflict in elevating the submission religion of Islam while they vilify Christianity. They do not care about the content of the ideas, or the inconsistency of their beliefs, but as Marcuse explains, they care about making it impossible to claim the authority of any one idea over any other. They seek creative destruction as a means to erase what man thinks he knows, so that we can somehow return to a mythical state before civilization where we lived all in

159

happy relative equality. Ignorance is their wisdom, and if they seem to push people away from deeper understanding of knowledge, then they would reckon that a victory as the inherently prejudicial nature of intellectual talent is elitist.

It will not surprise you that people so accustomed to weaponized hypocrisy have no problems with the many contradictions that accrue in their own lives. Consider the jet setting class who bemoan global warming yet fly to one of their mansions every weekend. As most revolutionaries have done, the rules that apply for the common folk still don't apply to what is no longer labeled thus but still very much exists as the emerging dictatorship of the proletariat. They believe it is their just due as brave comrades to enjoy the fruit of the evil oppressors, as the common folk who do not realize how their traditions hold down the other, and so long as they attack ceaselessly, they are praised by those who in their naïve idealism or delusional rancor promote these sickly ideals.

This is a religion because you can't prove these people wrong. They demand equality, and there is no amount of our people they will hesitate to sacrifice in order to achieve it. If equality were in fact part of the natural order, it would have been found numerous times throughout history. But so far, its only progress has been bought with mountains of dead, because as a notion contrary to the natural order, it can only be enforced through the death in which all are finally equal.

For Americans, if you want to understand why they believe in a world with no borders, or how they can reconcile two incompatible identities like Muslims and queers, as just one example, the answer is because each is a little chisel that chips away further at the idea that to be an American means something definable and meaningful. They say they support everything because what they need from the rest of us is to believe in absolutely nothing. They want violence, anger, and contradictions to grow, and to see America toppled and the world brought to its knees because their revolt is not against any one state or idea, but against the system of reality that exists in nature, reason, and good faith.

They believe in artifice, fantasy, and bad faith. They elevate hypocrisy to a fine art, indulge whatever insane definition people make up, and use the force of law with the threat of both economic and physical violence to enact their sordid dreams on the rest of us. We, who are decent, fell for their many false protestations where they claimed only to want tolerance or to be left alone, but we never have and never will see any such regard extended in fair equity back to us. They use our best nature and then use our attributes of kindness and fair play to create chains for us, by holding us to standards they will not only refuse to keep but despise also as the very roots of a system that keeps them from chasing their dreams.

I consider the philosophy pure evil and if you are so inclined, the relationships between communists, atheists, and occultists who aspire to Satanism is a dark and ugly road where much content can be found. Remember, Alinsky who wrote the playbook for progressives that has basically been in use in America since 1968 dedicated his work to Lucifer, and this was the man for whom Hillary Clinton had nothing but glowing praise. If you think we're just fighting a battle against naïve college kids and slightly misled intellectuals, think again.

There is hardcore commitment to death and destruction hiding just behind that row of rainbow flags, and we have seen this tried time and again in so many countries on every continent. Their thinking must be exposed, opposed, and obliterated.

What is being created in America is a combination of the Marcuse school of repressive tolerance in concert with the street radicalism that Che Guevara was practicing to force change from the ground up. When you see how blithely the elites are enabling these delusions on the basis they likely believe people cannot possibly organize around an idea so absurd, it becomes apparent this threat is real. One can and should argue that the inherent philosophy is delusional, but in the absence of an external threat which is precisely what our system allows, the ability of those who have taken charge of education and the media to sway people to something like these beliefs through selective use of information cannot be understated. The threat is real, and in some ways, the greater irony is the revenge of the Russians is not through Trump, but that so many of these loony ideas were long term plans of the old KGB to destabilize the West.

It's apocryphal, but there's a great video of Yuri Bezmenov, a KGB defector who was explaining back in the halcyon days of the 1990's what would be done if these people came to power. He spoke about how they would attack people for their traditional beliefs, how they would rise to control of the state and subvert it to darker ends. He warned that a figure like Obama would come who would invert the definitions of right and wrong and that worse still would follow until the people themselves would be so confused they would demand the destruction of their own country, abandon their families, and strike out for social justice.

We now live in their world. We, who are the majority, are the targets of their ire and anger, and when they become the majority – as they will so soon because the obsession of our ruling class and the selfish Right alike to bring people in to make a quick buck – all that wealth we amassed will be the kindling for the fire they seek to set to our entire civilization. Unlike the pragmatic Chinese, we have the zealots running our hardcore Left, and they will, as their faith requires, punish the Democrats through inaction when they do not toe the line, and work to bring in as many people as possible with zero loyalty to anything except to the idea of equalizing outcomes.

Our own decency blinded us to this threat. The tolerance we thought we were bargaining for peace was just taken as weakness and an opportunity to advance the agenda further. I want you to get it out of your head right now that there is a middle ground. You can no more reason with a cultural

Marxist than you could make a plea to a mindless machine to not chop your arm off if you get stuck. While it is true people can be rescued, which is why it is so important we understand this belief and call it out as the worst form of communism yet devised, an existential threat to the life of every American, we should be clear that the true believers are irredeemable and must be restrained from power by any and every means possible.

I know they have been permitted to flourish because they represent an attack in the culture war in defense of state prerogatives and against alternate spheres of authority, but just as with the French Revolution, the elites made a terrible mistake. In their hubris, they thought they could control the forces they had unleashed, and I very much fear they are making the same error anew with the consequence that our own civilization is being put at risk. They might destroy people very efficiently, but perhaps even more quickly than we who are sane can manage, and it irritates me that we have been placed into this conflict against them where those who pull the strings realize our very nature and desire for survival forces us from the Right into essential conflict to restrain this calamity.

Chapter 12: The Inestimable Value of Stupidity

Have you ever noticed that there are certain things that seem to make perfect sense when a smarter person says them, but become as clear as mud when someone who is less capable tries to parrot back the same concepts? Keep that in mind as we begin this chapter which is a profile about the useful idiots who exist in a strange place in idea space. They lack the full depth of understanding of the Marxists who have developed this deliberately destructive philosophy, but they either try to apply the same rules without understanding their deeper purpose, or there are also those who naively just believe the surface applications and support fantastic causes thinking they actually are intended to promote justice. The overlaps between the two groups are considerable.

Let's deal with an example from my home state of Maine. We have several well-funded progressive groups that have come here with heavy financing from places like Berkeley and Brooklyn to try to ensure we natives don't get too many ideas for ourselves, and they come in to enforce cultural orthodoxy through a monopolistic media and activists on the ground who are designed to shame people into compliance. One thing they get right is people in New England sometimes find violations of tact more offensive than supporting a harmful ideology as we are used to indulging cranks of all varieties up here. Yet, the people who came up here are clearly not on the A-Team for reasons I'm happy to demonstrate.

Maine is both the Whitest state in America at 94% and also the safest state in America if you measure by probability of your getting murdered. Be sure not to draw any correlations between those two facts as we add also to the equation that we have a homogeneous culture. So, when the progressives came up here informed by the efforts of Alinsky, Marcuse, and others, who instructed them to find intelligent wedges, they decided to primarily target White people as the problem in our state. Now, while this fits the basic strategy of trying to shame the majority into submission, it's also perhaps a bit bold to try to start from scratch and count on having enough influence to convince eleven of twelve people to experience self-guilt and hatred in sufficient intensity to enable oppression in a state where many of us are more likely to see a moose than a minority. Granted, we understand the dogma is disconnected from reality, but if you're going to use the guilt trip approach, it helps to have something people can relate to for the tack.

But this is what happens again and again, and the further you get from the money, the more you see those who are trying to apply a nonsensical philosophy to their lives attempting to debate others with decreasing effectiveness. Having had the unique pleasure of having angry cat ladies scream at me in German, about what a terrible person I am, and whose skin tone could be generously called albino demonize me for toxic whiteness, I usually can only shake my head at their lunacy and wonder if they understand their own hypocrisy. What makes it sadder is the less effectively the argument has been made, the more likely it is one is dealing with a true believer.

I suppose it is fair to admit that no person has a completely consistent worldview, at least whom I have ever met, because we balance competing interests and events often have positive and negative attributes that mean something can be helpful in certain situations but harmful in others. This perpetual flux can lead people to struggle to identify reality, but that's why the wisest people often have the habit of having more questions than answers. I would certainly prefer to invest my time in learning more, as opposed to sharing ideas that may or may not be of use to people, but as humanity is a team sport, it's necessary for people to understand some things I think for our own survival, and so I reckon a book like this is worth the cost of the persecution I will incur for sharing such heresy. But at a minimum, whatever contradictions exist, I hope my ideas hold together and in everything I argue, I try to present a rational sense of self-interest for the reader.

To return to our progressive flagellants, they instead have a very destructive tendency. Their job is to pretend they are suffering to show how virtuous they are, although the one thing the smart and stupid alike seem to share is the easy embrace of hypocrisy, but their truest delight is in attacking others who refuse to conform. It's weird to think of clean-cut college students and middle-aged ladies as the equivalent of gangs from the barrio, but the same basic psychology applies. They enjoy the feeling of power to label and brand others, and through the act of exclusion which they claim is used against them, they actually lay siege to a supposed superior moral status through abnegation of their own purported interest in favor of the interests of others.

They take pathological altruism to an unhealthy extreme where they proclaim it would be more moral to surrender their past identity, present civilization, and children's future to a more virtuous other. Such actions run counter to basic human programming, yet for certain people who are either sufficiently isolated, indoctrinated, or both, this appeal works specifically because it makes people who are otherwise uncertain feel special and superior. When you see the majority being accused of supremacy, whether on a racial, cultural, religious, or ideological basis, what is going on in the minds of most accusers is an inversion where they secretly indulge the feeling that they are better than you because they are willing to suffer more.

The cult of the victim is very dangerous and very deadly because it leads people away from achievement or investment in themselves, and toward a path of destruction that might begin with words but ends in the celebration of the awful. We look at whomever fails, assume they are not responsible for their failures, especially if they can create either a reasonable or interesting claim of oppression, and we make excuses for them. You'll note I do not exclude the Right from this behavior, as we have seen the same thing on our side for years, like how only Black conservatives go forward to talk about race or Gay conservatives about marriage many times in the public eye. It's the same basic phenomenon, different only in degree, that says we cannot talk about what we experience unless we are either directly impacted or we are greater victims.

In the ultimate race to the bottom in the victim hood Olympics, we actually finally end up fulfilling the long awaited Marxist prophecy of achieving equality because when no one is good, everyone is suspect, and not a single person stands for the idea that they can do better than the norm. Finally we settle into the squalor like pigs and revel in the triumph of the common man. If that sounds harsh to you, go watch a video of what is present on the streets of San Francisco, a place that in many ways is the epicenter of this earth-shattering ideology in America and tell me what you see. The streets have more shit strewn across them than a Delhi back alley, and more needles than a seamstress convention would carry. When no one is allowed to be right and no one has cause to celebrate achievement, all we see is the maddening rush to descent and escape as the only refuge becomes fantasy and the various physical pleasures of self-mutilation which remain open for everyone as an expression of approved dissent.

The problem is these people have become the least likely of all gangs, but considering they are never told what they can't do, how well funded they are, and the collective failure of our whole nation in refusing to call out these fantasies that motivate them, we are now all suffering the consequences of problems which could have easily been prevented had just a few people had a little courage a generation ago. Reason remains true whether we follow its precepts or not, but the ability of people to play make believe is as limitless as the human imagination, and now we're seeing a collective form of insanity spread forth from our education system to engulf the entire land.

Transgenderism is the perfect example of the phenomenon. People should have the honesty and integrity to tell someone that self-mutilation, even if it is as involved as changing one's genitalia and hormones to enact a fantasy, is still fundamentally an act of self-delusion. You don't have to like being born a man or a woman, and far be it for me to tell someone what they want to do with their lives, but what should be made clear is that there is no responsibility to indulge a mass delusion. Mutilation doesn't change your sex. Indulging a fiction like this is incredibly harmful to any sense of cultural unity, because when truth becomes arbitrary, it isn't long before people start checking out and numbly nod their heads as we all pretend how progressive we are. Most people obviously are not, but the mass of Americans have learned so well that the cost of speaking out is such a hassle they choose instead to allow the unreal to masquerade as true.

Here's the big problem, and this is very much at the heart of the American crisis which the elites understand, and the Left desires. When one generation allows a fantasy to persist as a joke, the next generation sees such as the new normal and then defends the fantasy as if it is true. Consider it Gramsci's revenge if you like, but the communists are succeeding in their effort to destroy normalcy, health if we are more direct, by creating whole generations who exist in contravention of old truths. Moreover, it's not like we have seen one truth replaced by another, but rather from hostile forces which were deliberately aimed just to reduce those pillars of our society which were most firm and beneficial. We end up with the worst of the worst.

I've long believed this is permitted because a group of people as ruthless as those with the means to enact a world order like we struggle beneath are confident their own health and decisiveness would allow them to dispatch any threat from the watered down version of the cultural Marxists with relative ease. On the surface, this would seem true, and they certainly serve a valuable purpose of both suppressing any nationalist impulse to actually help the people by creating a false moral narrative of perfection to oppose the good. They also manage to keep the majority in line by articulating a false equivalency between two visions of radicalism, that while they may occasionally consider similar means, have a vital disconnect in that one defends nature and builds upon it, and the other seeks to destroy it as the highest categorical imperative.

I admit to being guilty of the crime of smart people, which is to naturally assume that people will think like I do, and are capable of seeing things through a similar context of knowledge, but there are many people for whom this simply does not apply, and they are not critical in an intellectual light. I've learned that people who proceed through life act differently, often through empathy, and these appeals work especially well with people of feminine disposition and less experience. To them, the psychologically astute appeal of offering to help all people is like catnip, utterly irresistible.

This became clear to me when I was explaining to a friend who happens to be progressive why we cannot simply just take care of everyone who won't take care of themselves. She offered a series of statements about our supposed obligation to help those who couldn't help themselves, who had suffered so many slights, and that giving them a helping hand would not be so bad. When I asked her how she would do that without imposing upon others in turn, she stumbled along and eventually realized even though it didn't sway her opinion that if you give the victim power over the supposed assailant, you just flip the relationship and create a new problem.

It pained her to admit multiculturalism causes conflict, because it denies the idea of a commonly accessible standard, yet this is what happens when those who think more with their hearts than their heads take control. They try to have acrimonious ideas and identities co-exist in the same space, and then they are genuinely surprised when good will alone is not enough to reconcile fundamental differences in belief or behavior. They accept the end game of equality for all and don't realize that for one standard to exist, then all sorts of identity will have to be destroyed lest the supposed inequality which needs to be eradicated persist in service of injustice.

If people were logical, nobody would believe something so obviously contradictory and impossible. It's no accident the Left has more women than men, as the best traits of women – which are empathy and care – are perverted from their natural role of caregivers for the family to being actively promoted as chief decision makers. But empathy without reason is a recipe for civilizational disaster, and as unpopular as it is to state, there might be a reason why there is little evidence for any major matriarchy in history. It's because if it had been tried, it would have disappeared about ten minutes later, because nature doesn't reward kindness but rather foresight. I love women and I love empathy, but when we try to be all things to all people, a sign of someone who is feeling rather than thinking, we surrender any claim or possibility of judgment, and as such the first thing we abandon is any idea of goodness.

This affliction impacts plenty of men as well, so the commentary is less about gender roles than it is in how simple naïve kindness is actually one of the most effective means by which a policy that is cruel to both those it attacks and those it purports to serve can be advanced. A healthier society would be led be people who, for their self-interest if nothing else, would have restrained these tendencies. But as part of their war of demolition against the majority, our current ruling elite love the peaceful path to dissolution which calls itself justice. In the end, they know, as we should, that the people who just want things to be nice are ultimately going to go along with whatever, but we've seen our democracy rigged to encourage more people who think this way: That government should try to be all things for all people regardless of social or economic cost, and as such we will continue on the path to disorder until the frustration rises enough that a purge or collapse happens.

When it does, I guarantee the first people to be taken out by any new regime will be the loudest complainers from the previous cycle who offer nothing but constant angst and serve only as sources of discord. The new order always consolidates itself by purging the most offensive elements of its early proponents, in order to buy credibility with the center, so that means all those people who argued for identity politics as victims for their obscure causes will, having lost their effectiveness as wedges against decency, be left on the island of misfit toys to be abandoned to what is likely a violent and ugly fate. Their opponents don't want them, their allies will no longer find them useful, and the healthy state has no place for sick minds. What comes next is inevitable.

Ironically, I feel sad for these people. We on the Right who care for health are left with this problem because it's not quite as simple for most of us to just say: "blow them out of the way." The conundrum of how one deals with the inept who have been deluded tugs on our heart strings – not to continue their foolishness, but to nurture these people back to health. But in the same way people who have terrible behaviors listen more to those who will enable them as opposed to offer helpful advice and a chance to reset, we must also find in ourselves a sense of justice and sternness to not let our love for people distract us from our own survival and the race to reclaim sanity.

When I talk about the Great Separation we must contemplate, there is nothing we can do but leave the useful idiots behind to realize the consequences of their own actions. I do not see them as victims anymore, nor do I care very much for their opinions, as their own lifestyle choices make clear the folly of their thoughts. I reject the idea that their voices are as valuable as ours for the same reason that I would not listen to my pets about how to run the household. Leadership has to be demonstrated through insight and foresight for the future, and considering what these people support, they are simply trying to destroy everything around them to satisfy the emptiness they feel inside. It is a human tragedy, one we are likely doomed to repeat again and again, yet for all its predictability we should be even more upset that so many people will not merely tolerate what these empty people advocate, but desire it.

Democracy suggests we have no choice but to go along. It says that when everyone jumps off the bridge because the message of the week is that humanity can fly, that we must face the abyss together, in spite of knowing better. Join them if you like, but if you choose sanity and ostracism like I have, your chance of survival, let alone health, only comes when you understand you have to walk away for good. Because madness is contagious, and what starts out as a joke where you just don't want to hurt someone's feelings can all too quickly become a new reality where the price of escape becomes too high to overcome.

Chapter 13: The Media-Propaganda Complex

We are relentlessly taught that decent people are not supposed to closely study what the Germans were doing in the last big war, but those on the Left have never applied such prohibitions to themselves, and what they have done with the media is straight from the Goebbels play book. As the expert propagandist made clear, the key to telling lies is to repeat them often, speak them loudly, and make them bigger every time one is confronted. Our American media learned the lesson well, and now has become the premiere propaganda operation of the world, serving as the voice of the powerful against the common man in a dozen different flavors, but always to serve the role of keeping the thermostat of public opinion within control.

Fake news is not a new phenomenon, nor is the tendency of journalists to support the Left. As I make clear in each of my works, I firmly believe there is no such thing as an unbiased source, and usually only the most arrogant of people somehow believe they are capable of detached objectivity, which no human actually possesses. However, just that sort of hubris is rife within the mainstream legacy media which has always seen their job as gatekeepers who decide what you can and cannot be trusted to consider. Along with the progressive muckrakers who serve as their allies to help stories percolate to the surface, like the infamous Russian dossier which had no basis in reality but which Buzzfeed – yet another site obsessed with cats – was more than happy to sanctify so CNN, MSNBC, and the entire media complex was happy to parade before you.

There's this really neat trick the media uses where they know that simply talking about an issue causes a psychological quirk in people's minds to go off, where if someone hears a suggestion repeated with enough frequency or intensity, they will start to believe it. Couple that with the power of imagery and peer pressure and the mere accusation of a misdeed becomes a self-sustaining narrative. I would submit that the hunt for Russian influence is the perfect example of this, because the reality is Israel, Saudi Arabia, and increasingly China already exert far more influence on American policy – including through direct control of Congress through donor financing. Yet the media has shown zero interest in exploring how AIPAC, CAIR, or the Confucius Institutes are so powerful, but they will chase every Slavic shadow deep into the night. Truth doesn't matter here, and it has always been the first casualty in the culture war.

Let me give you an idea of just how bad the skew is in journalism today. A joint study conducted by Texas A&M and Arizona State Universities surveyed nearly five hundred journalists across several major publications like the NY Times, Washington Post, and other leading print publications, and 96% of respondents identified their views as Hard Left, Left, or Moderate. 59% admit to progressive leanings, 37% claim to be in the center, with the remaining 4% claiming to lean Right, most only slightly. In case you had any illusions, what you should now know is the media is a propaganda wing of the Left. The stories they tell always have a slant designed to disparage the Right, and furthermore, the truly negligent behavior on their part is best demonstrated through the stories they never tell and indeed, actively suppress.

Here's one interesting fact which will never appear in the mainstream media, as just one example, reported from our own Bureau of Justice Statistics, which is that in cases where criminal activity was threatened against homeowners by invaders, people with guns were far more likely to safely survive such encounters. It will perhaps not surprise people here to also learn that proportional to their numbers in the population, Blacks are disproportionately far more likely than Whites to commit violent crimes, including with handguns. In fact, you might learn that over half of the incidents that involve mass shootings were committed by this minority, despite making up only one-eighth of the population.

Why do we never hear how privately owned guns save the lives of citizens? Why do we never hear about mass violence, other than the absolute minimum possible, except when a White person is the perpetrator? Once it is ascertained that the perpetrator is White, the entire Left apparatus goes into attack mode to argue that the citizens must be deprived of their liberties for the actions of that one – and rare – assailant. Could it be that the media is not interested in offering information, but instead is simply propagandizing the public?

I would argue, as I did in *"Someone Has to Say It"* that the media has been doing this for many years. They beat McCarthy into submission when he was making progress and haven't stopped since then. Behind every foolish war was the supposedly objective media acting once more in dereliction of duty. They know how to ask tough questions of their enemies. They also know how to tell lies about people, and they slander and libel people who don't have the resources to compete with their corporate masters, working in conjunction with Left wing clearing houses like the SPLC to basically convert press releases into news stories. We see this up in Maine so clearly as the Beacon, the Portland liberal paper, is actually a paid product of the Maine People's Alliance, a Democrat front organization where they buy influence to win the information war.

It's despicable to pretend to be something you are not, and we have seen the media do that for decades in all their formats. Only in comparison to the sheer punditry that passes for cable news or the blogosphere could one call the print media restrained. With the dwindling example of Fox News to serve as counter balance, now firmly in the grasp of fully committed progressive James Murdoch, the entire network media now exists only to reinforce the talking points of the Left, a trend which can be amply demonstrated just by watching how the exact same language is used to describe the issue of the day. The Left always looks smart and caring. The Right always looks dumb and mean. You are not allowed to criticize the Left or you literally get banned from the conversation. But you can make enough redneck jokes to make a Jeff Foxworthy gag reel, and there is no problem because as we know, the hypocrites are at the helm.

As explained earlier, this is a perfect example of the false dichotomy between business and government coming to the fore. While the illusion is that the Republican Party is the friend of corporations, which may be true in the services they provide, the reality is that only six corporations own over 90% of the viewing media on television – with heavy influence in the music and online markets as well – and they do us no favors. Between AT&T, Comcast, Disney, 20th Century Fox, Viacom, and CBS, $386 billion dollars was made in collective revenue and in the creation of the content which you most likely are watching across a spread of hundreds of different channels and networks. You see what they want, and what they don't want you to see remains hidden. This can be seen in the way Disney owns ABC, Comcast owns NBC, AT&T owns CNN … and how biased CBS is, and how Fox is starting to shift leftward. It's clear there is no real choice anymore in the mainstream news circuit.

Things weren't always this way. As this book contends, it was the free market ideology of the Right which enabled such consolidation for the cultural forces of the Left. Go back just thirty years, and there were fifty different corporations that split up the top 90% of market share. Regulations which existed to encourage local control of media, and limited how many outlets could be owned by a single entity, were gutted during the George W. Bush administration. Deregulation was sold on the basis that it would increase wealth and opportunity, but the reality is that it has only exacerbated the tendency of these conglomerates to expand and assimilate their rivals in a march toward monopoly.

Lest we be accused of not sharing our criticism in a fair and bipartisan manner, perhaps worse than enabling the consolidation of the media was the decision made back in 2013 during the Obama Administration to allow the government to actively propagandize the people. The American military and State Department had long practiced overseas propaganda upon foreign nations such as the Voice of America programs with which you might be familiar, but he changed the rules to allow the government of United States to basically try to brainwash its own people. You heard very little outcry from the media when this was suggested under their beloved ally, even though they would threaten revolution if Trump suggested anything nearly so dangerous.

It's important you know just what contempt the government has for the people, because they will put out in plain sight just what they intend for us if you bother to read. For instance, if you support liberty, there are some agencies which would consider you a possible domestic terrorist for nothing more but adherence to our oldest and most treasured law. The media, which is theoretically their watchdog, has long been the handmaiden of the security state, having a perverse and symbiotic relationship.

If you were to tear apart the false duality between welfare and warfare that we used to be told was the "guns versus butter" question that separated the parties and their adherents, you would find a media that loves every war as good for ratings, to expand government, and to move another step closer to creating the need for global outcomes. You see a Deep State that plants friendly stories and coverage, using the media to broadcast their prerogatives above and beyond the elected officials, constantly attacking the Right, and branding nationalists as terrorists through selective dispersal of stories.

There are consequences to this level of deceit. When you see people on the Left marching as angry mobs through the streets and speaking about how much they want to offer their resistance, understand that it is the media that is primarily providing the animus that pushes them. The theatrical production they receive spins precisely the morality tale needed each time, including embellishment where needed, excluding those things which would debunk the narrative, and relying overwhelmingly on a heavy dose of emotion to ensure the shock narrative goes through as intended. Were I only to watch what they said, I might hate myself also, think this country was a rotten place, and act accordingly. But outside that bubble, where the facts tell a different story, people can find a better way to behave. The problem is that the media echo chamber is trying to swallow everything.

Numbers don't lie and what was happening, and frankly why Trump won in 2016, is because alternative media arose and leveraged the power of social media to get around this expensive barricade as nimble data often does. Certain major channels on YouTube and Facebook like Infowars, Joe Rogan, PewDiePie and others whom you may have never heard of, were able to reach new audiences in numbers larger than networks like CNN or MSNBC broadcast per broadcast. And when you factor in smaller channels that still garnered thousands or tens of thousands of views per broadcast, there was a vital and functioning media alternative that was crushing the competition. Only the excitement of the Presidential campaign and the perpetual shock of a 24-hour outrage cycle was helping keep the dinosaur of traditional media afloat, but after 2016, the Left determined such an outrage as preventing the coronation of Queen Hillary would not be permitted again.

With willing accomplices in Big Tech, including Google, Facebook, Twitter, PayPal and Apple as the worst of the offenders, a smash and grab campaign has begun to basically destroy the economic basis upon which the alternative citizen journalism model was flourishing. People were deprived of revenue on arbitrary terms, which in reality were intensely political. This can be demonstrated by the fact that every channel that has been either demonetized, delisted, shadow banned, or outright banned looks at important questions from perspectives outside what the official media allows. Lives were wrecked in this media war, and the biggest lie told in the process was to "disappear" the alternative narrative from the public eye. Those of us who knew where to look could follow the migration, but for the mass of people whose penetration of social media was only surface deep, they lost access to the countervailing narrative. Now, all they see is a steady diet of approved propaganda like YouTube feeds now read, with fact checkers telling you not to believe anything that doesn't correspond to the official party line.

The technique seems to be to so frustrate the alternative sources of media so as to bankrupt them or run them out of town. It is my misfortune to report this strategy is working far better than I would wish, as many people who were doing excellent work have been drummed out by selective enforcement against their messages. Furthermore, the new development as I write this is in the issuance of new rules that ban offensive content. Were I to post a video on YouTube, for instance, that was critical of the surge in illegal immigration, that video would be branded as hate speech and I would receive a strike against my account, with three such reported infractions leading to the termination of my ability to reach the largest viewer market in the world.

Comparatively, there are no Left leaning issues where a similar ban exists. They can say what they want, do what they want, and not only do they get to speak out, but they get paid for their work where we get attacked and often lose access to financial services. In these actions, we see clearly how the elites who control banking and business are tipping the scales to the Left thinking that their preservation lies in restraining nationalism in the name of ecumenical state-run globalism. They silence us because they fear what a morally awakened people in mutual loyalty could accomplish, but this struggle is one which is only getting worse by the day.

Even if the power brokers were neutral, the Left would still likely win this fight because they have no compunctions against lying in service to a greater cause, and because they punish their enemies. They organize mobs of people to get individuals doxed – to determine the legal identification of a person behind a pseudonym, and then viciously try to get them fired, bankrupted, or sometimes worse. They make clear that if corporations don't toe the line, a boycott and endless succession of hit piece articles will follow. They are nasty, but since they mean their threats, business acquiesces, and they are consolidating their control of legacy media at the same time they're snuffing out the other options.

Particularly disappointing, but not surprising is how the Republican Party has done absolutely nothing to help their partisans. They simply let it happen in oblivion, grateful for the attention to be pointed away from them for the moment, even as the very activists who are responsible for their success get swallowed up by this system one by one – never to return. They're content to lose the information war so long as they buy themselves more time, yet another reason I so hate what the Right has allowed to represent our position.

In this chapter, we've spent a lot of time talking about the direct media, but it's important to note, because the control of news and entertainment has become one and the same, that other forms of media which people consider purely entertainment follow the exact same formula. The stereotypes which are often the inverse of reality are aggressively reinforced, where movies are sure to endorse a progressive message and those who offer conservative dissent are inevitably blacklisted from access to further work. Predictive programming is the means by which people are conditioned to accept precisely what is wanted for the future vision of America, and we're told that we will live in a future of multicultural harmonious bliss where all benefit.

If people walk the streets for about ten minutes, the lie is abundantly clear. Yet, when no one can afford to leave their home and they retreat into the realms of fantasy, which is all propaganda really is. The hypnotic vision they provide bypasses the critical factor in the mind, and transfixes most people to such a degree that it's possible for people to believe anything, even something that contradicts what they see with their own eyes. America is a very big country, and those people living in the worst areas have reason to hope there are successes elsewhere. Others who inhabit places which are still nice will believe the worst and give power over to fix things so the ugly places can be beautiful too.

It could be a really great system, if it were rooted in truth. But just like everything else today, media is caught up in the great ignoble lie that we need to sack reason and truth in order to forge equality. So, they have become attack dogs in service of the mindlessness of the man they promote. I think many people in the field know this, and that's why they have settled into a shock and awe pattern of reinforcing existing bias and using a parade of color and imagery to whittle down popular resistance to their ideas.

I think it works better than we would like to admit, but whether one believes the news or not, I'll tell you what they definitely accomplish. They set the narrative, and if we win the day for our side by debunking some foolish claim, then what have we really accomplished beyond a rear-guard defensive retreat? We never get to push our issues, and in this war where we inhabit the perpetual defensive, we who are forced into being reactionaries are never given the opportunity to fully present our alternatives. We are told we never have ideas because we never get to set an agenda that will allow those ideas to be heard.

You can't win a war by only defending your fortress when the attack is unending. That reality is why the Left's control of the culture is so damning, and they win the battle to shape the noise each day such that we rarely manage to steal back the momentum. It's why I personally ignore them even though they don't return the favor to me, because each lie they tell is only a day wasted in distraction and diversion.

But it's hard to avoid that, and even against an old hand like myself, they still win more often than they should.

Chapter 14: Higher Indoctrination

In conjunction with a media that relentlessly reinforces a certain narrative message which is very friendly to both globalism and the Left, the entire school system is now structured to essentially serve as indoctrination factories whose primary purpose is not the education of children, but unfortunately to ensure conformity with the existing regime. This fact is why it is impossible for those of us coming from the Right to seriously contemplate the solutions we might like to imagine available to us of awakening youth to new possibilities, or a change in thought such that the trends expressed in demography and other areas might not prove so damning. The narrative provided by schools is so effective that the children and grandchildren of immigrant populations vote even more leftwards than new immigrants. Banish the thought of changing things through education ⊚⊚⊚from your mind, because whether one set of ideas is better or not means nothing when the only choices available almost universally subscribe to the dominant narrative.

We already know that teachers from grade school to the university tend to lean left, with the gap becoming more pronounced as the education level advances. Education Week conducted a survey of over one thousand primary school teachers which revealed they identified as Democrats much more heavily than Republicans and voted for Clinton nearly twice as often as Trump. None of this should be surprising, but what's even less shocking and potentially more harmful to the prospects of liberating our youth from the system is the overwhelming opposition the professional education lobbies have to any alternative to state schooling. It's predictable that as most teachers enjoy employment within that system, they would fight to maintain a monopoly that encourages the same sort of centralizing force that makes it so schools gravitate to just one set of opinions.

This gap only gets worse by the time minds have passed through their formative years to their final educational experiences in college, where ideological lenses become much more explicit. A recent study by Mitchell Langbert, Professor at Brooklyn College which looked into the affiliations of 8,688 of his colleagues at sixty of the top colleges in America, revealed a startling disparity in who is permitted to teach. For each Republican, there are ten Democrats, and over forty percent of the colleges have zero ideological diversity – where not even one Republican was allowed to teach. Consider just how vast that gap has become, and realize that colleges are not places our children go to get educated, at least when it comes to a balanced approach to civics. They are indoctrination factories, where social justice is creeping into every discipline, and the richest irony is we're paying tens or even hundreds of thousands of dollars per pupil to buy into this system.

Whether it is the always-rising property taxes that fund primary education and make home ownership an onerous financial burden, or the piles of debt required for access into the elite institutions and state schools alike, the genius of the

American education system for the Left is they collect so many billions of dollars to do precisely what they want: To control how we think. It is both remarkable and disappointing that private alternatives and school choice have not been pushed more firmly, a consequence perhaps of the collapse of the old parochial system from prominence on the one hand, and a short-sighted financial desire not to pay for a duplication of services when the state so gladly makes available their option which we all pay for whether we use it or not.

To fully comprehend how bad things have become, let's walk through the system as one of our children would have to do. From the onset, compulsory education has always been part of the socialist political platform going back to luminaries like Eugene V. Debs. The state has always wanted to take control of children's thinking away from parents, and long before technology ensured a screen was always before a child's face, schools were the first and best solution for managing how children think.

You have to send your children to school. While I think we would mostly agree that we want children to be educated as a basic value, what you discover is if you want any school that isn't the state school, you had better be prepared for major hassles. If your family is prepared or even able to make the economic sacrifice to home school, an option that is popular in some places, you will still be charged the tax burden for the service you don't use, and your child will still have to pass the tests that come from the same system –

meaning you must, at least to some degree, teach your children the lies of the dominant narrative so they can pass the tests. And in some states, even this option is not available. The same is true for charter and alternative schooling where each state is very different, but powerful teacher unions and ideological interests from the Left come together to deny parental choice or make it so expensive only the wealthy can afford it.

For many reasons, unless parents are already committed to trying to exist outside the system, a choice which often results in relative poverty and financial hardship, denial of access to resources being a major problem, most people just use government promoted statistics to determine what is or is not a good school and send their children along. Now, people will move and agree to horrendous commutes to find what is classified as a good school district, which is a common justification used that serves as a surrogacy to often avoid the consequences of what multiculturalism wreaks on other areas. That's another issue altogether, but assuming one finds a decent school, then what do the children learn?

I recently had the misfortune of reading a common core textbook out of morbid curiosity. I don't know how else to say this, but these systems are making our children dumber, and I don't think it is any accident. Instead of helping them acquire basic skills which will scale to solve future problems they might encounter, they learn tricks like estimation, and are instructed how to make use of sources around them to depend on their environment rather than to develop natural aptitudes. It is a system that encourages dependency and lowers standards to create a bar for success so low that if one could not pass, it would be a sign of serious mental deficiency for all students not suffering from some disability. Let's also not forget the creeping definitions therein of mental health where curiosity has become misdiagnosed as ADHD or a host of other disorders.

The politicians play a game where they say they no longer support Common Core, but who reads or publishes the textbooks? It's the same few companies who were doing so before, and as just a few publishers control that, you probably don't need me to tell you how far Left publishing leans as a field. That's why I'm self-publishing hard hitting narratives like this and living on the margin, waiting for the day when I get censored out of existence, while any progressive fluff piece gets massive promotion and free marketing from the major houses in New York. The process is no different in education, where the State Boards lean Left, and they make certain their agenda is being taught.

What children learn now is multiculturalism, a critical view of the United States, reduced and simplified versions of writing, reading, and mathematics, and they exist in a system where social promotion, especially in our poorest areas, is a reality of life. It's gotten so bad that I know students who have actually been suspended in some schools for daring to ask the simple question "why" about the story that is told. Instead of encouraging critical inquiry, once understood as the point of education, our teachers now do the opposite. They are forced to parrot the book, teach to the test, and should one of them diverge too far from the narrative and actually invest effort and skills to provide a broader view for the students, the consequences can be drastic.

You will never hear about a teacher getting fired for being too progressive in their views, but in this age of the social media inquisition, there have been many times where school boards have become aware of nationalist leanings in a teacher who was then released without cause from their position. I encourage you to check through the numerous stories that apply and see for yourself the reality of how the sanctity of indoctrination is preserved.

This matters so much because as Gramsci noted, these are the years where children through habit and experience gain their idea of what constitutes normalcy. Even the brightest of pupils, ultimately, are only a product of their environment, and what the Left has done so brilliantly and completely is control every element of outside influence in the life of a young American to promote, popularize, and moralize their message. Save for those lucky few who have families to provide a counterbalance, most adults much like myself only learn how deceitful these lies are through the ugly process of disillusionment from actual experience, the shocks of which some never recover from and retreat from the larger world altogether. But for others, the indoctrination sticks, and they follow a golden path set out for them where they learn early and well that conformity is rewarded and to sustain and bolster the message that we are promoting justice by taking down the old America for the new.

Our best and brightest compete against one another for the opportunity to be snatched up by a college system that opens doors to status and wealth in life, but only at the price of leveraging so much debt against one's future earnings that compliance to the system is nearly guaranteed. Attend an elite institution and the tuition bill for four years will extend well past one hundred thousand dollars. Add a postgraduate degree, and the cost could rise above a quarter million. It's now estimated students pay debt for upwards of ten years from graduating with a bachelor's degree, and even longer for those who get advanced degrees. I know because I'm still paying off the last of my loans from Swarthmore, a common and crippling affliction for our young people.

But what do our young men and women learn at college? They learn how everything is contaminated by whiteness, a definition so vague and expansive all at once that it has both the attributes of oppression and clinginess. It can be everywhere and can be used any time a person of color feels they don't have the advantage to cut down another from success. Did I say that wrongly? I meant; it exists to ensure that equalized outcomes are always achieved through the admittance that the accident of birth gives certain privileges to people who are habituated unjustly to better accept the cultural norms we must oppose as systematizing privilege in the legacy of colonial oppression. It's hard to speak that language – like the Orcish tongue of Mordor for the sane – but what they essentially learn is that everything old is bad, everything traditional must be opposed – and that their sacred religious duty is to wreck what existed before and celebrate the mean and the mundane.

You need only look at what gets protested and the movements which exist throughout this country as proof of that blanket statement. College has become a game where we try to identify new ways to claim victim hood, new means by which to attack reason and knowledge, and new fantasies which might be promoted. I genuinely wonder if this would work if not for the unhappy accident that as it still represents a way for young people to delay the onset of the working world. The alternative for noncompliance, which I know many thinking men and women have had to adopt as punishment for heresy against the new faith, is to revert to physical labor for survival as they have been deliberately excluded from the world of ideas despite having supple minds. But if you support the Left, you can be assured of a tenure track position, social status, and a comfortable position in society if you exert just a modicum of effort. A stroke of genius implemented in this system is that it rewards people as individuals for their compliance with the destruction of the group to which they belong, while using debt to keep them beholden to that system if their commitment should waver.

People who were habituated to critical thinking would realize such armchair revolutionaries who are subsidized and sustained every step of the way certainly do not represent any threat to an elite which proudly develops their mission. It's strange to me that this question never occurs to the young folk who think they are rebelling by doing just what they are told, but this is where that false narrative of partisanship where we're told big business is the enemy of the helpful government and the good Democrats oppose the bad Republicans is so useful. Having little context to understand the deeper problems, and being deprived of the ability to root critical thinking skills in reason rather than dialectical dogma, even smart people are led astray as their intellect is placed in service of false idealism; this faith that equalized outcomes are possible and that man can somehow transcend his nature to exist above our environment.

I actually wish we could have that argument on college campuses again. But we can't, because the Left only permits the people who agree with their views to gain tenure, using the linguistic attacks perfected by the cultural Marxists to ensure most universities remain an ideological monopoly. A combination of threats, protests, persuasion, and even violence is used to ensure alternative voices cannot invade the safe space created, a laughable term that conceals a far darker agenda. The safe space is the workplace where psychological conditioning is being completed, which we who still retain our sanity might find comical, but where our children are being lost, some of whom will never be recovered again.

If you don't believe me, consider some of the attitudes expressed by young people. A growing number think socialism would be great and that communism is a good idea. They vote overwhelmingly for the Left, and in people like Alexandra Ocasio-Cortez, you see the future of what these new Democrats will support. They believe government should run our lives because they believe our people are misled, that liberty is obsolete, and that we need to achieve "social justice" at any cost. Remember that this woman represents New York City, in part, one of the wealthiest cities in the world, which endorsed someone who basically argues to tax everything, regulate anything, and that we should return to primitivism lest an environmental calamity somehow destroy human existence. This shows the that the indoctrination lasts long after the pupil has entered the world at large, and that's the key piece: there is a lifelong continuity of information which exists to suppress opposing viewpoints and reinforce the conditioning.

The worst thing is our students and most of their parents have no clue this is happening until it is too late to stop. We sometimes will win a victory here or there against something so egregious that we laugh off the idea. For instance, there is a woman teaching at the University of Illinois whom I heard about yesterday for the first time that is a paid professor who argues 2+2 = racism because it represents the idea that objectivity leads to truth, and is the concept of objective truth constitutes a public expression of whiteness that is intended to oppress diverse viewpoints more concerned with the first essence of things. Somehow, I doubt she's conjuring up Plato for this case, and it's easy to laugh at someone like that as a quack, but she's taking in hundreds of thousands of dollars of tuition hours to spread this message, and while we fight away such clear stupidity, how many subtler messages are being passed on without being filtered out as the new normal, without our young folk even realizing the full depth of the lies being pushed?

There is hunger amongst our young people to hear a different message, as many smart people have enough reason and insight to see these ideas are absurd. This is especially true for those in college who went seeking to study hard sciences and other apolitical subjects who are seeing mission creep expand far beyond the nuisance primary courses most colleges require in general subjects to ensure the lessons in dogma are taught. These people are having to educate themselves, and they read heretical books like this and others to know there is another view, that Western Civilization wasn't always this insane, and there are reclamation and resistance efforts ongoing.

The Internet, for all its many problems, is perhaps our last hope. With ironic message boards and obscure places on social media, it's an irony that the counter-culture having been so censored from the legitimate spaces, and those legitimate spaces deemed as such being so neutered and controlled, that we have to count on sites like Gab, Minds,

Bitchute, and yes, /pol/ to drive the renewal of moral culture. At least they'll appreciate the irony of this situation, but in a world where your information follows you, what people think is how the culture war is won, and we are running out of time and weapons because in this numbers game, man is losing to the equality machine.

Chapter 15: Left Alone Death Will Follow

In this final chapter about the Left, I want to share why I deliberately took a different approach to how I'm talking about both sides of the conflict in this book. One of the challenges of writing a somewhat continuous narrative is to manage to cover information that exists in far greater depth elsewhere, as my explanation of the various institutions and interests in *"The Coming Civil War"* does, but which I am here only touching on briefly as we are fundamentally asking a different question. What unites the Left, what do they want, and how will they behave?

Our better nature compels us to seek a compromise solution where we can reconcile differences, which is why this book is trying to show you two things about the people who are the deepest adherents to their side. Firstly, they own the culture and they have no intention of releasing their grip even one iota. This matters because it means all the solutions to the conflict that we might imagine that involve education, a change in culture, or that we will somehow return to a saner center exist only in the realm of extreme improbability. Secondly, you have to understand how they understand themselves, and that they believe themselves to be on a holy mission to destroy normalcy so they can realize Utopia. They believe what they have been taught, and you really need to take them far more seriously than laughing at their absurdity, and see the threat they pose.

My father used to tell me that it does absolutely no good to tell a crazy person they are crazy. They won't realize the truth of the statement, and you'll likely only agitate them in the process. When you fight these people, they will hate you and they have no reason to back down as they control not just the narrative but through such, what the future America will look like. As it looks like them, it will act like them until we reach a point of no return, which frankly we might have already breached. When you accommodate them, hoping they might return the favor in a future reciprocation, I think we've now learned over decades of this advancing culture war that they never move backwards in their long march forward. This is why the most likely outcome is they will win, and their petty authoritarianism will either realize the debauchery of an orgy of state sponsored violence that wrecks America, or facilitates a more measured transition where the future United States will look much like the People's Republic of China if cooler heads prevail. Pick your poison, but this project will ensure one thing: As our population becomes like the rest of the world, so too will the way our government works.

As ugly as these proclamations are, my goal is to do you a service in destroying any false hope you have that gentle reform will save us from the consequences of dysgenic social policy. Our time is short before these trends are not only irreversible, but where we have an ever-reducing series of options which have less chance of success and require more radical thought and action. It's hard to make the argument

America can save itself, and that makes how we use the time before us a question of critical importance. More on this shortly, but let's talk about where the Left is going to go in the not too distant future.

Winners take a victory lap. Look for them to push harder to consolidate their control over the media and voices, and punish those who offer dissent. In advance of the 2020 election, it is obvious – or should be, if you pay attention – that dissident voices are being censored and blacklisted from every major social media platform. If this is not a coordinated effort, it should be even more terrifying to the rest of us. Because that means either the lobbies which spend all their time trying to destroy American citizens are that successful in pushing corporations into compliance, or that the rank and file of big business have become so indoctrinated already that they are independently working to remove anyone they don't like without any protest. The recent revelations from whistle-blowers at Google suggest the latter is definitely true, where social justice has become company policy. The former is also very much likely happening as we see certain lobbies, with the LGBTQ folks taking the lead, working to silence anyone who offends their ever-growing sense of injustices.

The Democrats do one very intelligent thing which is the opposite of their Republican peers. The Democrats use their left flank, that is, those who are far enough Left to be outside the mainstream, to do the dirty work that shapes the future, while the Republicans disavow even their most benign right flank, signaling their way into oblivion to please people who, if properly understood, are the enemies of all they say they actually believe. This is why the people surrounding the Obama Administration seemed so arrogant, because they knew they would have allies to expand their message into every corner of American life, and because they knew the demography was just a few election cycles away from realizing permanent victory. It speaks to just how terrible and corrupt Hillary Clinton was as a candidate that she could not win despite having every advantage, and that there was still some energy on the Right to oppose this agenda.

Don't count on it being there in 2020. It's easy to laugh now while the Democrats fight each other over who will be the largest social justice warrior, but when the final campaign comes, there are good reasons why they will likely win. The banks who do not appreciate being politicized will be sure to accelerate the economic downturn which was inevitable anyway to ensure a favorable environment to flush out the nationalists who failed to strike decisively. The media narrative will be to present whoever emerges from the Democrat primaries as a unifier, in the best possible light, and the campaign will ultimately be about arguing how to set politics aside. In the same way that "Hope and Change" was presented as moderate even though it was the most radically Left agenda in our history until what comes next, the media will sell the annoyed American public a message that electing a Democrat means all the noise and fury will disappear. Leave aside the truth that they cause all the noise and fury with their false accusations and active propaganda, two facts the average citizen won't understand, and you can see already how the map will look for 2020. Once the Democrats win, they will legalize every illegal the Republicans permit, which I bet will be all of them, and if they're particularly ironic, we'll be locked into the new America with a wall lest those of us who were oppressors seek an escape.

Maybe I'm wrong about 2020. Let's hope. But even if I am, this is coming soon, and every election brings us closer to that brink, which is why the Left is only going to double down on identity politics. They have stumbled into a situation where for the moment, they have created through intersectionality a coalition that unites every racial group against Whites who are presented, fairly or not, as latent Nazis in the making. They reinforce that message daily in spite of how many people on the Right are becoming aware of the threat because they have to remind their own disparate coalition of the justice of their cause, which is only held together by presenting a common enemy of sufficient stature to keep Muslims from throwing queers off buildings and prevent Blacks and Latinos from allowing gang wars to define themselves as enemies rather than allies under the deceptive frame of people of color. They learned from 2016 that the path forward is through organizing people into groups they can control, and so the attacks against the majority will become ever more vicious.

The Left is now a negativist religion whose doctrinal creed is egalitarian Utopia as the ascendancy, but which uses iconoclasm as the means of promoting itself. Predictably, the culture war will accelerate and attack those areas which exist outside their purview with greater force and urgency. The family will be targeted even more viciously, and if you look beneath the propaganda, you'll probably see those who are directly in the cross hairs will most likely be children. Look for new ways to emerge for the state to get involved sooner, more deeply, and be able to take kids from their parents on ever thinner justifications. As the ever-expanding definitions of mental illness develop, it wouldn't surprise me in the least if Child Protective Services evolves into a truly fearsome agency, far exceeding any mandate they already have.

There will be resistance to this agenda, but unless an organized front presents itself, what we will see is the threat of violence from both state and non-state actors will be used in conjunction to suppress those who want to defend tradition or morality. Law enforcement will be weaponized and politicized to an extent which befit the old Soviet regimes, with those who commit an ever-growing list of thought crimes accused of stealing from society at large. Look for these people to be actively shamed on social media, ostracized from access to basic finance, and reduced to a life of criminality which will be used as an ex post facto explanation for how they were really criminals all along. Lost in this convenient definition will be that it was society which criminalized their right of expression and in so doing, created a recidivist of every Republican.

Americans imagine this cannot happen here only because it has not yet occurred. Every country that has stood the test of time, which ours may or may not, goes through these phases. A prolonged period of wealth and prosperity leads idle minds down particularly unproductive pathways, and in overcoming opposition, we often become like those we defeat. In this sense, you could see the current problems as the continuation of the Cold War, where these last salvos of the Marxists that continued long past the demise of the Soviet Union are now coming to fruition. The security state both sides adopted always had the possibility to prove mutually destructive, and this idea that only nuclear weapons could destroy the future and potential for a people was always far too narrow.

In light of the larger framework we're using in this book, you can be assured law enforcement will eventually defend the elite's interest, which is just as well served by socialist egalitarianism as it is a capitalist variant. In fact, I suspect you will find the largest corporations are the most eager adherents to a common front to prevent their status from being threatened by true innovation, and the consolidation of new technology leaders into a single bloc is already happening as alliances are being developed to keep out insurgent information which could threaten the comfortable models people already use. The problem of bigness is you only stay on top so long as you squash those beneath you, so we know no matter what promises are made before Congress or the like, the information war that is culture will continue against the people.

In theory, the way one would have fought this previously is the way nationalists have done in the past: to take to the streets and organize on the ground. To some extent, the ongoing Yellow Vests protests in France represent one active and continuing variation of this approach, but the media blackout of these causes, the state crackdowns, and the deliberate support of Antifa organizations is also making this route impossible to enact.

To be frank, Antifa isn't much when it comes to a paramilitary force. But they serve the purpose of controlling the streets in order to assure that dissent does not emerge in a form potent enough to offer a threat to the evolving agenda. I suspect this is why they receive so much support and are permitted to leverage all of social media to spread their message and organize, and why the media villainizes those who take the opposite position which, despite the many lies to the contrary, is not the imposition of Fascism – a system of unity between the state and corporations that already exists under the current oligarchy and which masquerades beneath democracy – but rather the defense of traditional identity which has been attacked. The four groups presently attacked, who will continue to be targets indefinitely, are White people, straight people, Christians, and country folk. To the extent a person fits any of these categories, they will be suspect, with people like myself who embrace all four being branded as domestic terrorists for our very being. You see this already if you watch how they speak on the news or are actively involved in social media.

Antifa exists to threaten us every time we organize. Allow me to share a recent story that played out here in Maine with my own group, Maine for Mainers. We were holding a family picnic last month, and then these mysterious letters appeared for all the neighbors adjoining the property where the picnic was scheduled. The letters stated that we were having a "White supremacist" gathering, and that they could leave their hoods and robes at home. The media jumped into the fray to accuse us of sending these postcards, which we obviously did not, as not only do we not believe these things, but we also would never do anything so obviously harmful even if we did. In response, we asked the State Police to investigate, and we discovered that these cards came from some anonymous mailer a hundred miles away in one of our larger cities. What makes this more impressive is the location in which the event was held is such that it was not possible to simply send mail to the people living on the street, as PO Boxes were used in this rural area, so someone got paid to look up tax records to send out these hit pieces. We know that's how it happened because of how many maiden names were used, a sign that old information was used to determine how to reach that particular street. I'm telling you this so you understand that people literally are getting paid to go this far to disrupt a family picnic just to maintain the narrative.

As the story evolves it gets worse, because the media appeared, and had the presumption to ask why we espoused the views on the post cards. From this it is clear that the media are connected at the hip with the progressive nonprofits who advertise in their rags and who are ideological allies. So, I had the joy of explaining to deaf ears – for the thousandth time – how we are not Nazis, while the other side says we are. How does one win such battles, even when the evidence is so overwhelmingly apparent? We held the event four days later and I'm proud to say our group grew our online presence by 20% that week thanks to people being fed up with the same tired narrative, but Antifa sent three armed people out to the country to threaten, harass, and stalk the property. I am certain it is no coincidence that the media just happened to show up five minutes after. After doing a bang up job reporting on the "White supremacist" picnic, they all disappeared when the local police came along, and we could get to the question of how the twelve of us who cared could somehow stop a system where the media, politicians, finance, and street thugs were all aligned against us.

My experience with a simple family picnic is only a microcosm of what any activists opposing these people face, because while Antifa might not be impressive in isolation, they exist as part of a broader cooperative effort and as the useful flagellum waving about that allows the Left to leverage its control of so many other areas into perpetuating and advancing a false narrative that most people don't bother to question. Some never get that far, some are inclined due to empathy to support them, and a great many who know better go along because they reckon it not worth the hassle. In that last group, we find the true danger of what they represent and why odds suggest the Left will most likely succeed in owning the future.

When we watch the protests happen on a larger scale than what I recounted from my own struggles in the field in Maine, the same basic facts hold true. Just this last weekend, there were competing rallies in Portland, Oregon, and the media was already out there attacking, and I kid you not about this term, multicultural White supremacists from the far-right in the Proud Boys group. In reality, they are primarily a Christian organization who has been forced into paramilitary posture by being constantly attacked, not just by their opposite number, but by lawfare in terms of members being threatened with lawsuits, as well as the Democrats who run Portland trying to help their Antifa voters who dress up like terrorists in black and go assault the streets. The good guys turned a nice trick by not showing up leaving the media to run stories about the far right protests where the actual images were of Antifa clad goons attacking the police when they fight they hoped for did not materialize. But it just shows how anyone opposing the Left is always going to have to overcome being set up as the villain.

It's probably too much to ask when people are as passive as they are. Those who act and lean Left have a huge advantage. But those who take no action, which is the lesson most people are supposed to learn and where the elites want us to be, are also facilitating the rise of the Left. Now, I have no doubt these useful idiots who insist too far, such as the Antifa goons, will be removed once the new order is declared, as Alinsky told the same to radicals in his day that liberalism in the classic sense was a system that allowed its enemies to get away with murder. We see that now and today, to be honest, and considering the costs of speaking out are almost becoming more painful than the costs of committing such crimes, one wonders how long America can endure.

There was a time when many Leftists would have been bothered by such an outcome. Not now. Workers of the world unite is the spirit of the time, and as we are overrun by newly undocumented future Americans, remember the future of equality is where these people will the means by which those of us who are now obsolete are pushed aside. An invasion by any other term, the Great Replacement is both a demographic and cultural attack for which the Right has lacked the moral vision to even attempt to offer an answer. If you aren't worried, you should be.

Chapter 16: Money Can't Buy My Love

In the classic morality tale with heroes and villains, this would be the part of the story where having presented the dangers from the Left and having excoriated our negligent and prideful elite, that I would tell the story of the happy agitators who are offering noble resistance. I wish this were that sort of fable, but alas, reality is disappointing and so much more banal, hence the next stretch of chapters is going to obliterate the Right for how it behaves. These attacks are intended less for the adherents, although we all should take our fair share of responsibility, but more for the thought leaders, institutional actors, and those we put into power to advance our cause. And this is my message to the thought leaders and institutional actors of the establishment "Right:" You have all failed us miserably and before your cowardice costs us our entire civilization, you need to get out of the way so people willing to rise to the occasion and offer a forceful rebuttal to the Left and to globalism can emerge. If no other appeal works, consider your own survival is likely just as dependent upon this happening as ours.

If someone attacked you and said your family was awful and ugly, I bet you would have the instantaneous response which is natural and proper to say that your family is good and beautiful. We define conflict in moral terms by our clarity of opposition and strength of resolve. One could call these faith and passion in a broader sense. So, when we were told that the people who make up the majority of

America are wicked and harmful, the response from the Right should have been to defend those attacked as good and essential. However, the moment the Left played their game of linguistic programming and issued a modifier like White, Christian, or Straight, somehow the Right short-circuited and went into a mechanical repetition that identity doesn't matter. The consequence of this is that the demographic replacement of America is creating an ultimate path to total victory for the Left, that our moral leadership from the church refuses to go anywhere near political issues (except in those cases it is willing to adopt the Left), and families themselves are defamed as sources of oppression. Love is literally seen as less preferable to the state in some quarters, which could only happen when people became so craven that they would not defend the essential, which is precisely what has happened.

It's a terrible analogy, but it's sort of like a brow-beaten husband whose wife is truly a terror to behold, one of those shrews who so dominates her partner that he shrinks from being, and when she yells, he goes shopping just to escape. In a moral sense, that's what the Right did starting in the 1960's as they retreated into an amoral bubble of libertarian free market bliss where toys and tools became their refuge because the heat in the cultural conflicts became too much. We ceded the question of morality in the public sphere to the Left who would go on to impose their ideals in the synergy between the state, university and media. And thus began what we could ungenerously call our long retreat. We abandoned our cities, our schools, and by now, even our children into escapes in a world of merit, a self-sustaining economic bubble. We did become rich in material status, but at the cost of moral bankruptcy, so when we wonder why young people have such little interest in what is promoted in respectable circles, it's not hard to understand why an amoral philosophy of humanist relativism, also known as capitalism, is clearly morally inferior to a moral philosophy of humanist relativism, which is what communism is.

The reality is both systems are insane because they suffer from the same defects of seeing humans in purely economic/materialist terms, and of assuming directionality in history. Capitalism might not be as doctrinaire as Communism, but the obscure moral core of the belief system has always been toward acquisition and consolidation, so the argument that more is better becomes the imperative for those who want to demonstrate their good character. Do I believe Capitalism is better than Communism? Marginally yes, only because the best producers understand that innovation and growing new markets create value, and this requires the ability to think of novel approaches that have social utility. Yet, economists have long understood there is a corrosive tendency toward the commodification of things that places concerns of material and capital acquisition above the interests of people. As a result, there has been an awful negative feedback function such that as America has become more morally empty, capital has become more rapacious in how it balances short-term gains over long-term investment. The problem of bigness and the search for profits has stomped out the idea that work itself is a moral value, and we see instead proof of this in how every aspect of law and regulation helps the big company at the expense of the little one.

An easy example to prove this is the case of a local brick and mortar business versus Amazon, something very relevant to small towns. The brick and mortar inherently costs more to put products to shelves because of the economy of scale issue, but if the government truly supported entrepreneurship, they would want a diffusion of business and opportunity to push the a society of ownership and the idea that work has value, both of which ideas have long been Republican rhetoric. In reality, what happens is the small business has obstacles to financing from the banks, has to tack on sales tax, almost always pays property taxes, and has none of the subsidies for shipping which Amazon gets from the Postal Service which allows them to thwart any rivals. Walmart employed the same basic strategy with fewer perks for the preceding two decades, but was there ever any complaint from the Right about small businesses being closed? Nary a peep because we were told that was the price of competition, that the moral position is for us to descend into a surrogate war like Hobbes' Leviathan of all against all with any action taken by those who survive being justified by virtue of whatever their victory required.

I cannot imagine why the ideology of Gordon Gekko did not appeal to young people who, primarily motivated by idealism, wanted to create a world better for people. We might have won all the cutthroats, and perhaps we won the contests which were chosen about who had wealth and status in society, although the former does not always convey the latter, but only at the cost of destroying any belief in anything besides stuff and status. Having exhausted that, we just have a shell of a movement remaining which ultimately is going to surrender all its toys and hard-earned wealth anyway, so who really won?

The history of how this happened is interesting and relevant and something with which I've only recently become familiar. We have to go back to the 1950's and to the Establishment coup of the Right through the Republican Party. After Franklin Roosevelt ran the country like a king for close to two decades, bringing socialism and dependency into the American mix, smart people started asking why the communists were catching up so fast. Although the media derides these efforts today, what the House Un-American Activities Committee did, and what Joe McCarthy truly discovered, was that the far Left littered the entire government. They were trying hard to root them out and having successes. They discovered what Diana West shared in her excellent work: that there was a conveyor belt straight to Stalin from FDR through Harry Hopkins for all of our most sensitive technology and ideas, a sharing of information and material which was both illegal, and I would argue proved directly responsible for the War in

Korea with all the American and allied lives lost in result – not to mention the destitution of so many Korean people.

McCarthy's team were doing good and honest work, but the media was able to derail the effort, and the Establishment came in under Eisenhower and decided to calm the storm and let the Security State which Truman catalyzed in 1947 with the National Security Act come to the fore. As is often the case with radical change, what the Democrats implement, the Republicans solidify, so by the time Kennedy got elected, the idea of a permanent military state had become de facto reality, and we can look to Ike's Farewell Address as the warning that now the soft power of economics and hard power of military capacity were welded into a new America on a very different basis: Security not liberty.

Against this backdrop, America remained mostly a moral nation whose values were rooted in the traditional Christian faith of our people with church attendance high and civil society in good order. However, after the assassination by Kennedy, LBJ led the coup of the government against the people in attacking the moral foundations of the traditional state, including working to use tax-exemption status as the means to force churches to abandon political dialogue, a selectively enforced prohibition that has never silenced churches on the Left or figures of the Al Sharpton variety. State alternatives to services traditionally provided by churches and charities were forced, as a taxpayer owned mandate designed to compete with and ultimately destroy the voluntary civic alternatives which were the core of American moral resistance. There was opposition forming against the Great Society and those elements that sought to solve the Civil Rights issues not through division, which is what multiculturalism spawned, but to integrate more fully through unity in belief and purpose.

At the time the cultural revolutions of the 1960's went out of control, the Right was talking about an idea called Fusionism, wherein the moral actors of the Right, informed by people like Russell Kirk, would be a counterbalance to the market forces which came up through the Goldwater Campaign and who sounded like Milton Friedman. The stated theory was that this would maintain a balance between industry and morality that needed to be finely tuned so that work had redemptive value but also served the higher purpose of community building and sustaining the nation. Organizations like the John Birch Society were there to ensure that liberty and community would be the basis upon which it would grow, but what happened was that the new establishment types like Bill Buckley jumped in from the Ivory Tower, and plotted a different path, a more material approach to freedom that sought through amorality and materialism to create a quantitative method to success.

Our weakness for many years, which endures to this very day, has ever been to want to convert moral questions into numbers so we can prove we are right on a comparative basis, and I think this oversimplification is crucial to the failure of the Right to sustain a moral counterbalance. What happened is the original good faith of the moral faction was betrayed by the market faction as the investment of the people went into what would make them more money versus those who argued for restraint. By 1970, the cultural revolution had decimated the academic Right, quarantined the churches, and had consolidated control of the media.

The response of the Right was to retreat, make money, and treat that as a moral end unto itself. The riots of the late sixties, like that which infamously took Detroit – then among the wealthiest cities in the world – down a much darker and angrier path. These riots met with the decision to bankrupt American industry through a strategy of outsourcing and flight, which was followed by capital and commuters alike. We learned not to fight for our civilization, and that habit of turning our backs on the fight has become so ingrained today that Americans accept moving multiple times in the course of our lives – just to stay employed – as a national tradition. Do we realize how profoundly unnatural it is to accept being people without a home who have to constantly move in search of new opportunities instead of building roots and networks to sustain ourselves, our communities, and multi-generational families who can influence value and meaning? Do we not feel how inhuman it is to become fungible and movable commodities in service to economic forces, rather than being rooted where the support of our extended families can make us strong and resilient?

It's not something people on the Right readily consider, but the moral cost of being materialists has been immense in terms of all the time we have sacrificed from other ideals, all the opportunities we have not explored, and in asking what it means that we define success by financial or material status alone. I get why the Right likes this approach, because it creates an objective metric that avoids the thorny questions of good and evil, or right and wrong. It also allows the difficult questions that emerge from race, sex, and other issues to be bypassed altogether. After the drubbing they took in the 1960's, they no longer had the stomach to argue the biologically provable fact that races are actually different – not better or worse, but products of different environments that instilled different attributes which could serve as advantages or disadvantages depending upon the situation.

The institutional leadership of the Republican Party, despite paying lip service to a captive conservative base which was stuck voting for them as the lesser of two evils, lacked high level figures arguing that feminism was a disaster because it placed a financial demand upon child-rearing, the essential responsibility of all human societies, but which ran counter to both the Left's narrative of liberating women and the Right's pale alternative that they needed to make money also... as we could now only be treated as atomized individuals. On the surface, the moral message of capitalism seemed perfectly suited to liberty as expressed – a free market of ideas and opportunities that allowed any person to succeed, but it missed that there were certain inescapable foundations that are necessary to uphold any society.

The single biggest thing the free marketeers missed, which both sides ignore today and is one of the three deepest roots of our national degradation, is that individuals are a social dead end. The smallest self-replicating social unit remains the family. A man and a woman are required to produce the next generation, and when we separated one from the other, the cynical and deliberate act of feminism, then we both lost the future. And even for those who did come together as nature demands, we lost so many of our children as they became subservient to the needs of the system. Couple this crisis with the problem of having abandoned any pretense to objective morality, and to the loss of faith that will come to define our previous century, and it is self-evident why we face catastrophe today.

We live in an age where the individual is paramount. People are alienated, isolated, and adrift. There is no moral compass of sufficient authority to guide them, there is no leadership speaking to the disaffected youth who are able to emerge and present a counter message, and yet we continue trotting out the worn out bromide that playing the tired game that competing and driving ourselves to always get more will be somehow redemptive. Forgive me, but I don't see it, and I think as people from generations which follow those who made these choices look upon the impacts both to the country and to the people who choose to sacrifice themselves to the system, we ask rightly what good was this? Is a richer America better? Or is it just the case that playing a winner-takes-all game is the root of all our problems, because what we really wanted was not to have more stuff, but to have more meaningful connections?

I talk to many young men who fear and hate what the Left is offering. They are told they are the would-be oppressors even as they live with their parents, in poverty and often without companionship. And who speaks to them? Do you think telling them that working two jobs for menial pay is a compelling message to get them to fight for the future? Or do you think they long for a society where men's lives have meaning, where families are rebuilt and where women no longer have to prostitute themselves for attention – as they now very much do, falsely branding this degeneracy as liberation – but instead were valued as mothers and wives?

It would mean that the Right would have to invest in the family instead of in making money, and it hasn't been willing to do that for a very long time. We see other countries, primarily those in Eastern Europe, are righting their ship this way. Instead of arguing that they need more people to feed labor into the insatiable machine of capital accumulation, they accept living with less stuff and financial progress is a better deal at a human level when it allows for building families and deeper roots.

If we were not driven by purely materialistic concerns in service to a system, we could stop replacing our people with outsiders and instead encourage our young men and women to believe in the future, together, as happy partners. But that would require the profit engine to stop, and as we as know, that profit engine is now so concentrated in such a few hands that it will continue to invest in these dysgenic policies until America collapses because capital will gladly flee these shores.

Our new elites have earned their way above the nation, but what will happen to our people or our land for those who either made other choices or who lacked the capacity to do otherwise? The Left has an answer for this, as impossible as it might be. Do we? Because if the answer is the Koch Brothers, buying every race in Congress to ensure that we keep the supply of cheap labor rolling, then the battle is already lost. If the answer is more stuff that ends up in landfills anyway or more money in the hands of those who don't care for us, then the bankruptcy that cannot be avoided will kill us all.

But if we believed in something again, if we believed strongly enough that we could justify fighting evil with good, then we might have a chance. Forget making America great again. How about we make her good again?

Chapter 17: Strategy Without Objectives

If politics truly is war by other means as Clausewitz posited, and the nation is the moral resonance of a state – a people who self-identify based upon common identity and purpose – then what strategy can we develop to win this moral war before us that the cultural fight offers when we have no objectives? The market foundation of the United States is the ultimate exercise in transactional subjectivity, where all values are negotiable, and all substances may be modified. If we go into battle with our opposite number who are willing to embrace and expand upon any form of relativism unto literally degrading humanity itself into an amorphous nothingness of primal mediocrity, how do we win that battle? I do not see it as possible, because we have a strategy that has no objectives.

The moral statement we would have to make is that we want to be free. But even though I share that noble aspiration, permit me to ask: what constitutes freedom? Is it the freedom of having to succumb to the ubiquitous threats of nature from which we must daily shelter ourselves? Is it the freedom of knowing we have the security of loved ones around us who will provide succor and support should things go awry such that we might take greater risks? What are the foundations of this freedom we want, and without which we realize less potential because we are forced to devote so much of our time and attention to mere survival that we cannot express our mindful desires to explore the luxuries that can only be properly considered once we meet certain needs?

What things are so objectively true that without them we cannot look for freedom? This was the moral question we once asked as a regular course of being, up until about one hundred years ago, in the time before technology, urbanization, and mass logistics, when agriculture was still paramount to our survival and shaped our way of life. These questions arise from instincts which are hardwired deeply into all of us along with our hunter capacities. If we are to develop a strategy to fight back, we need to decide here and now what values we will use as our bedrock principles, and we need to be unrepentant in claiming these values as both objective and the legitimate foundation upon which either renewal or rebirth shall occur.

Before we discuss these in depth, let us consider the case before us which is being presented as the counter-narrative. The Left is making the argument that they will realize ultimate equality by ensuring all ends lead to the same outcome, a status which inherently must be destructive at all times and to all good ends, but which does appeal to the well-developed and cultivated sense of guilt that people experience for their successes. More accurately, I would say they use a trick of infinite regression to sell their philosophy, where every halfway jump to the final goal is sold in isolation as a moral success against some oppression. But if we really understood the big picture of what they are doing, it would be clearly seen as an attack upon our reason because they exist in a vacuum of objectivity.

Relativism is an attack upon the mind. It's why capitalism works so poorly as competition to the communist mindset, which has at least the rhetorical trappings of the communal mentality, which acknowledges the value of people other than as economic units. In truth, they are just fuel for the state to mold us into a hive, which is why they so often use the word "collective" to describe their goals, but this too is a willing act of self-destruction. A person has to agree to be less than they could otherwise be for this system to work, to make themselves subservient to others on a permanent basis, and this attack suggests the most obvious means of reply we could offer as one point.

Where the Left's goal is to support becoming the least, we should retain our idea that we on the Right aim to enable the best. Where they try to be all things to all people, we should recommend that people can be what they choose within workable constraints. The touchy part here is we cannot be relativists like them lest we fall into the market trap of subjectivity, but to allow our searching realm of possibility to be linked to a series of objective goods which benefit us but transcend the material. We need the reclamation of truth to liberate the mind from this hellish descent into fantasy which we have fallen into, and to fight that will require strong language, painting in bold moral colors, and to pick many ugly fights moving forward.

Addiction is a good comparison. Once someone becomes addicted to a drug, and fantasy can be amongst the most alluring of narcotics as Marxists have ever known, one often has to be shocked from a reverie and then nursed back to health. Each person is obviously different, but so often the key to treatment lies in the twofold approach to putting sound fundamentals beneath a person to sustain their reintegration into sanity while also giving them a clear moral framework to beat their addiction and find self-worth. America needs this sort of thinking as she is racked by doubt, self-hatred, flashbacks, and frankly, a host of parasites pushing this disease who are not being targeted in an effective manner. At best, America is receiving palliative sedatives and reprieves, but we need a much better strategic plan to compete.

When in doubt, I look to our Founders for guidance because these men really did think deeply on the problems we would face. Had we not allowed our evolving ideas of justice to so transform, corrupt, expand, and pervert the many limitations they put into the system, we likely would not be in nearly so much trouble today. But they understood the core values that were needed as a system which operated on reason, which was rooted in an actual understanding of man's nature, and which encouraged the search for Grace. Liberty only makes sense in correspondence with these three principles: the ability to reach common conclusions, the understanding of a shared common reality, and the desire for a universally accessible higher outcome. Absent any one, the balance fails as we sink into discord, despair, or depravity.

Start with reason. If we cannot agree that anything is ever true, we cannot build a society which is sane or functional. Any person who has even a rudimentary appreciation of logic understands this premise is the foundation of communication and human co-existence. When one and one no longer equal two, language diffuses into meaningless gibberish, a succession of words devoid of meaning save as abstract expressions left to the subjective determination of the speaker and listener. We need to again assert that we inhabit the same reality and the same sphere of ideas and push back hard against the assertion that all ideas are subjective and equally valid. Instead, we must demand the recognition that truth is real, and has value as such. And we cannot be afraid to admit there are both truths we readily understand and others which still elude us but which we want to seek because we want to exist in the world as it is, believing happiness and meaning comes from having who we choose to be correspond honestly and with integrity with the world.

Nature is the second attribute we must attach for this very reason. Between truth and fiction there are many degrees of meaning, but while we recognize there are exceptions, we need to also use our reason to fix our mind on trends so we can intelligently understand our world and know that when something is mostly true or mostly false, that we categorize and act upon those basic tendencies in how we interact. We need to understand ourselves that way in a world where change is constant. The attack which the Left uses to point out exceptions to invalidate general tendencies is worth opposing because we need to learn to demand that exceptions prove themselves through habit or conduct instead of subscribing to false and deceitful optimism to draw conclusions which will inevitably prove wrong more often than not. Looking at nature is about understanding the world as it is, not as we would wish it to be, and it is an inherently moral statement to suggest people will be happier when they exist in concord with both their internal nature and their external environment. Realism is the wedding of nature to reason, and should be the foundation from which we operate, refusing to allow ideology or doctrine to keep us from questioning anything and also sharing honest observation.

Grace is the final component our civilization requires. Instead of using the inescapable doubt of a subjectivity that can draw no differentiation between right and wrong as excuse to succumb to the moral and mental attack upon our ability to make judgments and interact with any sense of self, we can instead forgive ourselves in advance for our mistakes and trust that an honest effort made in good faith is better than the submission to indifference and despair that comes from a mind which believes it cannot understand, interact, or positively influence the world which it inhabits. We know the nature we see; we use reason as best our faculties allow, and we assert that we search for truths yet unknown to us in hope we will live better. The failures we will inevitably make will become stepping stones to the success of new achievement, grounded in the common desire to offer grace also to one another who share this quest not as opponents or adversaries, but as fellow wayfarers in the quest to revitalize our now stolid civilization.

I would love to take credit for these ideas, but decency compels me to share they were there in the Good Book all along just waiting for us to remember that we don't have to discover every truth on our own to find the big answers. I submit to you that a little humility goes a very long way, as we have the great fortune to be descended from a line of brilliant men and women who conquered a continent, understood much about the world small and large, and asked questions both profound and minute. Do not assume such achievements only began with the Enlightenment either, as those so-called "Dark Ages" were often responsible for brilliant thinkers like Thomas Aquinas who argued for the natural law that is the foundation of the West today. In so many, they best understood liberty properly as the balance between those divinely bestowed attributes which we all share and those choices we have to make as best we can in accordance with our unique and particular natures, which if we understand, we can seek objectively better solutions to express.

Fighting the culture war on this basis: Reason, nature, and grace gives us tools we desperately need for the fight, and an objective framework with which to most directly and honestly attack the moral onslaught which has so corrupted our ability to resist. We can call out their fantasies as corrupt delusions driven by the desire to create a nature in us which would reduce spiritual and thinking man to just another animal in the herd. We must reject their assertion of not just the equality, the sameness of all people, but also of all things, and assert our right to value some things as greater than others – not just because of their exchange rate, but because some ideas have intrinsic worth which makes them more important than others. Like our families, as but one example, as a source of liberation from the state and its corrupting centralizing power through the transformative power of love between blood and kin. Lastly, we must allow ourselves sufficient grace to overcome those doubts which will be thrown against us, the secret success of their attack as our opponents have always used our superior moral sense against us.

We will likely have to remember some ugly truths which the many intervening years of civilization have given us permission to forget, but these include that the future is not decided merely through acts of persuasion and generosity, but also through the exercise of force in defense of those ideas which people value most, and that this moral struggle is inescapable and timeless. Even God had to put down a revolt in heaven, which shows just how eternal these battles are, and we have the blessing or misfortune to be a generation of warriors who are called to these lines once more in defense of humanity and our future. Do we have the courage to risk failure to become better beings and regain control of our future? Or will we succumb to those who would see us reduced to mouths to feed? Should we win that battle, can we build a framework to unseat those elites who set us against one another, and build a greater and more blessed unity built upon tranquility and integrity where we remember we exist not just to enjoy our rights, but also to honor our responsibilities?

Let us end the age of conservatism with this honest admission: Conservatism conserved nothing. The strategy of endless retreat, with ill-defined and diffuse objectives has put not just America but the entire West at peril. We have lost the sense of ourselves, and to recover from this sickness, we must do a few things. Obviously, we have to destroy the source of the infection and with a better understanding of cultural Marxism as the child of positivism, this idea there is a final outcome to history, and an obsession with humanist equality as a cult, recognize what has corrupted our reason, perverted our nature, and removed our grace. But we also must understand this doctrine is being promoted by people who realize how corrupt it is as surely as those who agree with the conclusions of this book, but who have made the decision to set them against us so they can escape to just a newer and fancier form of escape in transhumanism and world domination. Here's the good news: One truth really does destroy a thousand lies, and when we root ourselves in truth, in good faith and loyalty to one another, we can, and we will overcome all these obstacles.

I call myself a traditionalist because I honor the past and search what we knew before for wisdom to learn so we do not repeat the same mistakes anew in the future. I do not seek to merely make what existed before endure a little while longer, but instead to build a new beginning rather than a last stand. I seek to build a future where we are unafraid to promote our values in our new ways, and understand that both the state and market should be seen as tools for the benefit of the people who keep asking this one question: What is the good and how do we find it? Even if we don't know the answer, the story of civilization is really about the search for those answers, and those nations which succeed best are those who choose certain values for which to live, die, and kill and who, because of good choices shape our direction toward a future which benefits those people who believe and live their beliefs. This is an accessible and fairer definition of morality, which allows for the survival of we who dissent, and which will not see us trade away tomorrow to buy ourselves relief for today.

We are not habituated to courage because we have lived in a world of many comforts. The inescapable reality of such success is that the unfamiliarity of failure likely ensures that when the disruptions which will come from the problems with which we began this analysis soon arise, many people will not work to survive. Some will die. Some will simply retreat into shells of themselves. Many will be led along whatever path is presented to them, and given what those who have been allowed to organize offer, either despair or domination, these might prove even longer and more painful outcomes. Few like to write about the morality of collapse or submission, but you need to think deeply on these things now as you make choices for you and your family as to how to avoid these different levels of calamity. Any action you take will likely have a cost, which is high now and will probably only rise as the time becomes shorter.

Until we get to a place of health, all choices are bad choices. But if we surrender to the despair in the false belief that we have no choices, then the battle is lost because you can't win a war without any strategy or any objectives. My objective in all my writing is to awaken you to new possibilities, explaining that there is always a way for people who want to live as better men to find a different path. If we cannot still save America, perhaps we can at least save ourselves, as we should take heart that millions of us are still here in this country, and millions more around the world who desire something better than what we're being offered.

But the moral trap we have to escape, which is why I devoted fifteen chapters to explaining why the West is screwed, the elites are psychopaths, and the Left is criminally insane, is to tell you that we cannot liberate ourselves from them if we still consider our fates bound to theirs. They may influence us, they may oppose us, but either through the subjugation of government or through the force of arms, they cannot be permitted to control us, or intimidate us. Our very existence has always been the most basic moral cause, and we have a right to our future. This is the message which has been lacking, and as we honor our past and become a people driven by belief, we can once again lay claim to a future for our people. Who are we? We are the survivors who honor the good, seek what is healthy, and protect one another in fellowship and, if necessary, through separation. Only then may we have the chance for survival.

Chapter 18: The Failure of Identity as Alternative

This will likely be one of the most controversial chapters in this book, but I want to share with you what the Alt-Right, as it came to be known was thinking, what sort of alternative it posited to the existing system, how and why it was subverted, and ultimately why this model not only failed but will also continue to fail to serve as a viable alternative to the model being presented by the Left.

As a movement, there were many heretical ideas embedded within their thinking which the status quo ruthlessly suppressed, and it will be helpful for you to understand why they think what they think. For clarity, although I am frequently lumped in with these beliefs, my views have always been much more culturally driven which has important differences and allows for certain flexibility that the more doctrinaire thinkers of the Alt-Right would dislike. But my goal here is not to present my personal views or to endorse any position. I just want you to understand them as they understood themselves, and my critique will be functional in nature.

There has been an undercurrent percolating throughout the West that we took a wrong turn going down the egalitarian trail. We have already deeply discussed how the Left has seen this manifest through a vision of compulsory state control, and how the Right instead adopted the cutthroat free market standard as their own. There have been people for some time, with a deeper current going back to Europe that posited a different view. Sometimes called the Dark Enlightenment, or neoreactionary thinking, the idea they had was that the supposed progress that civilization was making had, in fact, been a great failure that had alienated men from one another and from a higher purpose. In some ways, the thinking was akin to classical spiritual traditions, except it was a secular variant that in certain forms elevated the object of reverence to the people themselves, looking out for the good of the tribe as the highest categorical imperative.

Thinkers like Mencius Moldbug, Guillaume Faye, Jared Taylor, Kevin McDonald, and many others who you probably won't know, who exist either at the fringe or who are now banned, have written much in a similar vein where the common attribute was that the way to challenge the existing system was to present a positive case for White identity as the primary counterpoint to the Marxist struggle. Recognizing the many challenges in organizing the morally driven components of the Right to unite around a common creed, this approach was fundamentally different in that it sought to break the paradigm and the systemic mindset, and instead encourage young Whites to adopt their identity as politics to provide a direct defense to the ongoing cultural Marxist assault.

Skip to 2015 when the Trump candidacy began in earnest, and it is very true that the early adopters of his campaign were heavily populated by the people who would become the Alt-Right and who recognized a few truths that were both politically incorrect and inconvenient. First, they recognized the inherent demographic problem which we've discussed in depth in this book, which is that non-Whites vote overwhelmingly for socialist solutions to problems, and furthermore, they support redistribution on an identitarian basis like the reparations we see actively promoted as policy by nearly every Democrat running for the highest office. Second, they wanted to apply the ideas of science and reason to understanding the differences between races not as a question of supremacy, but rather to root questions about interactions on a factual basis instead of the assumptions forced upon us by the cultural Marxists. The Alt-Right called out the hypocrisy where we had to assume all were equal when it served to the benefit of the institutional Left, but where government policy fundamentally allowed special privileges and protections for minorities against the majority. Each of these ideas is fundamentally correct on a factual basis and, if popularized or implemented, represented a major threat to the existing status quo.

As a disorganized movement which existed as an organic creation of the interaction of primarily young men who were dislocated from the system and the political discourse, the ideas developed in a way that was very scattershot, heavy with trolling and satire, and relentless in pursuing those in opposition as these people had long been used to being targets in the culture war for many reasons. They brought a hard edge, much frustration, yet needed energy in asking questions that we have not been permitted to ask for a very long time.

To give you a better feel of who fit into this movement, I want you to imagine a young man who grew up in a family where perhaps there was no father, just a single mother, and he had to overcome challenges to succeed. He went to college, and he earned a degree with high marks despite having to hear propaganda each day about how he was to blame for all that is wrong in society. Being socially awkward, he watched all the women go to the popular guys, and he simply wanted to earn a place in the future. When applying for jobs, he was passed over because even though he had higher marks and aptitude, he didn't fit the right profile and a quota sees the job he struggled for handed to someone else who only real merit is they're not White ... and he is. An outcast, a pariah, alone in the world and without friends, this is what the system wants to make of the majority, and they are succeeding in radicalizing a generation. A seminal event in the evolution of how the Alt-Right launched was Gamergate, where social justice even inserted itself into video game development, one of the last escapes for these guys, because a woman slept her way into conferences and leveraged her position to try to force change to comply with the rest of the culture.

The story is so absurd in some ways that it must be true, but what resulted were vast numbers of a generation of dispossessed young White men who were told they would have no future and needed to be ashamed of their past decided to fight back.   As the joke often goes, all they wanted was to be left alone, but the religious imperative of the social justice warriors who poked the bear of identity literally created the reason why the Alt-Right mobilized. That term, coined by Richard Spencer who became probably the leading voice in the movement, was designed to convey that what was being tried here was an alternative to the Right, a moral case for survival based on the idea that Whites were targets and should organize collectively in reaction for self-defense.   During 2016, it appeared the movement might grow massively, and when we look at the impact it had in the meme wars of the unlikely success of Trump's campaign, do not for one second believe the Russians or anything external was responsible for his deep and talented Internet support. The core of that faction was pissed off White guys who just wanted to know they had a say in the future.

We need to talk about the opposition that the Alt-Right faced, who runs that opposition, and how they operate. For those not familiar with the trenches of political warfare, the story will likely sound a bit like a cloak and dagger novel, but that's closer to the truth than you'd believe. I've had people stalk me, engage in car chases, and pull weapons on me for my own views – which are considerably more modest than what many others advocate. But that should give you a feel for just how far this goes, and how real the cultural battles are as the first stages of this coming civil war. But what you need to keep in mind for this discussion is our common understanding that the media tells a narrative driven lie, and they often receive marching orders from others in the Deep State, finance capital and other places.

Nationalism has terrified the elites for decades, and their fear is demonstrated in how vigorously they opposed the comparatively milquetoast civic nationalism of Trump. It should be clear that they will not hesitate to throw every brand and slur, or tell any lie about people who try to organize a political movement on a constructive identitarian basis. Whether this is civic nationalism, the weakest form rooted in symbols and law, cultural nationalism, a stronger variant which I personally support based upon ideas and institutions, or ethnic nationalism, the most exclusive version which draws upon race and identity as means of distinction … all are attacked with the same zeal because the threat of leaving systems based logic does two things. Firstly, it wrecks the ability to synthetically control the course of intellectual development through false dialectical choices. Secondly, people who act upon the interest of identity outside the permitted cultural Marxist framework begin to look at those who oppose them, not in the sterile context of ideology which removes people from their ideas, but rather by looking at the identity⊚⊚⊚ of the people promoting those ideas.

It's no secret which institutions exist and are incredibly well-funded, often by foreign dollars, and are given gold standard status by the media, by law enforcement, and by the established system. Groups like the Anti-Defamation

League, the Southern Poverty Law Center, and others exist basically to prevent the development of an alternative the Marxist egalitarian agenda, to protect their allies and attack their enemies. Yet these private, very ethnic and clearly Culturally Marxist institutions claim the imprimatur to be above the fray, and to be able to objectively and justly point out figures who are potential threats to commit hate crime. Let's break down that bit of Orwellian double speak in light of their agenda, which is to protect the smaller at the expense of the larger. Their job, understood properly, is to protect the most destructive forces of the egalitarian deconstruction against any organization by the majority to defend itself which passes a certain level of efficacy. It does this by smearing and branding any group with ideas that effectively oppose their agenda as hate groups.

Yours truly enjoys the honor of being on that list for arguing two things. I argued that Islam doesn't fit the model we enjoy of separation of church and state – which any person honest about Sharia law would recognize in about five seconds. I also argued, perhaps more infuriatingly to them, that White people have the right to feel pride in our identity and to work toward our collective interest. For that heresy, I was fired from my job, branded with a scarlet letter, and literally have people paid to detract from everything I say including the pithy one sentence reviews you'll see on all my writings to scare away potential buyers. It's not enough for them to attack their enemies, they need to destroy them into silence and submission. Who hates whom again?

And that is just my own personal experience, as an entirely reasonable and moderate advocate. The lengths they have gone to take down and destroy others who engaged in such simple acts as collecting second-hand clothing for White babies, or reading Anderson's Fairy Tales as a podcast go much further.

Here's where the story gets complicated and a little uglier, but you need to understand these facts so other things make sense. We can describe the ideology of groups like the ADL and SPLC as fanatically progressive. We can describe them institutionally as members of the larger cultural Marxist and Democrat leaning framework. But what you also discover is that these groups designed to delineate which groups are allowed to claim positive expression of identity and which groups are barred from positive identity share another thing overwhelmingly in common, and that is that they have an incredibly disproportionate number of leaders who have Jewish heritage. Across the media, throughout academia, and most certainly within the most radically Communist organizations, the representation of Jewish members compared to their proportion of the population at large is ten to fifty times more prominent than would be suggested by a standard distribution of people. The Alt-Right saw this also, dared to comment upon it, and were branded as Nazis about ten seconds later. These facts are branded as anti-Semitic to discourage commentary on what is real, but that does not make them false.

In the interests of furthering a productive dialogue about this question rather than what has descended into one side screaming that the nationalists are trying to plan another Holocaust, and the other which is so frustrated about their ostracism from legitimate debate that real people are getting hurt, I want to share an observation about this. My observation is based upon conversations with many activists from all sides and many Jewish people of good character who understand the need for this movement, as well as a few remarkable Jews who are even deeply involved with it. Allow me to preface all I share here by saying this is just commentary on my part, with the full understanding it is up to people individually and collectively to figure out their own paths toward positive interaction.

After the fall of Nazi Germany, to prevent another incident like that from happening again, victim status was essentially weaponized in the Jewish community with anything that threatened their interests defined as potentially another Holocaust in the making, including nationalism itself. As the far Left has often attracted many intellectuals and academicians, fields where Jews have traditionally been drawn and excelled, this became part of the Leftist framework. The ideal of egalitarianism suited the specific Jewish interest of preventing identity-based nationalism in countries outside Israel which largely practices the opposite, in which exclusionary ethnic principles impacts legal status. The desire to never again see a Holocaust happen has become a categorical imperative to the Jewish elite, and so they actively disrupt, brand, and tarnish anyone who appears as a potential threat, and they came down hard on the Alt-Right as both ideological and identitarian enemies.

As such, it's predictable that this drove the more eager and less sophisticated members of the Alt-Right directly into the narrative of blaming Jews for everything. The hypocrisy practiced by the groups assigned to monitor hate groups being so extreme that some people adopted symbolism and ideas from the Nazi regimes of the past to make clear they saw who was responsible for trying to destroy the movement. Through both controlled opposition outfits where the Left masqueraded as the Alt-Right to present a false view of what spawned this movement, and the authentic channeling of frustration into efforts which were incredibly unproductive, the Alt-Right was eventually neutralized by turning dissidents into Nazis in either the public eye or, occasionally, in fact due to their marginalization. But where a group like the Black Panthers which originated in a similar fashion would be celebrated, these guys were painted as the villains, by which the entire cause of White identity has been tarnished.

Charlottesville broke the back of the movement. It was always a stupid tactical idea to go to a college campus, but these young men wanted to be where they were being most vigorously attacked, and so those events took place. A criminal act by one man destroyed a movement, and his conviction conceals the reality that the report commissioned by Charlottesville itself informs that the law was broken by the police, the counter-protesters, and the local government to create a violent situation specifically to advance the narrative. The Left succeeded, Heather Heyer is dead, and her blood became martyrdom for the cause of the cultural Marxists.

After this, the media branded White identity as domestic terrorism, and with the exception of the President, the Republican Party gladly jumped on board. Instead of addressing the legitimate questions of what it means for millions of Americans to live in a country where one set of ideas is being swapped out for another primarily through a demographic swap, this became another of those forbidden questions we see black listed from public discussion, and that's when the censorship and demonetization purges began. Radicalism and alienation increased, which fits perfectly into the larger civil war narrative, and instead of having the possibility for open discussion of the issues of interactions between groups, you now see the media purging those who offer dissent and those who think otherwise going deep underground as they lost any faith the system will ever serve them. What do you think will happen when potentially millions of young men who have little hope are pushed to the margins?

A few shootings later, you have the answer. I'm certainly not here to justify, condone, or apologize for senseless acts of criminality, but the public deserves a better and more useful explanation than just to attack the Second Amendment. The reason these shootings keep happening has everything to do with the media which tacitly supports demonizing Whites in America as one of the four groups Americans are encouraged to hate which I remind you are Whites, straight people, Christians, and country folk. It is no accident those are the forces I see uniting in the future conflict because when you tell people they are not allowed to survive for who they are or what they believe, can you blame them when they decide that they can't live with you?

I know how these guys think because I talk to them often, and I work hard to present a better way. My Christian conscience compels me to find hope and to prevent senseless violence, and to let them know there are other ways to deal with these issues. These books are a big part of the appeal I am making, to find a peaceful path based on truth, mutual self-interest, and separation to avoid all these zero-sum games of ethnic conflict that identity politics alone portend. A fairer time would understand what I am doing is a brave and dangerous effort to keep the peace, but the primary narrative will say I am a villain also, guilty by association of thought crime, even though those few like me are the last tenuous threads holding the fringe together and preventing much larger calamities from occurring. Because people need hope.

Let me conclude this chapter by returning to the Jewish question for just a moment because it's going to be relevant going forward. Many smart people within the Jewish community already realize the embrace that the Marxist left has made of Islam means they will eventually be a threat, as comments made by Representatives Tlaib and Omar reinforce. As someone with no animus whatsoever against Jews, and as evidenced by actions from the current President, and figures like Matteo Salvini in Italy and Victor Orban in Hungary, the movement to advance and defend nationalism is not trying to attack or slaughter anybody. All it really wants is to see the people survive who represent the old majority and to have a future, because if we're honest about who the real minorities are, Whites are the least common of all races at a global figure of 8% and dropping, and we are the ones taking in people from everywhere else at the same time we are actively discouraged from having families of our own.

Jews could choose to be White and end these arguments for once and for all. It's up to them to define themselves, but in the same way that Jews vote 70/30 for Democrats where Whites on average vote about 60/40 Republican, excluding that tribe, I genuinely believe the greater danger for the Jewish population lies in serving as the mouthpieces for so many of the cultural Marxist entities that are wrecking all that is good in the name of equality. If they do not call out their own people since no one else will be permitted to do so, I fear the consequences will be suffered by all if this comes to a fight.

They should also realize that the Marxist third-world coalition they have assembled will not consider Jewish claims to victim hood compelling against their own self-interest; already they do not. Please do not twist my words into being some sort of threat, but rather consider them the analysis of someone who wants to escape the cycle of retribution that has so defined history between Jews and Whites in the West. I'm very well familiar with the many difficult details, and I hope and pray that those battles will finally end. It's time we stop being victims and aggressors and consider working as partners in common cause against a threat which is larger than either of us and which requires new thinking.

There are cultural solutions to be had which work for everyone, and that's the point of this chapter. White identity is not going to prove the magic solution, although if things go hot, you should not be surprised if race becomes the quickest and most common identifier of who represents each side because the Left already thinks that way. The Alt-Right was honest in seeking out the problems, but it didn't understand how to solve the issues that were presented, was boxed out of political relevancy, and perhaps could have been more useful if guided by saner hands toward constructive approaches. Unfortunately, the institution which stopped that, and previously sidelined every potentially productive movement of the Right from the Tea Party to the Moral Majority and many others going back for decades, remains the Republican Party.

Chapter 19: Republican in Name Only

As any grassroots activist on the Right already knows, there is no greater enemy to our cause than the Republican Party. Literally every time a movement has emerged which offered a possibility to resolve some of the larger issues this book questions, the Republican Party has co-opted the narrative, adopted its cause as its own for a season, did nothing to advance the agenda, and then moved on to the next big thing. Promises are made, but they are never kept, and the nature of our two party system has served to preserve this least faithful and most feckless of organizations in power because they understand that their own voters are held hostage by the desire to prevent the Democrats from succeeding in finally pushing through their progressive agenda.

An entire book would not be enough to fully explain just why the Republicans are so pathetic at defending their own supporters, but for the purposes of our analysis, we can look at this in terms of three factors. First, we should look at the history of the party and understand that it has been heavily impacted by its roots in Northeastern classical liberalism. Second, we should understand the party has added people who are discontents that have been left aside as the Democrats moved more toward progressive orthodoxy, but whose appendage to the Republican effort is an odd construction that has built a Frankenstein Party that is ineffective because the regional interests it represents are too much at variance with one another, a crisis in this time of centralization where the inability to articulate a new common national belief has proven elusive. Thirdly, most simply and most tellingly, we must always remember that politicians as a whole are a bought class of people and it should surprise absolutely no one that the party of free market ideology would be the easiest to sell out.

Before things got confused after the 1950's, there was a time when Rockefeller was the name associated with Republicanism, and the Solid South was a Democrat bloc that had voted that way since the Civil War. The history of the Republican Party was as an abolitionist party that also supported tariffs which the agrarian South opposed for many reasons, which had displaced the old Whig Party, and upon its first successful and highly divisive election, was in power as the country descended into Civil War. After the Union Victory, the Republican Party became the de facto party of the land for a generation and established deep roots among the states of the Northeast, Midwest, and California. The party essentially espoused classical liberalism, which was a combination of a market driven system with some government intervention and eschewed heavy social involvement from socialism. They were free marketers and the party of the tycoons back during the Gilded Age and into the 1920's as the Democrats underwent their own transformation from the Party of Southern Resentment to that of more universalized discontent in the person of Franklin Delano Roosevelt. It's easy to forget now but works like the Tennessee Valley Authority were efforts to promote old school Marxism of class resentment in a nation where the possibilities of cultural transformation which technology and communications revolutions would permit had not yet been fully realized.

Anyway, by the time the 1960's came to pass, the parties began a titanic shift as the Democrats made the decision to abandon their traditional southern base in favor of a new coalition of the discontent where race would be used as a means to provoke ongoing conflict, and where racial disparities would be used as a moral argument to justify further growth of the state beyond what they had already done to elevate the rural poor of the South. These rural poor were now enjoying more prosperity, and were not so sympathetic to these other classically Marxist appeals. It's worth noting that even back then the Democrats put their agenda ahead of the needs of the people and their wishes, a trait which defines them to this day, and why any success they enjoy is undone by their religious zeal of seeking out the next person to help and abandoning those who facilitated their rise as predictably as a metronome.

I suppose that might seem less bad than what the Republicans did, which was basically buffet themselves around in a purely reactive and responsive measure to what the Democrats suggested. For about sixty years, it seems like the end game has always devolved from a posture of principle to a plea to not to move forward quite so quickly with the cultural revolution. Whatever the Democrats gain, the Republicans enhance. Eisenhower only solidified the many social programs of Roosevelt and the security apparatus created by Truman. Nixon didn't undo any of Johnson's reforms from the Great Society. Reagan voted in gun control and a major amnesty. Look beyond the rhetoric and the narrow window of finance and economics, and you will see every Republican who has been in office has done more to help progressives in terms of both policies and advancing the rise of the state than the Democrats have achieved on their own.

Remember the roots of the GOP. It is a party that supports industry in the market as it did at its founding, that had no compunction about intervening against state interests as a highly Federalist party, and which was never particularly driven by social issues. However, as the parties evolved, and as the Democrats pushed aside those people in Dixie who had been the core of their support for a century, what happened was the weird transposition where a series of clever operatives like Lee Atwater, Roger Stone, Paul Manafort, and others worked to bring the discontents from the South on board into the old hated Yankee Republican Party to build some new golem. The Republicans had found their conscience and the first group to join their ranks were the Moral Majority who took their cue from people like Ralph Reed and Pat Robertson.

Christianity and capitalism are an odd fit. One belief espouses that the love of money is the root of evil, and the other argues that pursuit of money is our moral imperative.

Promises were made to what was then called the far right that values would be defended like reversing abortion, stopping gay marriage, and protecting prayer in schools – a vanishing trend against the secularization of the progressively controlled school system. The right things were said, and the votes were counted, but when the time came for promises to become policy, the GOP held true to its roots and voted to protect the economy while refusing to act on social issues. Never liking a culture fight, the Republicans went just far enough to lock down the votes of the discontented, but never with intention of honoring their commitment at the highest level.

The challenge that Pat Buchanan launched represented another viable thrust that could have transformed the Party. Imagine the dynamism that eventually brought Ross Perot within reach of victory in 1992 encapsulated within the framework of the GOP, organized in what was still then a much more culturally and ethnically homogeneous country, seeking to offer an alternative to the free trade agenda and instead articulating a moral vision of excellence for America's culture. The movement proved popular and gave former CIA Director and northeastern liberal George Bush a run for his money. But Republicans went with the money as per usual, and the eventual failure of Bush because he sold out to the Left on his taxes pledge gave the White House over to the Clintons and their lascivious parade to which our country has now been subjected for decades.

The Contract with America which Newt Gingrich carried forward in 1994 was a clean vision of a less corrupt government and the first time a sound policy basis was listed in many years. It even got off to a good start, but once again, it tuckered out for the same reasons these movement kept failing. Grassroots energy never amounted to institutional development, as the free market forces of the Right inherently disliked government doing things, and so they would pass prohibitions but never put any deeper roots to defend changes made. In short, every good idea was an election away from erasure.

More recently, we could talk about the efforts by Ron Paul to end the Federal Reserve Bank and get us out of endless wars. We could talk about the Tea Party which demanded limits to how much power government seized for itself and to honoring the Bill of Rights. We could even talk about the Alt-Right whose basic message that the government was importing people that are creating an inevitable one party state are all pleas and cries for some opposition to arise within our government to suppress this slow rolling steamroller of a cultural revolution. But despite all the shouts from the people, the response from our elected officials remains the same. An inscrutable smile and vague promises conceal that they will do nothing of the sort.

The Republican Party exists on the back of its donor class, and these are wealthy industrialists and finance capitalists who believe in the free market agenda for one reason. They like making money, believe in opening up whatever new markets are required through force or through trade, and while they do not care about what trade imbalances or overreach the American government or people incur, they jealously protect their corporate prerogatives. Due to the stranglehold they exercise on campaign contributions, their moral framework which elevates material acquisition as the highest value has long been the doctrine of the Republicans, going back to a donor base that had decades to define the party long before the occasional and ever shifting voting blocs came in to win victory. Next chapter, we'll talk precisely about how this was done with the incipient nationalist movement and has likely drained the energy from the most optimistic of all solutions left to avoid the larger conflict, but here I want to talk about why this happens in a structural sense.

I've been a campaign manager and a candidate before. What you learn very quickly is that politics is a very expensive business, and no one takes you seriously unless you can write big checks. One could argue, cynically, that it is an opportunity to demonstrate your networking skills and the chance to meet the various ridiculous requirements that govern a campaign. Like any other business, this guild also has its barriers to entry, and what everyone who has any real experience in politics understands is the people who can write the biggest checks represent the structurally permanent interests which are to be defended, and about which politics is not allowed to talk. Look for the bills that get no attention, much bipartisan support, and where all your taxpayer income goes, and you'll discover who our elites are, as the information is mostly a matter of public record.

But people ask the reasonable question of why our politicians don't represent us, and the answer is more complex than assumed. The first thing you must know is that trying to build a career off grassroots support, unless one has the good fortune to sit within an ideologically uniform district without ambition of higher office, is that people change their opinions constantly, and those driven by passion are also the quickest to turn on you. It's not a popular opinion I express, but the reality is we get self-interested politicians who seem scummy so often because people themselves are fickle and inattentive. This goes to the heart of my critique of democracy and why the elites love to spread this system everywhere because it creates the illusion of popular consent in the vacuum that emerges as public neglect. This being the actual truth of politics, the politicians learn quickly that if they are to survive, they need friends who will stick by them, and so the loyalty of the oligarchs trumps the passion of the people.

This tendency is far more mitigated and contested on the Left because their base consists of believers who both pursue their course across multiple elections with religious ardor and who build institutions to leverage their power to elicit change, whereas the Right sees our big movements vanish like farts in the wind after the last election. Since these are often oriented to prevent government from doing something, whether victory is achieved or not, people go home without ever realizing government is still there. This is why conservatism is an inherently flawed and defeatist philosophy, because unless the Republican Party had been willing to undo what Democrats had done in entirety, to draw the conclusions which spun off the doctrinaire Libertarian and Constitution Parties who made just that case, they could only ever succeed in being the political equivalent of a paperweight.

To be fair, there are some lobbies on the Right who have some sway. The gun lobby is one. People against abortion is another. But they have never had the ability to shape the party because they didn't rise to a high enough power level since the cultural sway works against both constantly, and also because they have foolishly tried to have it both ways and to push both parties and be above the idea of the fight. That the gun lobby doesn't inherently appreciate why Democrats who teach that liberty is an abomination are not a problem so long as they don't vote to restrict cartridge capacity shows precisely the narrow, self-interested, and short-sighted thinking that explains why despite having facts in our favor, the Right loses again and again.

The ultimate microcosm of this conflict is, in all these variants, from the Republican Party to its various spin-offs, the idea that the individual can eternally overcome the collective. It's a good story and sometimes true, but when you let the collective forces put their thumb on the scale and make the hill ever higher to climb, the appeal to merit alone seems clunky when you give a handicap to help everyone on the other side who says they need more help than you. If, on an individual basis, perhaps even this would be acceptable, but have you noticed how the Republicans have surrendered so deeply in the cultural fight they simply adapt to whatever media standard is promoted? Like trained ponies, they walk in circles as the proud opposition who is respectable because they never stray too far from the comfortable ring of capital driven amorality.

Activists go insane fighting battles on the ground only to hear politicians through their staffers tell them how the time is never right to fight their issue. We're not allowed to say truths about immigration because that might cost Latino votes. We're not allowed to oppose gun control because soccer moms poll that they like protection. We're never allowed to say anything, or offend anyone. We just have to vote harder until the country dies, but it will be fine because at least we won't have voted for the Democrats. What a load of crap this is, yet we keep buying it cycle after cycle, because we have given up on the idea that we have better options, and we understand how badly we suck at organizing that we accept this as our best option.

We relent to neoconservative subversion, a Trotskyite variant of ideology that sees our men and women used as mercenaries around the world, and where America is expected to defend every moral interest except that of our own people. We can fight an invasion anywhere around the world in 36 hours but can't even put a wall on our southern border in 36 months. Worse still, these traitors didn't even try, although they literally funded building the same thing in other countries like some of our Middle Eastern allies. I do not know how to hide my contempt for their betrayal so I will no longer pretend to do so.

The Republican Party will likely survive the coming conflict in the role of "loyal opposition" if the submission scenario happens. If the new regime is particularly adroit, they might even let them have an occasional victory just to maintain the illusion of choice and keep the edge off dissent. But these are people who have no moral core, who will sell their souls to win election, and sadly, too many think of this as a moral act. The moderates, rightly branded as RINOs (Republicans In Name Only) can always be counted upon to not be there when needed, and to betray when expedient, so why do we wonder that a party rooted in disloyalty has proven a mere shadow of what we truly ⊚needed to save the republic?

I invested many years in the Republican Party, and I'm using this year and this election cycle to make one final futile effort where I've literally been arguing the only hope of having any use of this party is to vote everyone presently in office out of their comfortable sinecures. Because the system is broken, the party is owned, and whether through the desire of those involved or not, they have become nothing more than controlled opposition. They are the Washington Generals, paid handsomely to protect the reputation of the all-star Harlem Globetrotters and to lose the fights that could change things where the only victories they are permitted are those the elites already wanted.

The donors are there for a losing policy, and they will certainly get what they purchased. But what does it mean when the same people are buying both sides? Doesn't that reveal just what a sham our democracy has made of this once proud republic?

If you don't want to believe what I am saying, allow me to further strengthen my case by considering in depth what Trump has accomplished since becoming President, and then see if you still want to keep that Republican voter card in your pocket. I know I do not.

Chapter 20: The Nation Betrayed

Like millions of other Americans who somehow managed to overcome the odds, I had hoped the election of Donald J. Trump to the Presidency in 2016 would represent a seminal moment in our history, a reclamation of the nation and the beginning of a genuine movement to undo all the damage that had been done. Whether it was said precisely this way or not, I think most of us hoped we were essentially electing a revolution into office with the mandate to do whatever necessary to unmake the systems which had made government so elitist and corrupt. We had high hopes, but three years into the Trump Presidency, it seems like all we have actually gotten is another politician. My disappointment rises to the level of sheer despair because when you take a moon shot like this and miss, the consequences are dire.

I will try to write this chapter with a little more sensitivity than my writing usually connotes because I know many of my readers are fans and apologists for the President, but in the same way that I laid out the factual cases for America's problems at the structural, institutional, and partisan level, I would be a terrible hypocrite if I refused to apply that same logic to the President in terms of how well he has reached his stated objectives as well as those implied developments that fundamentally moved the crowds to support him in 2016.

If you recall that election cycle, there were three chants which were guaranteed to be heard at every single rally. "Build the Wall", "Lock Her Up", and "Drain the Swamp". Furthermore, three of the bigger promises that candidate Trump made were to see our departure from the endless wars with a new age in diplomacy, to work to redress the ridiculous trade imbalances where we lose hundreds of billions of dollars annually in net trade, and to bring manufacturing jobs back home. Let's look at the results before we move to explanations just so we are on the same factual basis.

Once you move past the partisan political rhetoric, every person on the Right who is sane understands immigration has been a disaster. Not only is there no wall, and no funding for the wall, but we are seeing an invasion which is accelerating by the day. The Border Patrol reported catching 400,000 people illegally entering the United States in FY 2018. While President Trump publicly claimed they were catching 90% of the people trying to enter illegally at the time, most common surveys claimed this number only represents between half to eighty percent of the people entering. However, if one researches further, there's an interesting project by Princeton Professor Douglas Massey, who runs the Mexican Migration Project, which collects statistics from the migrant side rather than through government agencies that suggests far worse numbers. For the last recorded year in 2016, only one in five illegal entrants were caught, with the government never succeeding in finding more than forty percent. Depending on who you believe, that means somewhere between 500,000 and 4,000,000 people illegally entered America in 2018. and the rush is no slower now that the Democrats control the House.

I'm not even going into the devastating statistics for legal immigration that we described in the first chapter. What we see is a country that lacks the will to enforce its laws, a failure to provide security on the Southern Border, and a proliferation of sanctuary cities that flaunt the authority of the Federal Government. Trump's Administration has been so hogtied by the media, the judiciary, and the Congress to the point where we actually, painfully, have to say based on raw numbers alone, Obama was more effective in controlling the flow of people entering the United States illegally. How depressing is that?

The second chant we heard all so often was to "lock her up," a cry against Hillary Clinton and her decades of theft and malfeasance, as a symbol of a much larger concern of corruption. While the rule of law never permitted such action absent an investigation, I find it telling there has been no public inquiry by the Department of Justice into any of the questionable actions of the former Secretary of State or that foundation that she ran with her husband. Everything just went away very quickly, and to the extent the Department of Justice does anything, it seems like they have only had an unending succession of Trump campaign officials they targeted from General Michael Flynn to Paul

Manafort to Roger Stone. One distracting effort after another has run out the clock, and here in the few weeks after Jeffrey Epstein somehow "committed suicide" despite being in a secure facility, Americans should be realizing that justice will never be applied to certain people who are above the law.

Trump might have spoken about the need to "Drain the Swamp", but he's been floundering in it since the first days of his Administration. He surrounded his administration with Deep State flunkies and neoconservative retreads like Nikki Haley, John Bolton, and Reince Priebus. Not surprisingly, nothing happened in terms of government reform, and we've seen the Federal Bureaucracy essentially assert imperial prerogative against Trump by proving so ineffectual that the government neutered his administration. Such institutional resistance was inevitable for any nationalist, but Trump's failure to have a plan to work around this most predictable enemy is a strategic disaster from which America very likely may never recover. We have finally proved that our true government is not ruled by those whom we elected, but considering that they and their patrons have the power and the biggest guns, this is no happy revelation for our citizens.

One could argue, except for the border wall, that it is unfair to judge Trump by the desires of his supporters. If the need were less urgent, I might even agree, but in the interests of fairness and balance, let's look how he has done in other areas.

With respect to foreign affairs, it has been a mixed bag but there are some good developments. I think the President did very well to de-escalate the situation with North Korea, as well as the complete destruction of ISIS for the moment. That said, firing missiles into Syria at the request of a questionable media narrative and getting so close to war with Iran remain threats to be avoided. America cannot afford another theater war with our country falling apart at home, and I hope Trump ignores his advisors and the rapacious donors behind them and continues the path of peace which his core voters want to see enacted.

Trade is less good. Leaving the Trans Pacific Partnership was a good start, but the USMCA trade agreement is only a slightly better version of NAFTA which is not what the people had in mind. More importantly, our trade deficit with China jumped another $75 billion dollars according to government statistics in the last year alone, so we're obviously not solving that problem yet. What bothers me here is that Trump campaigns on these promises and expertise, but anyone who takes five minutes to do the research can see he is lying. I get why these changes will be hard to enact, because it requires the profits of influential corporations to be compromised in order to improve the national bottom line. But rather than giving false hope, he should just come clean about this fact. And while he is at it, he should explain that China could choose to cause other problems if we were to play tough. But, he doesn't, and so we are stuck always speculating about what we are actually getting and what it means while we give the corporate lobby a free pass.

Manufacturing is another example. The corporate tax break which was the singular accomplishment of the Republican Congress did encourage some on-shoring of capital, and the hope of seeing some industry renewed domestically was long overdue, but the long-term trend lines are still moving away from jobs returning to American industry due to automation. That disappointment is clear in the President's flagging poll numbers in places like Pennsylvania, Wisconsin, and Michigan, where even for the companies who came back, the jobs just didn't come home. Trump seemed to have more success in the energy sector in both mining and extraction, but these will likely prove less helpful at the ballot box because of the geography involved.

In the end, what has Trump achieved? He's pissed off the Left quite frequently, which amuses some of us to no end, but other than in forcing that culture to reveal its truest character, his accomplishments have been few. Trump would claim the tax cuts helped families, which depends entirely upon their particular status, but I think it did far more to help advance supply side economics and corporate profit margins. I think there was some economic benefit to the one-time inflow of capital created, but as the national debt continues to spiral out of control with inflation sneaking up ever more quickly, and tens of millions of eligible Americans still permanently outside the labor market, we sit here as I write in late summer of 2019 on the verge of a recession which seems likely to hit well before the next election day. To be fair, that's not Trump's fault, but considering that his case is now defaulting to economic competence, he will be judged by that criterion – and probably not kindly – by independents who tire of the incessant drama.

Only the sheer ineptitude and insane antics of the Democrats who are still slightly ahead of pace for the policies they are supporting give me any hope that they will be defeated in 2020. Despite their many problems, I would still bet on them at this point because the fundamental demography is moving more their way each election cycle, because Trump is losing independent support and core support behind supporting issues as foolish as limitations on guns. In short, he's become a politician, and that might earn a vote, but it won't earn the passion of 2016 once again.

I personally think he failed because he surrounded himself with the wrong people, including Establishment hacks and listening overly much to his liberal family. He seems to have approached the whole enterprise like running a business, where his dictates would be followed, not realizing government with its independent bureaucracies is a whole different animal. Trump took too long to get to his agenda and allowed himself to be drawn into tactical warfare at the cost of any strategic vision. Lastly, I think he failed because he was unwilling to cross certain lines which might have been necessary when judges overstepped theirs and bureaucrats refused to listen. No politician would have been able to overcome this by playing by their rules, and whether for good or bad reasons, Trump has done that unceasingly to ineffectual results.

People often ask me why things went this way. Was Trump serious and legitimate or was he controlled opposition? Did his many years working for mainstream media show he was a deep plant? Was blackmail used to control him? Or, was it just the success of the Deep State in showing how no one could succeed? Did Trump refuse to shut down the government because he loved America too much to see people hurt, or too little to have the fight over our border which was needed? These are just a sampling of the questions we could ask all day and never answer. We must be content to say we may never know the full story of these years, so rather than speculating about what reasons exist for these outcomes, I'm going to jump past this armchair quarterbacking to share the more important results. Trump bought us time and greater awareness of the cultural conflict, but at the price of the elites advancing their control over dissent outside of government to such a degree that an attack against the system like his campaign will never be viable again, and with the reality that we still face the same problems we attempted to address by voting for him, but with slightly worse odds than before.

Trump needed to come into power and force an America First agenda into being which was unapologetically and explicitly nationalist, galvanizing his support into an active base engaged in the retaking of America. Instead, he outsourced the agenda, perhaps at the urging of Vice President Pence who had deep connections on Capitol Hill, to Paul Ryan and Mitch McConnell. They avoided immigration, failed on a health care reform that likely would have been unpopular anyway, and passed a corporate tax cut Jeb Bush would have signed. The Establishment Party helped the establishment cause, and when the time came for the quid pro quo on immigration, their standard bearer John McCain flipped one last bird before descending, and they did nothing. Trump's final opportunity to shape the government came in early 2019 when after the midterm elections cost the Republicans the House, likely because their failure to address immigration demoralized the once excited base, he had the chance to shut down the government to force the issue. He did not, and since then, government has been utterly ineffectual.

Absent some massive change in events between now and Election Day, it seems highly improbable anything can be accomplished in Washington. Certainly, from the legislative perspective, the Democrats owning the House means nationalism will not get another chance to adopt new laws or statutes. It also seems President Trump is content to fight the election over issues like immigration rather than solve them, which means we American people will have to see another few million people pour in here so that political advantage can be played out. More than most, I understand the need for political theater, but not when it comes to facilitating an invasion of this country, and that vacuum of leadership will ultimately prove destabilizing and no asset to what happens in 2020.

In the end, the Republican Party killed nationalism. Just as it killed the constitutional fervor of the Tea Party. Just as it killed the desire to protect moral authority back in the day, as well as the last protections for native industry. I told you that they represent the money and the power, as they have since after the Civil War, and they honored their donors over their base as they always do, because they make the bet which is both true and cynical that you'll vote for them anyway especially as the Democrats go more insane. They choose the short-term victory over the long-term cataclysm because they figure the big problems are beyond them and they need to survive. It's an entirely rational solution, consonant with free market thinking, and the reason why nationalism will not get another chance and why we will have a one-party state even sooner than I originally feared.

So many people tell me that Trump just needs more time, and that he will be able to do more in a second term. It's an optimistic thought, but one which runs very much counter to the history of lame duck Presidents. The political process quickly moves past them to the new cycle, and with no nationalist movement going forward beyond a shrinking cult of personality which Trump has insulating him, the institutional GOP is going to pick someone like Pence, Rubio, or Haley to resume their push toward being the respectable losers in the new global order. Any victories will be erased, and the joyful nostalgia people have now, which perhaps so many needed enough that they think it worth using this time that should have been better spent, will give way to an awareness of a terrible and inescapable situation all too late.

The way Trump came to power is being closed off. The far right has been exiled. The media has clamped down on the ability to even talk about immigration, as has social media where even mentioning illegal immigrants on YouTube will get you banned. No one else has the money to do what he did, and the ringleaders of the plan to save America all ended up in jail. He might be permitted another term, if only because so many other attacks are succeeding outside government that should have been resisted, but I echo those who believe Trump will be our last President who even paid lip service to the Right.

The death of nationalism and populism along with the disappearance of viable solutions from the ballot box at the Federal level is an Earth-shaking development. It changes everything, and it forces us to think radically more differently than we have about this battle before now. Where we could legitimately ask before how we should fight for control over our government to push our ideas, the shift in our thinking which the Right will have to make if we decide to honor our values will entail a different question: how do we fight against our government to preserve ourselves and our ideals? This paradigm shift is one most will not be ready to entertain, but we need to see the truth: The government will be going to war against the people to restrain our liberties to ensure they can maintain constant control. The elites want this. The Left wants this. Demographics demand this. The economic crisis will permit this. The question, of awful import, is how do we prevent this?

"The Coming Civil War" speculated that militarism and nationalism were the most likely way. We needed Trump to assert executive authority and conjure up his inner Andrew Jackson to overwhelm the Court, the banks, and to represent a new wave of freedom for the people from the heartland. It was a one-shot opportunity, and unfortunately, as should be evident to everyone reading this, we still live in an America under their control. That means our next approach becomes significantly harder to develop and implement.

I write to you on the Right because the burden will fall upon us now to fix this, and it will require us to go far beyond our comfort zones if we want to offer contest, because we won't win by voting harder or being more reasonable. Those doors are closed. We must think differently now.

The solution will be something better than we have now, which honors our heritage and principles, which has the ability to sustain itself and enough support for the people to live and offer meaningful defense of our people and our beliefs. It will not come from the Federal level, it will not come from the Republican Party, and it does not presently exist. We will have very little time to make this happen, and it will be viciously opposed. It brings me no joy to share these revelations, but the only promise I ever made was not to lie to you about the problem we face.

It is not yet beyond us or beyond our abilities but let me pause for a minute to conclude the useless endless war of the Left and Right might be too far gone, and with it, so too might be the America we've known. We can love the ideas, the beliefs, and the liberties, but we need to recognize and admit that the monster on the Potomac is not part of that country we love. It is the devourer which, if we let it, will now swallow us all. But we also cannot panic, because if our only answer to the hopes of the other faction is our fear, we will fail out of despair. Against their vision, we must forge a greater hope all our own.

Prognosis: Where the Odds Now Stand

In *"The Coming Civil War"*, six scenarios were laid out which represented those possibilities which seemed most likely to resolve as America completed its transition from a Constitutional republic into something new. In this reassessment, we will take some time to consider those options anew in light of recent developments and their ongoing future potential for success. No one should be surprised that this analysis will prove far less optimistic than my earlier work, but pragmatism is our ally as we do not have time to waste on fruitless efforts moving forward.

My previous analysis rated **submission**, or victory by the Left, as always being the most likely of outcomes. As insane as their ideas might be, they have several major advantages which they continue to compound. Firstly, the inherent demographic shift in America favors them heavily, and no serious political actors are willing to work to resolve this, let alone publicly comment upon this. You would not believe the number of people, and the positions they occupy, who privately are fully aware of the situation, but they are so well-trained and frightened by the media complex into silence that they essentially operate in a world of lies.

I understand the price of speaking against the machine, which is why I will probably be, absent a political revolution, forever unemployed, but when you agree to fight your culture war in a realm of lies, then you've basically conceded the culture fight as well to the ultimate relativists.

If our lies are any less than the fullness of reality and all its problems, why would people choose our fictions which will not work, as opposed to a more fantastic story about how anyone can be anything and each choice exists apart from consequence? You might laugh at how ridiculous that sounds, but cultural Marxism works so well to allay resistance because it indulges every fantasy that separates people from one another and weaponizes them in support of their own isolation.

Furthermore, even a cursory study proves true the axiom that politics is downwind of culture. When you look at what is on television or the most popular websites now, it has been a fairly consistent evolution that the ideas expressed in these venues get codified into law within a decade or two of their appearance as the new order. Young people come up through the indoctrination state of entertainment and schools enforcing the same moral message that equality must be forced and the old ways pushed aside, and as older folks die off taking their antiquated ways with them, the war of the young against the old offers a clever symmetry to conceal the continuation of the status quo.

We already know the Left owns big media, big tech, controls the message of big business, and inhabits big government. The Ivory Tower flies the Rainbow Flag and the bankers have given them an unlimited line of credit. They're winning, and if they're obnoxious now, it's because they know it. We should be united in calling them out, but between the delusions of what we want to be true, and our own subversive leadership, this does not happen.

In the same way that minorities vote seventy percent of the time for the Left, their odds of success having now thwarted the nationalist revolt must also rise to that frightful number. Given their control over culture, their superior organization, the many local governments who support them, and the likely course of events, prepare for a **70% likelihood** America is beaten into submission.

Even a well-designed strategy like **militarism**, the idea that a nationalist leaning right could take control through force in defense of its prerogatives becomes incredibly less likely once that angle of attack is launched and fails. To be fair, I think many of us were hoping Trump could read between the lines about what was necessary, and that he had it in him to become the man the moment required in service to the Constitution and the country. We needed transformational leadership which would have held the Left to account for all their crazy ideas and undone the elite power structures, but the moment he decided to play ball with them, which may or may not have even been a choice he was permitted to make, the nationalist dream flickered.

If you couple that with the decline of the identity movement which could have advanced nationalism, a brutal cultural and economic take down of dissent that is destroying lives for advancing free speech in defense of survival, it has become clear that the future choices we will be permitted for our nominal leader are going to be much more constrained. The Internet will be a smaller place, with dissent exiled to areas where it can be monitored and controlled until assimilation is forced, probably on a pretense of helping with mental health not too long from now. I look forward to my own appointment with Big Brother in Room 101 which will probably be mandatory in the not too distant future.

The small option exists that the military might unilaterally exercise its own prerogative as solutions from other countries have sometimes undertaken, especially in Latin America. However, this seems highly unlikely as the many years of both Bush and Obama saw the creation of a politically correct army with leadership chosen on the basis of adherence to certain political dogmas. Moreover, the makeup of the military has become far more reflective of American demographics, and I've had many older veterans correct me about the makeup of today's forces. There are many patriots and we should honor all who serve, but they tell me half the rank and file would be just as glad to fight Americans who claimed the Constitution as their means to resistance as they would be to fight in the sandbox overseas. Do not expect hope from there.

There remains a small chance for something exceptional to happen, and maybe I will be proven an idiot and the proverbial 4D chess will illustrate the limits of rational analysis. Perhaps a transformational leader may arise to upset the balance, or events may decline so rapidly that a sea change in thinking happens. It's nice to imagine these outcomes, but they are severe outliers now. Pray for mercy, but those of us on the Right should now expect that a national solution only has **5% likelihood** of seeing militarism, the force of will applied to the restoration of America through direct action by part of our Federal Government.

There are many more people rooting for **collapse** than we saw just a few years back, with the hope being that since inaction leads to terrible outcomes, at least a shuffling of the deck necessitated by a collapse would undo the likelihood of victory by the Left. I think much of the Right which is really paying attention has shifted to this mindset and this hopeless sort of hope in preparation, survivalism, flight, and the bunker mentality. Far be it from me to criticize as I sit ensconced in the comfortable wilderness of rural Maine for playing the odds, but I think the idea that we can only hope to be the last survivors of a mess to come while others suffer the consequences of a fantastical ideology coming into conflict with the reality of nature is not a brilliant path.

Admittedly, there are many versions of collapse scenarios ranging from the complete and instant breakdown, where little centers of order will need to re-establish themselves rapidly with prepared individuals and communities being rewarded, versus a long and punctuated breakdown where there are moments where the system gorges itself on the healthy morsels of civilization remaining to try to survive as it takes us all in its death throes. We can't know that future and trying to predict such chaos is a fool's errand. While it might not, sadly enough, be the worst of all outcomes given the track record of mass murder under unopposed Leftism, it's certainly not what we should embrace if any other options remain available.

Oddly enough, as bad as things are getting, I actually have reduced my likelihood for the collapse scenario for two reasons. One big thing required for this to happen in many permutations would be political conflict between two sides, and the cuckoldry of the Republicans we're going to see in the near future will be truly staggering. As such, we will see a more militant and aggressive government that will be willing to use force to survive disruptions and problems. Authoritarians can more readily survive economic disruption as they will use power to suppress dissent and solve economic equations the ugliest way: Less people equal less problems. That probably sounds as ridiculous to you as it would have to a Russian in 1916. Things change quickly.

The second reason I think collapse less likely is because this whole thing feels like an elite take-down to transform America into just another nation. It's painfully evident the conflict is being pushed to facilitate victory by one side, yet they want the fight to be against those who fundamentally push for loyalty between people and who still defend the idea of citizens having liberty and families having validity. Understood properly, this is an attack against non-state authority, and seeing those deeper tendrils make me convinced that as bad as things might get, they won't become as bad as they could.

Could a force from the Right change this by acting upon the many vulnerabilities within America to allow no other option? Absolutely they could, and this outcome is probably the fastest rising likelihood of collapse. I guarantee you patriot groups and militias have such conversations regularly about how to save the republic, but the problem is who wants to be the one who pulls that cord? It's one thing to say you want to fight the government; it's another thing to ask people organizing in defense of the morality of liberty to basically pull the plug on America and force all the millions of people who would perish to be held to account.

That's what happens if the power stays off for a few weeks. It could happen because of internal politics. It could happen, just as easily, because of external politics as perhaps the Chinese could use such a subtle strategy. It could happen because of nature also. Given the sanitation crisis in California, maybe the bubonic plague will take us down. There are plenty of collapse possibilities that have nothing to do with the people, but my point is just that there will always be many people who for self-interest will fight to restrain these. The odds are still considerable in my opinion, but less than they were before as I rate a **15% likelihood** of a near future collapse.

In the earlier book, I separated out three other scenarios as thought pieces where I did not rate any as particularly likely, but thought the ideas of **decentralization, separation,** and **secession**, needed to be considered. Those attentive readers who are skilled at arithmetic will have already noticed I've left aside a **10% likelihood**, which represents an increase from my previous predictions to be assigned between these three options. The failure of nationalism to penetrate the political framework at the highest level has so reduced faith in the ability to see one American solution, that it forces those of us approaching the question of the future from the Right to consider other opportunities to live in preservation of our lifestyle and liberties.

The core problem being the rising tyranny of the majority that is gathering ever more power to the swamp on the Potomac, the question becomes twofold about how we who defend liberty can resist this. Two answers become obvious. The first is that we must stop giving authority, wealth, and power to the central government and work hard to make decentralization a reality if only for our own defense against the inevitable demographic reality which will only accelerate. The second is that to oppose those powers, we need to quickly forge pathways to actual political power that is capable of resisting what the DC legal, New York financial, and Hollywood cultural machine will bring to bear.

When America was previously threatened by tyranny from away, what happened was that states organized themselves in resistance. It's easy to forget now, but when Massachusetts organized itself against taxation without representation, one had no idea whether Virginia or Nova Scotia was more likely to join them. As it worked out, enough states saw a common interest in forging a new path from the government far away in London which said their prerogatives had no meaning and threatened the use of force to enact compliance. War was ultimately required for victory, but the moral claim was strong enough to bring over two hundred years of prosperity with greater peace than not to our young continent. That model has now been tried twice and has shown its efficacy to offer resistance, whether in victory or defeat.

Separatism would see the destruction of the Right from one political party at the national level which is corrupted anyway into distinctive regional and state level parties. Instead of our nations now being America, perhaps they might now be New England, Dixie, Cascadia, and others. Instead of being lumped into one size fits all solutions where the Republicans from one region are stuck in these odd alliances, we could return to natural regions based on culture and economy and build identity as a new force with energy and vitality outside DC, and work to see our resources stay within our region and our efforts directed to our people. People laugh occasionally at this line I use, but I am now a Mainer before an American, because the United States are going to be wrecked by socialism, and I think many states have enough sane people who might choose not to go down with that ship.

We have firm legal ground to stand on in the Tenth Amendment, and we should fight these battles to reclaim revenues and righteousness back to our regions and our states. We should start making red lines we stand behind instead of playing hopscotch with them like the feckless GOP. But to do that, we need to start winning states over, and build governments therein that defend the people not just in liberty and prosperity, but against the likelihood our Democrat tyrants will come to snuff out the last vestiges of the Tenth Amendment as aggressively as they're silencing the First, Second, and Fourth.

As someone doing this on the ground, I can share with you this is a vision of hope and opportunity that excites people to escape the deep corruption and unnatural consolidation that is being forced upon all Americans. I know what we want up here is not what others want elsewhere, and the great thing about this plan is we don't have to agree upon what we want, just to work together against those who want us to act as they do, and then accept that our different constituent nations may have their own futures to find. We can move between the lines to find satisfaction for ourselves in an America of many nations, and we can finally offer the fight to DC on equal terms when we take back our states and make clear we will not live by their rules.

It is a peaceful path of defense, an honest one for which we can hope, and if the fight is picked against us, we will at least know why we are fighting. If this could succeed in just one state, let alone several, what was best of America might survive. And as the consequences of the terrible decisions likely coming from Washington, I believe if a healthy few can manage to quarantine themselves and endure, that they will be the core from which a reclamation of the entirety of this continent may prove possible within just a generation or two.

My head says the odds are not with us, as I rate the Tenth Amendment Plan as having a **10% likelihood** of success, but the future that leads to Constitutional secession in defense of our enumerated liberties stirs the heart, honors our best traditions, and respects the divine natural law of liberty. Oddly enough, I agree with the progressives on one point: The world does eventually tilt back toward justice, and this fight, a moral battle for freedom, family, faith, and fidelity asks more of us, but what it does not ask is for us to support people who lie to us.

I'm ready for a crusade for truth. I would rather see that than our country debased any further. These last ten chapters lay our first thoughts on the vision of how we who still value liberty can ethically fight this cultural war to whatever end required, knowing that we picked the right cause and that which gives us the very best chance of survival at this moment. My revolutionary ideal is liberty versus democracy.

America was always about these ideas. As long as they live in us, whatever nations we form and whatever states defend these beliefs, the true spirit of America shall live. Moreover, if we practice what was intended, a hopeful renewal awaits which is a most exhilarating prospect for us all.

Chapter 21: Identifying Our True Enemy

Before we can win this cultural war, we need to fully comprehend and make clear what we face. We need to understand not just what has been done to our country but start also anticipating moves which will be made against us before they happen. We need to become active instead of reactive, and the way we do this has to begin through better knowledge. As brilliant strategists like Sun Tsu made clear, to understand your enemies without understanding yourself is to ensure defeat, so these next few chapters are an exploration in depth of what we will likely face and what we will need to become to make that ten percent possibility into a one hundred percent probability. Should we fail in this endeavor, you already know the consequences will be devastating. Since we must not fail, I take it as an article of faith that we shall not, but these final chapters will lay out the challenges and a method we can apply openly, publicly, ethically, and hopefully peacefully toward victory. What it requires from all of us is to forget everything we think we know and start anew from the beginning.

The Fourth Generation of Warfare stresses the importance of the moral actor in finding victory. In this world where the sides are uncertain, where people have false motives and false agendas, this suggests we must know what our enemy offers as their claim to leadership, and also define ourselves most clearly who takes the field in opposition to their plan, and in defense of essential truths. For too long, we have just been attacking at the fringes of their power or operating within their system as subversive elements. We have been conservatives in a losing battle for our civilization, and reactionaries hoping to discover a magic formula to undo what is being foisted upon us. But like a hydra, we define our enemy in a hundred different ways, and when one of our allies or unknowing fellow combatants slays one head, the beast comes back with even greater fury with the ninety-nine remaining heads. Win at politics, lose at culture, media, and street conflict. Win on information, get controlled by finance, leveraged buyouts, and smear campaigns. We face a foe that always attacks from multiple fronts, and that is our first hint to the true nature of our enemy.

Call it men against the machine, as we fight an ungodly system devised entirely of artifice that has many layers against which we struggle. Ultimately, it is a vacuum that sucks up all that comes into its orbit, then shreds whatever is decent, good, and moral into something different. If you have wealth, it steals your money and charges you interest. If you create a new idea, it tempts, corrupts, and perverts it into a mockery. If you have liberty, it degrades the words of freedom into meaningless securities that people rush to give away. Our enemy is a system and that system is evil, wicked, and inhuman.

Try those words out on your tongue and practice them in the mirror until you feel comfortable speaking them with force and vigor. You have been told for many years that you have to believe the best of those who oppose you because we all share something in common. You can keep that lie, but the price of it will be the loss of everything you love, and everyone that you love. Have we not seen over years how our every kindness, our every effort at tolerance and compromise has eventually been met with nothing but scorn and contempt? If you do not believe this, put this book down now and go read how the elites talk about the regular people in their preferred publications, or go visit the Twitter hate machine and assert some moral value and wait for the response. You will find no quarter there, and you will find only people who are lost and ravenous for the next decent voice they will consume.

We are fighting against a technological totalitarian form of tyranny whose very goal is to end history. They work tirelessly to reduce humanity to our basest and most easily controlled emotions, destroying beauty and tradition without pause, and seeking to convert us into a hive species which they can manage one terminal at a time by controlling the flow of information, of resources, and by remaking the language itself. Newspeak is here and those of us who honor the old ways, happen to be born the wrong color, or who try to have families are thought criminals, and you need have zero doubts that the system will get to each of us in turn. It will consume us, correct us, and delete us because the future is not one of liberty or freedom, it is of conformity and correction until we become the ideal efficient drone.

If that sounds too harsh to imagine, then you need only look how man is merging with the machine. Is it not true that so many of us are perpetually connected by this tangled web they weaved for us already? Look how people are adding technology to themselves to augment their abilities and better fit into the world of things which respond all around us. We imagine they're watching us to be helpful, but who programmed the programmers? We know what big technology is doing, and we know why capital has invested so many billions into their efforts: They want to transcend humanity, they want to become more and to do so they will spare no expense and could care less what happens to those of us beneath them. If you have to ask the question, then that is you.

The revolt of the elites is very real, and they attack us on every front. We are born into a financial system that has multiple stages of debt servitude, a trap from which one cannot easily escape unless one delves even further into debt bondage for social mobility. Millions of our people are trapped by those commitments, and whether wisely or foolishly entered into, the question now must become: can we free them and awaken them to new possibilities? Can they be awakened from programming so subtle and subversive that tens of millions of Americans hate themselves based on a fictitious view of history and a twisted distortion of victim hood as virtue?

Those who avoided those traps through hard labor, or the providential planning of others still face the state and its many tentacles. If you own your land, you still pay rent as property tax. If you own your business, how many rules must you comply with to not be thrown in a box? Do we have our freedom, or are we permitted delusions to keep us from rallying too hard? Is that the real purpose of all these wars, to take men who might otherwise ask questions with their patriotism and exhaust them in the theater of the absurd overseas instead of working to liberate our homeland from the enemy within?

Try to turn away from these terrible thoughts for just an hour or two and what options do you have? Would you listen to the radio where every song is a paean to indulgence and recklessness? Perhaps you would like to see the sanctification of the newest depravity on the television? Or maybe you want something more real, so you surf the Net hoping to find whichever guilty pleasure keeps you sane. You can smoke your weed, drink your wine, or enjoy either the prescription drugs or the discount variety available on most every corner. All of these vices are permitted – encouraged even. Because they keep us from caring too much, and the moderation of indifference, tolerance toward everything, and diversity in defense of mediocrity is good citizenship.

In America, all roads now lead to Washington. Compare the roads with potholes we have in so many of our communities with the gleaming new houses in the environs of DC. Our stagnant wage growth has no meaning to people who swim in pools of wealth, like those who get fat off contracts earned through corruption and cartels. We see our law enforcement serve as hired guns, we see our military used as mercenaries, we see our political parties for sale to the highest bidder. They don't even have the decency to pretend shame as each rushes to collect more money, like points in a video game to please their masters who print the money at a touch of a button that you and I are forced to bleed for.

Look to the banks, as has ever been the case, for where the paper trail goes. Look to the trillions they print, derived from nothing, and rule by fiat that each and every one of us subscribes to like some dark transfixing magic. The blood of the system of systems, finance is the chain that wields the state against the people, and the bonds through which so many of us voluntarily surrender our humanity for the promise of just a little more comfort and a little more security. We serve the wrong masters, and we find that our world collapses around us because of our poor judgment.

How they must laugh when we fight between two sides about whether people should make ten, twelve, fifteen, or one hundred dollars per hour! What difference do these battles into which we pour such blood and sweat even mean in a system where those who are in control could easily print a billion dollars into being? And they aren't limited just to the illusion of paper, but can also create a hundred different instruments of credit – only some of which we see – and for which those that the intrepid amongst us can view are descriptive enough. The charade of the ever-changing colors of who supposedly represents us on top loses all meaning when the hooks in the back of the representatives all flow from these same hands.

Do you live in their world of systems? Are you a liberal? A conservative? Are you a Democrat? Are you a Republican? Are you a communist? Are you a capitalist? Are you here to stop the other side? Fight on, win the battle and lose the war. We have loans to help. We want you to win. We want you to play. We love the game. We are the game. And we are the players, being played again and again by turn.

Full stop.

Are you angry? I could write on for pages if you need, but if you're not angry by now, you probably never will be, and you will not understand. If not, this book is not for you, because you should be mad. You should be incensed that our entire lives, our struggle to survive, our sincere professions of morality, our search for meaning, is just a game to these people. It has been that way for a very long time and playing divide and conquer was the game that both built Rome and killed it. It will do no less to America, and I fear we have already reached the point where that is our national future. It fits the novel international dictate from our invisible masters, as the borders and lines on the map mean nothing in how we speak anymore.

To the communists who run the Left, the current favorite of the power brokers, borders are just an opportunity to draw in new people to advance the universal cause of the eternal revolution. What can be more evil than to revolt in perpetual pride to advance the idea that a being of lower intellect can make a better world in his image? Be careful not to cast your stones too quickly if you come from the Right because have our capitalists ever refused their thirty talents for a better deal? I wonder when we let our entire species devolve into this ludicrous fight about how we can best turn ourselves into something else, blockheads to be the pieces with which others would build their imagined future.

When was the last time we got a new tool, toy, or technology and asked if it was any good for us before consuming the next big thing with voracious and unending hunger? Can we not see that we undertake debt which forces us to work endlessly in service to the things that are supposed to be for our pleasure, and yet our entire lives are sacrificed to their needs? How many hours is your commute? How long are you kept on the phone? On the Net? When was the last time you saw your friends, your family, or remember who you were as something other than just what life forces you to be?

Money again, I know. We think ourselves virtuous when we work hard to earn it, but can that be the case when it comes out of thin air from people who need not work for it at all, but they can nevertheless use it to control us? Look at those little symbols and phrases on the bills and realize they are not there by accident. Deeper truths await discovery by your intellect if you have the stomach for it, but you need be no scholar of the occult to realize that when you make a possibility into a concrete value, much is lost. Does a picture convey the full beauty of a smile in a warm moment? Does a dollar bill warrant how much we put in service to it?

The enemy is certainly the system, and I pick just the most obvious point of control to show you how you may have forgotten how to be a man, or perhaps never learned, because you – just like I and just like the rest of us – have been slaves to a machine. We want an enemy to fight, and we can blame the elites for their cleverness, or the radical progressives for their folly, but what you don't want to hear but desperately need to know is that the enemy is us. We are the crazy people who are ruining our world, because we refuse to think, to choose, to exercise judgment, and to show restraint.

Any power these people have over us exists solely because we forget ourselves, and their entire system has one fatal weakness. The mirrored heart of the many-headed hydra reveals the reflections of our own attacks against one another. If, instead, we refuse to live by their rules and imagine ourselves a new future, we may escape the control they exercise through their many illusions.

I'll admit this book might have tricked you. I brought you in to this world with chapters chock full of graphs and figures, safe and sterile analysis that you could share with your coworkers. Prudent, rational, and very much true. Those are the types of solutions we want, and the sort of solutions that we are conditioned to seek out, because they work within the system to find a gradual safe correction to a manageable and predictable world. That's what our elites do. They stay on top by giving you two reasonable choices, counting at every opportunity that you will be reasonable and do what they expect because as talented as they are, what they cannot anticipate is when people choose collectively to break the narrative and go against the odds. This is why they fear the nationalists, because they might choose passion over prudence, and in the heart of living patriotism there exists the potential for victory.

This war will require spiritual men. My goal here is not to proselytize you to the true ecumenical faith but to remind you that absent faith, one does not take risks. Without belief, change becomes impossible, the province of other people who have not given up on their ability to make this world a better place. Our final adversaries are those who have abandoned that search and who instead seek only to control and condemn men to become less so their comforts can become all the greater. It is a hateful thing to make men less than they are, and to see us turned to servants, slaves, or mere synapses is cruel and wicked. We are not victims when we stop thinking of ourselves as such, and we must be born again if our nation is to be renewed.

Our enemies say we must accept all and judge none. They masquerade this as social justice, but they forget we have better intellect than that. We can reason what is true, live with the nature of ourselves and this world, and plead divine grace for the mistakes we make, as is necessary of those who are seekers, confident only in the knowledge that such an easy truth presented for us is false and reeks of death. The only way we can exist as full equals is when our animated clay returns to dirt sufficient only to be fed upon by worms and carrion.

Do not let your spark be extinguished. Awaken something better in you, and ask those questions not expected from us. Break your loyalty to the system, and return your loyalty to your fellow men, your family, your homeland, and this world. We need you, brothers and sisters, for the fight coming will be ultimately about preserving humanity, and we need as many victories as we can muster because should we win this war against the Left, this war against the elites, and abandon the dreams of living as machines ourselves, we should not delude ourselves into thinking the fight has ended.

In truth, it will just begin anew because we fight our nature, fallen as we are into deceit and depravity, and we must rise again to escape that. We must understand we cannot break the cycle, and that for all our cleverness, our only hope lies in wisdom and humility. We must remember ourselves, and a time when we understood things differently to have a chance. A people without a past has no future, and so we start our fight against our many enemies both without and within, by remembering what worked so well for so long: Liberty.

Chapter 22: Embracing the Timeless Cause

What is required will be far more difficult than anything you have been asked to do, or what any other politician will request or desire of you. As we understand that we are fighting a system that encourages helplessness and operates at many overlapping and interacting levels of control, we then understand the first step toward liberty must be our own liberation. You need to free your mind from not just the ideologies that constrain the potential solutions you can consider, but more deeply embrace a truly revolutionary mindset where you assert your personal independence as a sovereign individual who has both the ability and the authority to make decisions about your own life.

To invert the famous saw, we have to be willing to sacrifice security to regain liberty. This means that choices from here no longer have the same guaranteed outcomes or safety nets which buffer us like overgrown toddlers for our entire lives. I cannot assure you that this will end well, and I'm pretty certain that the repression of people who resurrect the Founding impulses of a very different time will be targeted by the most violent lackeys of the system, and will be the most denounced public enemies of an increasingly politicized judiciary. Do not expect most people to offer support either, as they will find the idea of being denuded of their happy comforts far more unsettling than the idea of living under state control. For every person who can think outside the system, it is likely at least ten or twenty would prefer not to have these struggles.

Liberty is never a popular cause in its own time. Everyone serenades the heroes after the long battles end should they succeed, but they would just as gladly spit on the corpses of the last free men, and we should be very clear this cannot be a popularity contest. While we can and should strike with an idea accessible to all, the timeless idea which says men can choose for ourselves how we should live rather than being told, it should be understood that even this is not a majoritarian proposition.

The Founders understood this. They understood that liberty could not be entrusted to a majority, which is why the leadership of the fledgling United States were so restrictive of suffrage. They knew that unless stakeholders were the decisions makers who balanced responsibility with rights in equal measure, that such a republic as they devised could ultimately only fail. I share this because our revolution should be one that tries neither to adopt nor abandon any specific form of governance. The Founders selected a system that made sense in opposition to the challenge of their time: A far off tyrant whose oppression was economic and military in an agrarian state of rising prosperity but wide geographical separation. Without doubt, the Constitution was a brilliant document worthy of veneration, but we must be unafraid now to seek out solutions that honor liberty but fit our own circumstances. We need answers for a technologically minded future with much higher population density, a far smaller world, and the ability to deliver force instantly to a person's doorstep.

Those questions are hard to answer; impossible for any one man. Because of this, we've fought for years about the right way to proceed in a world changing ever more quickly, and we've lost the initiative through such uncertainty. We must evolve past thinking we have or need a singular answer, and instead revert to basic principles we can agree upon in good faith and mutual trust that when these battles resolve themselves, the answers can be found. It took twelve years for the Founders to get from Revolution to Constitution, and we should expect whatever we attempt will take some time to adopt. What matters now is that we must begin these conversations and get ourselves thinking – not of ourselves as subjects or servants, doomed only to vote harder or seek exile – but instead keeping always at heart that we have agency and can choose different pathways. If America closes those doors for us, then we must open them where we are for ourselves. As a matter of faith, we must unapologetically assert that we have basic rights which we shall neither surrender nor suspend.

These are fundamentally both moral and legal actions. The Bill of Rights is the most important part of the highest law of the land, and any government which abrogates those guarantees has so violated the social contract established through centuries of practice to have rendered itself illegitimate. By both the letter of the law, regardless of what any robed figure in black may claim, and the spirit of the law, it would be an abomination to all that America's founders ever intended to simply permit this to pass absent resistance. Moreover, it is inherently a good act to preserve inviolate for men the conditions that allow us to understand our nature and explore our reason, which we already see is being boxed into ever smaller arrangements to reduce our nature.

Furthermore, these values have increased significance in a world where the power of the state is not merely notional but has become familiar and actionable. We need to ensure the freedom of thought, of assembly, of worship, and choice of association in order to be able to thwart demands of compliance made against us. We need our weapons lest our government decide that this experiment should end because the people prove too inconvenient. Privacy should be defended vigorously so we can continue to offer dissent in a time when thought crime is becoming a popular concept, and no sane man should ever be forced to self-incrimination or be deprived of a jury of his peers. In truth, even the rights we uphold now are not enough to defend the attacks before us, but they are a start from which we cannot retreat and still hope to survive.

This is why liberty must be the essential value. All great accomplishments in history begin with a thought and with words. More fundamental than identity even, in its transcendence, the word has ever been the beginning of civilization and of man's ascent from the herd. It is a challenging cause, yet an open one, to recall that we can seek to be better than we are, and that we could use freedom once more to advance ourselves morally, practically, and physically. Frankly, it is the last common denominator we have left, because once we surrender the enumerated rights and the implicit additions which so connect, all we will have is a tyranny of force sanctified by the majority with no common opposition to be found. We will have the appearance of choice without the possibility of truth, as our system will allow us our illusions but no actual agency.

This battle is for free will versus predestination, a complex and paradoxical struggle which has exhausted many a great mind and surely will do so again. Yet, we who adopt the choice of freeing our wills now make a profound statement of also asserting our worth. We cannot know what we cannot know, but we can choose to move toward those values that are presently ineffable as an act of good faith to demonstrate our desire for understanding, for advancement, and to strive not toward celebration of our bestial nature, but to overcome it as a spiritual transformation into something greater. We could become men and women worthy of our strong and proud ancestors, refusing the facile compromises where we are promised safety, a meal ticket and the promise of scant provisions from those who reckon themselves our superiors. We can resume the question of how we become more than we are,, and perhaps even rekindle the fading hope that the nation itself may renew.

America is still a young country as these things are reckoned. At two hundred forty-three years old, we have enjoyed times of prosperity and of peril. We have achieved great things in the world, some of which were terrible but necessary. We built ourselves from nothing, but now we have come to the identity crisis which many nations reach at this point in their development. We must decide whether or not to continue the American experiment, and whether a free people are desirable once a certain standard of living had been met. Our ancestors made their choice favoring liberty and its accompanying responsibilities, hoping thereby to escape the many different broken systems they knew had never allowed them the chance to succeed beyond a very modest level. But we, their progeny, also enjoy comforts and status they could not have imagined. In truth, the wealth of even the poorest American and the guarantees they functionally enjoy regarding access to the implements of the state would make them among the most well-kept people in history compared to the standards of just a relatively short while ago. It's the question we're asking now: Is liberty worth it, or should we just tell the white lies of peace in order to exist just a little while longer?

Perhaps our decision is eased by the reality that an insanely radical Left is out there promising to enact full equality, and that the purge they will eventually deem necessary seems to have the tacit approval of the elites. But let's imagine our oligarchy was more benevolent in their expression, a conclusion which is very possible given how they too have needs for which they will find people useful and a desire for order as the final outcome. If we could have a benign authority run a tranquil existence, would we choose that outcome thinking it the happiest of all outcomes? Is peace and plenty enough if we have to sacrifice the search for meaning and the evolution toward excellence and new ideals as the price of escaping the perpetual war?

If we answer that question in the affirmative, then I think nothing of what America once was will ultimately survive, because a moral case to be sufficiently compelling to those who understand the purpose of such articulation must be objective, it must become a universal imperative at all times. Ironically, it has to exist as the goal which can never be reached, because the very instant we stop climbing toward achievement and look down, we will inevitably fall from the heights we seek out into the fear and despair of our minds going where our mere bodies struggle to follow. This is an inescapable consequence of the human condition, to allow our cerebellum cause to hide us in the corners of thought and existence, and this is where those of us who come from the Right now find ourselves. We look upwards with temerity, seeing all the noise and fury around us, occasionally daring to dream but rarely risking our deepest hopes, let alone trying to stand amidst the rushing torrents of people who hate the idea that we would rise above them.

I think it important to also understand that this is an intersectionality which allows us to work with one another even as we disagree on certain fundamental issues. Uniquely, liberty allows flexibility for the men who are driven by moral causes to work toward a better future. In this way, such men are not required to endorse ideas with which we do not agree. Defining goals in terms of aspirations can sometimes create problems of essential unity. But the commonality of liberty is also an achievable goal for a system such as ours where the creation of the sorts of commonalities other nations enjoy through centuries of kin bonding or institutions of such veneration is not automatic. Our American mythology which has more currency than I think people sometimes realize, honors pursuit as part of our founding principles, and this approach recognizes it as such.

There was a time when we understood our differences as far more useful than today because those differences seemed to be merely different paths in pursuit of commonly desired outcomes. This narrative tries to redefine our cultural totems as reason, nature, and grace, to reset our actions in liberty toward a common set of values from which we have historically benefited, and which recognizes the overlapping traits of those people most likely to act in defense., The distinctly American concept of Liberty has worked fairly well in pushing these thoughts toward new and productive outcomes. In addition to being an idealistic philosophy, something important for a polyglot nation such as any region of America now has become, liberty also remains a practical option.

Just as the last chapter was about understanding our opposition in this notional war we are imagining; we need to be very clear about who we will have to be to fight on these terms. Are we willing to impose our wills in this time to see the restoration of a system where liberty is properly balanced with responsibility? Through action rather than words, we will inherently have to provide an answer, taking it upon ourselves through personal resolve to offer these alternatives and see them brought into being. I live in the painful glare of a hostile media, and I will tell you it is extremely unpleasant. Do you love the ideas enough to see your friends abandon you, your family attack you, and the system brand you with every horrible insult they can manage?

Would you be able, as the Savior himself once reminded, to form a new family of those brothers and sisters who through common faith forge a new and deeper bond to experience a rebirth in our lifetimes?

As expressed throughout this book, I draw inspiration from the Gospel for our struggle of good versus evil, and I use those terms with the clear understanding that liberty is good because it allows us the chance to freely approach both a better understanding of this world, and to voluntarily walk toward greater wisdom absent the force of compulsion, whether by state or by religion. Our Founders spoke about divine providence supporting this plan, and it is a matter of faith that I believe that if a sufficient number of people stand for these ideals, that help will come in forms unseen, as reality will bend to the wishes of those who act with divine sanction.

Do not discount the reality of things we cannot understand because the cause of the cynic is never won. Had our own Founders reckoned the struggle they launched in the 1770's against the full might of the British colossus in terms of just men and material alone, they would have never found the courage to even take the field. Instead, they understood the reason for their fight transcended their likelihood of success, and they issued their earnest appeals not just to one another, but they also called upon divine providence to bless their efforts and bring allies to their side. In the fullness of time, their courage inspired many British to distaste against their own government for fighting men who only sought liberty, and inspired the French and Spanish, perhaps for their own selfish reasons, but nonetheless to enter the side of the war to assist the colonials in securing their liberty and sovereignty. There are times a long shot made in service of a higher cause cannot be measured as a simply one in ten proposition, and when we look at what the world will suffer should some corner of liberty not endure from the American experiment, we would be well within our reason to ask if this is one of those times. Sometimes, the battle is worth long odds, and that is the attack which has a real chance of success Because nobody sees it coming.

You really have to be born as a new man, a free man, to fight this fight. I'm not fully there yet, but it is an amazing thing to feel alive, to have agency, and to not merely have to go along to the next obligation. Embracing a different way of being is a challenge that does not happen overnight, and it's something you have to seek deeply inside yourself in order to understand that you can be more than just a summer patriot when the threat of a long American winter looms ahead. I think you might like this better, as I know I do, but the question is if there are enough of us, and if this fight where we agree to make ourselves better as opposed to the same is the ground upon which we are finally willing to make our long-promised stand.

We will find no better ground, so the question becomes: who are we willing to be? Can we remember our better selves, and do we still share those dreams?

Chapter 23: Fight Them Like They Fight Us

Books written about politics, history, or social commentary in our era are written with a degree of detached reserve that is a product of our times. We seek to draw upon authorities greater than our own as if they somehow add credence to the rationale of our conclusions, and we hesitate to paint our visions in bold colors. We care too much about respect and too little about content, I fear, which is why my work represents a much-needed counterpoint to the sterile and safe discussion originating elsewhere. It is a different way of looking at history, and we need to escape the trap of accepting reasonable solutions or living within the academic bubble.

It's worth taking just a moment here to think about how our Greek and Roman predecessors understood history. I assure you most did not actually believe that Zeus and the Olympians were battling for the right to conquer Troy, but instead they were instructing their young men in how to approach the questions of the world and warfare – not through abstract theory, but rather through concrete experience. Whether reading the accounts of Herodotus and Thucydides who present history at a remove, or looking instead to Cicero and Caesar, the objective was always as much to present a moral case for history to recall and learn from as to share the reports of various challenges and conquests. Now, we like to pretend we are detached, and I think the practice of such indifference toward ourselves and thinking that those who know what happened should have the least say has served us very poorly.

We need knowledge for the fights ahead of us because if we had that understanding, we could better predict what challenges will arise. If instead of meekly accepting that the law will magically serve as some sort of constraint on bad behavior in a cultural war like this, if we better understood how these struggles work out, we would accomplish two important outcomes. Firstly, we would much better understand the urgency and the immediacy of this fight, as there are several excellent examples of the cost of allowing a revolution like the one being launched by the Left in deceptively slow motion to succeed. Secondly, we would also better understand the methods by which our culture has been deliberately, not accidentally, deconstructed to accomplish ulterior motives. Our blind spot caused by false idealism and a misplaced sense of equanimity would dissipate and we could see our enemies and their tactics much more clearly.

This matters because we are entering a time when idealism is a luxury that must be held close, and we must be painfully realistic about the decisions we make in times when the only choices available may all have flaws. We have to unlearn the habits of a self-destructive movement that knows too well how to hesitate and not well enough when to strike. We need to abandon conservatism in recognition that conservatism failed so badly that whatever we would wish to conserve is now gone, and instead remember what we want to recover and strike out as traditionalists to reclaim our past and thus regain our future. We need to be able to take chances again and accept the good over the perfect. This is why I've spent so much time in this section encouraging you to rebuild yourself as a moral fighter, to find those values which you can hold dear through dark days ahead, and to make them be the light to guide you through hard times with uncertain ends.

But using reason to articulate better solutions is only half of the equation, and frankly, it is the easiest part of what will be required. The harder thing will be to recognize the fallen nature of those who oppose our solution, and to treat them with the same disregard with which they treat us. Such teaching goes against years of instincts and the philosophical retreat which we have all been long accustomed to making, where if we do not succeed in the practical application of our beliefs, at least we can cherish the moral victory of being of an uncompromising nature.

Such a luxury was possible in a society where choices were less constrained, but people must recognize now that to adopt the position that the struggle is beyond individual action is a retreat rooted in cowardice for those who truly understand what we face. If we continue to permit one set of rules to be applied by our adversaries against us, where they wield government as a weapon and justice as a cudgel, we will make the most immoral decision of surrendering to defeat rather than being willing to genuinely present ourselves for our beliefs and stand upon them.

For too long, I believe the West has been in retreat because we've tacitly accepted this idea that it is nobler to die for a cause than to kill for such. I challenge that assertion specifically because it is far more challenging morally to admit sufficient belief in something to not only surrender oneself but to exert force also upon the world to shape the future to your belief. Except for those who are sociopaths, of which there are a few (and disturbing number in politics), this is not ever a choice which should be happy or easy. However, the idea that violence in self-defense is reserved merely to the state is but the modern articulation of slavery, and we should remember our Founders left the Second Amendment with many writings on this very subject as a reminder that they understood the force of arms is sometimes required for our preservation, and not just for soldiers in sanctified missions chosen by the state for its own interests.

We have allowed patriotism to be defined as criminality in the common discourse by people who commit the very same types of acts in service to a more heinous cause but who are permitted to get away with such hypocrisy. No more can this be permitted, and we need clear understanding and articulation that we will be prepared to meet force with force, and to assert as a matter of preservation and justice the will to exert force in self-defense. We remain moral as we link our cause not to some capricious pursuit or individual ambition, but to the defense of the nation as articulated in the ideals that generated such success.

Do not take my words to mean sanction for individuals to go off and arbitrarily pick fights with their foes who irritate them. A Hobbesian war of all against all is not what we want or what we seek, and such acts would inherently be both criminal and counter-effective in nature. Yet, we believe in proportionality, to mutual defense, and to the right to organize in legitimate defense of our beliefs and liberty, and to ultimately create institutions willing to stand and seek out our separation against the tide of injustice being used against us.

I fear things will ultimately come to a question of force, and absent our ability to organize from the Right, we will lose the battle, our nation, and our civilization. This is the most likely of all outcomes, and for us to change this, it now becomes incumbent upon us to act proactively rather than in reactive defense, and that means organizing, articulating, and separating with great speed.

We can be assured that efforts will be made to disrupt us, and we must thwart them. If people come after us, we must learn to punch back with enough strength that they do not do so again. Responses should be proportional, measured, and useful, but when we get called every horrible name in the book, we cannot be afraid to brand our enemies as wicked, evil, socialist, communist scum who would sell out their own people. All these things are true, and we do not have the time or luxury of always being better than them when survival is on the line.

It is a painful thing to learn, as it has been for me and my family, but the time we waste in trying to rescue people from their own foolishness is a lost opportunity for us to work toward our own survival. I understand we all work to reach family and those closest to us who don't have the faintest clue that a war is already happening around them just because bullets aren't yet flying, and it is good and just to reach those who can be awakened to act toward their survival. However, for the time well spent on those initiatives, how much time do we forfeit jousting with useless idiots who exist only to trigger reactions and delay another day away toward the ultimate cultural and demographic victory our schools are facilitating, and our porous border is welcoming?

Imagine if our President spent as much time and energy solving problems as he does talking about them, how much more he might have accomplished by now? I submit the same option and opportunity exists for each of us to focus our efforts where they will be useful, and that is in leveraging the individual excellence of those who lean Right into a collective framework where whatever our disagreements, we can work toward mutual survival from a position of respect and in deference to liberty which serves all our interests.

Not only must we not equivocate against those who we must begin to understand as our enemies, but we need to be incredibly aggressive in destroying those implements by which they attack us incessantly. The fake news should be targeted for destruction as the propaganda machine it is, with local and state governments being bold in willing to revoke licenses, to reduce this corrupt consolidation, and allow the people's voice to re-emerge from beneath the noise of those who drown out legitimate dispute with their scorn and who censor away alternative options. Each man is guaranteed his free speech as an absolute, but these corporations are no men, and for so many years how much harm have we allowed them to do by giving them rights which they, as corporate institutions, do not deserve?

We must be willing to reclaim knowledge from those who have shepherded our children and young adults astray. All of us know the colleges now exist only to push a certain agenda, so why do we continue to fund them with our tax dollars on one hand, and a combination of hard-earned money and usurious loans on the other? Would we not be better served to speak up to reform education in favor of principles which benefit the nation and destroy this ridiculous tenure system that is used to protect the worst sort of thinkers who only do harm to our children? Why is it we only defend liberty when it does us harm, but never when it serves to the good?

The answer is because our enemies, just as Gramsci predicted, Marcuse elaborated, and Alinsky codified relentlessly use our system against us where they hold us to the standards we believe should be true, which we endorse, while they adhere to the opposite code to destroy all that is healthy by using every contradiction without regards to how hypocritical they become. I will not pretend that fighting against this will allow us the ideological purity that has long been our bailiwick, but what it might allow instead is a chance at survival, to disrupt those institutions and actors which are so hostile to America and the West, and make clear for those people who can be awakened that there are better choices to be made.

We must win the fight to use language well again. Go back and read the Founders or men of that generation and look at the precise, morally imbued, and well-balanced language they use to describe the challenges before them. Their rhetoric displays they knew their place in the world, a cultural framework that made sense rooted in logic, reason, nature, and grace, and their appeal stirs timelessly across the generations to today because of its unapologetic boldness and simplicity. Can we not find the ability to speak so well once more and refuse to allow the prostitution of our very words to these false causes which we indulge thinking them a harmless exercise in applying tact, but in reality represent a surrender of the mind to fictions which only lead us even further astray?

I do not recognize made up pronouns. I reject the language of oppression, domination, and control that causes the perpetual war. Equality has no appeal to me absent value. I don't have to understand, to accept, to tolerate, and I will gladly discriminate, judge, and act upon those beliefs because those are the consequences of rational thought. No two things can be equal unless they are the same, and the eternal reduction of the West to the lowest common denominator must be confronted, opposed, and fought.

As someone who has been called a supremacist, racist, bigot, xenophobe, Nazi, separationist, villain, secessionist, and various forms of bastard, I don't care what these people think because I know myself. I share with you these values of truth, nature, and grace, because they are the virtues that made our past and can rebuild our future, but only if we are willing to be honest in our application of their demands to ourselves, our society, and our opponents.

I might feel empathy for the people, each of whom has a divine spark that could be nurtured into something greater, but I respect the validity of their choice and am all too willing to hold them to account. If people choose to become part of the machine, if they let their fears turn them into the pedestrian monsters who are the enablers of the very system of their subjugation, do we have such a moral obligation to rescue them that we sacrifice ourselves? I argue we do not, and when we sacrifice those who count upon us and our strength of resolve and action to preserve the future from their twisted visions, we are derelict in our duties if we continue to allow ourselves to be blackmailed into serving those who choose their own helplessness.

Yes, so many of the people we oppose are caught in a mental trap where their best impulses are corrupted into service of a wicked system. They believe the rhetoric whereby they are taught equality is the uplifting of all peoples to overcome contradiction, ignorant of the frequently repeated reality which demonstrates the precise opposite. They get caught in the web of information that is more damaging than a thousand missiles that traps the infinite potential of the human mind in enigmas which cannot be puzzled out and render them inert. In all times, all men are always subject to these snares, and each of us will likely get trapped in unsolvable questions of our own, but our task is not so complicated here in this battle.

We simply need know based upon what we believe that we are better than those we face, that what we intend will lead to better outcomes, and as such, give ourselves grace enough to act with moral sanction to oppose them by whatever means necessary. We know they will play dirty, and if you need any deeper understanding, I highly suggest you take time to familiarize yourself with what has happened to so many of the White farmers in South Africa. These tragic stories display the worst and most aggressive displays of bestial cruelty against families including young children who are beaten, raped, dismembered, incinerated, and other actions for the crime of mere existence as an affront to a regime which claims equality as its mandate.

Equality is death, the time when our spirit fades and we either lose life altogether or surrender such to some idea that reduces us to cogs in a system or serving as motors for a short season before our expiration. We must be better than that, and to ensure that such an outcome does not result, we must be willing to do whatever is required to survive and build a space for ourselves in which security comes from the active and common defense of liberty, with an awakened citizenry who is educated to these dangers through learning and experience, and which is unrelenting in winning the war of words, institutions, and organization that precedes the state.

The days of blackmail where the best of us surrender so much to those who have nothing to offer but excuses for why they constantly fail must now end. We will help the helpless out of love, but for those who only make up stories, we must understand they are only holding themselves back and we cannot waste another moment on those types who could do better. We must trust our judgment to become better through practice about that with which we are dealing, and to recognize whatever mistakes we must inevitably make, it's better than allowing this system which would make us all into nothing would be far worse.

With this mental preparation always close at mind, and with a clear understanding of ourselves, our opposition, and the need to fight this battle to win, we give ourselves the best chance of survival, which should be our goal in the culture war which might go hot at any minute. It is essential to understand why we must do these things, to ensure our survival and to claim a space in our future, but now we can begin to consider the more challenging question of how we must act to give ourselves the best opportunity at success.

Chapter 24: The Building Blocks of Victory

War is a numbers game. It's true for militaries in the field in a hot war, and it's true for activists in the streets in this warming culture war. While smart strategists can and do leverage their forces and the environment around them to create opportunities by employing nature in service of a bigger plan, the reality is that we need many more people to awaken if liberty is to have any chance. We should not try and do not want to replicate the plan of democracy, which is to have a middling effect of using passive absentee support to create a veneer of legitimacy in order to sanctify the existing system – a system which fundamentally operates upon debt usury, large scale corruption, and the selective application of violence. Instead, we need people who understand why they are involved, and for each of ours to be worth ten of theirs. We need men and women who can decimate the facile arguments of the system with logic, and who through nature can persuade allies to our cause by offering the promise of a better future.

The nature of the cultural control that is exercised against us ensures that the opposition will always have an advantage when it comes to disrupting our efforts. People will be economically banned for speaking truth, silenced from popular platforms for disturbing the peace, and some will likely be targets of the legal system for standing up for rights that our Constitution guarantees but that the government sworn to uphold that very Constitution would rather ignore.

For decades, a quiet decapitation strategy has been used to discredit and de-legitimate possible leaders, and destroy whole movements, as happened to the Alt-Right. This strategy has been in effect, and we should only assume that these efforts will be in overdrive given the accelerating course of events.

However, we have to overcome these challenges and build organization of our own. What form it should take is entirely dependent upon the direct objectives needed in the moment, but instead of thinking in terms of permanent institutions that will be targeted for destruction by the lawyers from one end, the activists on another flank, and the so-called hate group watchers in another layer, we must think differently. L Specifically, we must operate on the basis that we are fully enacting an insurgency. Our uprising of ideas must be as fast as information itself, redundant in finding new ways to flow, and be the whispers that hide amongst the shouts we will surely hear used against our efforts toward reclamation.

To win, our cause must be more moral than our enemies, and we have to remember that in all we do. As an example, what we do in Maine is aptly demonstrated for the public to see in all clarity on the Maine for Mainers page on Facebook. We assert unapologetically that the obligation of our state is to the people who are here who have legal status, that the resources of our state belong to and should be dedicated to our citizens, that we accept no inherent responsibility for outsiders with no prejudice for or against them, but that we stand against those who make the false claim that our lives and our ideas have less value just because someone else claims to be a victim. We honor the legal equality of opportunity for those who share citizen status, but reject the idea that our lives should be held in involuntary service to enabling the indolence of those whose only contribution is an unending series of complaints.

We are hated because we speak truth. We make clear the attacks upon so-called "White privilege" and "supremacy" are not only attacks upon straw men that don't exist, but are also just the latest in a series of hypocritical attacks whose real purpose is to bypass reason. We talk about race, frankly and unapologetically, admitting that no two men or no two groups of men are equal, but we also recognize that even though two groups may have different values, that does not make either without value, without the need for improvement, and without the natural human right to claim pride in heritage and identity. We break down false division through honest discussion of nature, and we do that to disrupt the comfortable corrupt coexistence between Democrats and Republicans in order to openly explore why certain questions never get asked.

A few people love what we are doing and are excited and engaged. More hate it because they're told by the full force of the local system what bad people we are, and they never bother to invest the effort needed to pierce the illusion, since they have no incentive to do so. Two commie potheads run what counts for local media in Portland up here, and they basically give each other a reach around about how the broader media lets them say whatever they like while they plot to destroy a healthy culture. No one dares to oppose their open plotting because people are more scared of being called racists, sexists, or xenophobes than of seeing their whole state turned into a mockery of what it once was. Their friends in the larger media who find them useful are only too glad to use them as a wedge against the people, demonstrating how radicals are leveraged by the system to defend its own prerogatives without having to claim responsibility, thus demonstrating another tactic which we need to learn with great haste on the Right.

The days of punching Right because someone doesn't sufficiently adhere to our preferred ideology must now be over. This has to be the single stupidest habit we see repeated time and again, where we literally hurt people who agree with us on most issues because of one disagreement, and instead give power to our enemies to separate and divide us. The energy of activism is constantly repressed by the stolid arrogance of the Republican Party and those so-called "respectable" leaders who want to be gatekeepers. We should start recognizing these folks for what they are: the collaborators of a regime that is turning against the people, and we should show them no more consideration than we would for any other occupying force. We should understand that these "respectable" leaders don't gain that respect through service to truth, but rather through the fact they are given deference due to the service they provide to the very people they claim to oppose. In truth, that is what purpose they now serve, and while I do not support infighting generally, one exception worth making is to exclude those disloyal idiots who place themselves above the cause and try to sow division.

You must accept from the outset that every horrible thing will be said about you. Every activist already in the field knows this, and every Republican from President Trump to an establishment hack like Mitch McConnell is already perceived this way by our opposition. It's lunacy to continue to give credence to their linguistic programming attacks by trying to thwart them on their own territory using rules they change whenever they wish. This failed approach is rooted in the idea that the way to continue to win the game is to appeal to some amorphous mass of independents in the middle who somehow have a wisdom that transcends the rest of us in their commitment to either conformity in one group, or unfathomable indifference in the other.

America is failing because we have an identity crisis. We have competing incompatible visions, and the answer cannot continue to be to seek out the least damaging forge of schizophrenia, which essentially is what the centrist path will boil down to if you consider their logic. Moreover, such thinkers will choose the path of least resistance, which fundamentally means they are the great mass of enablers who will choose democracy over liberty and thereby facilitate communism, because ultimately, they care too little about the results to engage. Instead of seeking to appeal to those expressed interests, we must evolve our message to help the apolitical understand how they will lose what they love if we continue down the path they favor, and to reach the centrists by making clear the extremity most threatening to their future is not posed by those of us who seek to constrain government, but rather by those who will facilitate intrusions into every aspect of our daily lives.

When we play the systems game, we lose. We have to be unafraid to work outside the system and be willing to come in a form which is not expected. That means the days must end of gathering permits so a bunch of thugs who are well-informed in advance can be bused in to fight us, and where the media has ample opportunity to craft narratives in advance to presents us as the villains in a wrestling match. Just as a general doesn't announce his attack in advance, and he avoids a cavalry charge through a swamp, we who fight the culture battles need to get away from this mindset that paints us as just two sides in a battle of equanimity that is "politics as usual." This is wrong – we must see ourselves as a force for the liberation of our people, our lands, and our minds from a system which is always trying to collar us toward its ideas of "respectability." Respectability in this case meaning, in essence, surrender.

I believe the strength of the idea being articulated here is that each person yearns, at least in part, for free expression. I think most people also understand that certain limits exist beyond the imposition of men that come from nature and logic itself, and that when we adhere to those restraints, we better accomplish our desire to achieve goals and fulfill ourselves. We build solid foundations in this way, based not on fantasy, but on practicality. We should ground ourselves in reality with whatever ideals we express and focus on taking one concrete step at a time, always moving forward in a direction that makes sense. We must learn to act instead of always reacting, and to force the cultural rhythm to move to the beat of our choosing.

The cornerstone to success has to be overlapping networks that go to the ground. Instead of just fighting in the idea space of whatever particular issue motivates us, we must seek our broad foundations rooted in the places we live and the people with whom we interact. I know how gauche it is to talk politics and culture, but we must have those conversations now, and bring our families and loved ones on board. Now is the time to be having those challenging talks where mutual understandings are reached, and even if not another soul knows that you are preparing, even these preliminary actions will have tremendous value in allowing to you to prepare, persevere, and prosper in the uncertain days ahead.

In all my writings, I emphasize third way thinking which gets past the Left/Right paradigm and posits the question about what is the good, and how do we reach it? There are different variations which my other works explore, but the universal constant that we need to remember here, as we build our insurgency into something effective, is that loyalty matters most. We must act in good faith to the common ideals we express, consistently work to deliver options that bolster those results to the public, demonstrate why our ideals represent a better way forward, and live those ideals in our personal lives in each and every interaction. This is most important in how we treat one another as brothers and sisters who are willing to join this sacred fraternity in common defense. We are here for people, and can admit some differences as long as we share broad commonalities that give us faith that those discrepancies can be resolved later once the crisis is past.

I think we also need to be very careful of our own greatest weaknesses which are two-fold. Many people who would fight in defense of liberty well understand our tendency to regress into ever smaller camps in defense of our own highly unique and individual forms of perfection. By keeping our cause basic and our solutions universal at the national level, while allowing and encouraging diffusion and differentiation into multiple aligned entities at the local level, we can turn this weakness into a potential asset. But the biggest problem, to my mind, remains this idea that the last chapter spoke about in that we care more about those who fight us than they care about themselves or us. We have hearts that care and are passionate, and as such, we are too easily swayed to restraint with the promise of optimism.

Against that, so much of what I've written herein is designed to help you steel your soul against these spiritual diversions, and to remind you what we are doing is fighting to envision a future whereby we don't have to always make awful choices. There are possibilities where we live in health and we can be optimistic because we will have sounder foundations in the future, but those cannot exist today, and any concession we make to the system only prolongs the misery. I hate to describe what we must contemplate like euthanasia, but it's closer to the truth than not. We do no kindness to see a nation so despoiled as America has been by those who now pollute our halls of governance endure thanks to our cowardice or misplaced empathy toward what we fight.

If your heart is moved to help people, then by all means, do so, but not by investing in a system which destroys our humanity. Instead, work within your community or perhaps your church to provide the alternative and demonstrate that liberty offers ways where the strings aren't attached. I've often thought one of the biggest mistakes our system made was in creating tax exemptions for nonprofits, because this well-intended idea basically turned charity into a tax write-off for big business, and corrupted selfless acts into being a way to cheat on taxes for far more people than most would like to acknowledge. My goal is not to argue for or against the policy here, but to elucidate that charity should be its own reward, freely undertaken, and not in service of some hidden agenda or financial gain.

Having that impulse reveals what will likely be our biggest challenge, which is that to do this will take not only will and organization, but a lot of money and the exercise of sufficient power to resist the state. There are two models I believe which exist that could manage this. One, which I think incredibly unlikely, would be if the institutional church remembered itself and awakened from its long slumber to reclaim moral authority over its own flock. The reason this seems unlikely absent intervention from heaven itself – not an impossibility considering the signs of these times – is that the Church too has succumbed to the doctrine of humanism and rather than being "in this world, but not of it" is awash in the world of men and money, with any desire for change being diverted to a passive desire to wait out the second coming. This topic is important enough to me that I literally have an outline sitting next to my computer for a book explaining why Christians practice bad faith when they abandon the struggles of this world in order to sit apart. It is bad faith when they are unwilling to act in support of the struggle of good versus evil here, when this is still very much a world where God remains present. Allow me to cite Matthew 25 and leave the rest for another day.

But the second model, and the one I am arguing for here, is to see the states themselves mobilized as authorities against the national regime. Just as we have seen how effectively civic governments have been able to exercise civil disobedience against Federal power in basically harboring an invasion of this country and re-branding illegal aliens as undocumented citizens in a truly mind bending delusion, we know that those corrupt entities also offer both payment and protection to the radicals fighting to unmake America. The need for resources and a canopy of legal support is very real, and has been woefully absent from the Right for a very long time. As bad as it is now, we know it will only become so much worse once control of the White House shifts, and if we do not prepare for that with full knowledge of how aggressively those who posit dissenting views will be attacked, we have only ourselves to blame for such lack of required foresight.

In the war of the government against the people, the citizens will be hard pressed to win because of a lack of preparation, difficulty in seizing the initiative, censorship of our ideas, and the political prosecution of our leaders. But if the war shifts to a war of government against government, with our side sitting as the legitimate defenders of our Constitutional liberty and expressing a collective will of defiance in organized civil disobedience, then we might just have a real chance. It is a lot to ask in an age when we are so accustomed to thinking all solutions come from the center, but a necessary revolution in thought as nationalists to become local again and recognize that we can only fight for that we can maintain in unity with those who share our concerns.

Beyond this, the tactics and strategies will need to be loose and flexible, but always mindful that we are trying to remind people that they have a choice to be more, and to realize as we are asking for more that we must give reasons for our cause. We must be better than our enemies when not fighting, but more vicious than them when we engage. And ultimately, we must not fear hope. We must hope for a better future, paint a vision that carries us through the long days and night ahead, and end with the promise that we are doing all this not for our mere selfish benefit, but so that those who follow us will not be subjected to this stupidity again in their lifetimes, and God willing, not for a very long time after that.

We fight sickness with health and let that serve as our guide going forward as each of us has to navigate hard choices and uncertain compromises, as we hope not for salvation to come from without, but from within. In our minds, and in our actions, America lives, and from there we must seek restoration and renewal. Even if the form has to change, and it very well might, at least the essence might live on.

Chapter 25: Hope and Renewal

If these last few chapters have felt unbearably heavy to read, imagine how much more so it must feel while I'm writing them? Although this is quickly changing, we still live in a country where you have the right to read whatever you like without incurring any penalty for doing so, but putting thoughts like these in this book carries serious consequences. I am quite aware of how dangerous some of the things I am sharing might prove, fully cognizant of what I am promoting as necessary, and am willing to stand in front of a movement whose time has come but which will face massive backlash from an entrenched system. This is utterly exhausting, in thought as well as in actual deed.

These last few chapters have been about the mindset we need for the tough days ahead, and a fuller comprehension of the battle. The next few chapters will be about technical details of how we, as Americans, can still work within the system to undo the worst elements toward either restoration of what we have lost or renewal in new beginnings that are truer heirs to our republic than anything likely to emerge from DC. But this chapter is deliberately a breather for our minds and a chance to see the struggle in a different and healthier light.

Take it from someone who gets attacked nearly every day by the media and activists alike, that if you listen too closely or care too much about what others think, the only thing you will be assured to lose is your own sanity. What we fight is a spiritual attack against our minds, and as such, we need hope and tranquility to repulse those challenges as we march away from the abyss into which everyone else seems so content to jump, and shake ourselves awake from the hypnotic promise of destruction where we are not forced to stand alone against the tide of the time.

As much public speaking as I do these days, I spend much more time imagining in my head and indulging a vision of the future that is very different than today. I skip over the ugly days which will be in the near future in any scenario, and my mind drifts to a happier future. Families are together, playing in well-kept and busy parks once more, with children everywhere as a blessing to those couples who now have time to appreciate life. I imagine small towns have come alive and small businesses offer quality goods once more as we escape the bustle for a simpler life.

Happiness isn't about having more, but about doing more with what you already have, and if we have to take a few steps away from consumerism in order to recover a sense of ourselves, such a life would appeal to many. I consider myself truly blessed to have had this unique opportunity at the middle of my life to ask questions usually only left to the very young and those about to depart, and to realize the biggest obstacles we face are ones we can often walk right past if we can imagine something better. We need to be unafraid to dream, and to allow hope for a much improved and optimistic future.

It also seems like we have reached a time when we should no longer count on others to provide solutions for us, but recognize that we must get there on our own. It sounds daunting to fight the entire system and it's more than we are told we can achieve, but trust me also when I tell you that the terrifying apparatus we face is made of people just like us, who leverage networks, just like we can, and whose control depends entirely on the consent of those around them. They encourage people to invest in their own mental, financial, or moral degradation, knowing the most powerful weapon they wield is the self-hatred people feel when they've allowed themselves to slip into lives unbecoming of their fullest potential.

A message of hope could reach out to these people who are not permanently lost, like the zealots we must rebuke, but who seek to belong and be rehabilitated to this world. It is a tragedy how readily we discard our own people, as we've sadly experienced in my home state of Maine. Our government found millions of dollars for refugees imported here who broke the law to enter our country, but they could not even find a tent and warm clothing for our homeless veterans who have suffered in some cases for years. Such disloyalty should be punished, and if you become the leaders who reach out to those who need some help and provide succor and kindness, people will notice the moral difference.

It will not be so long before they realize we are the good people who are fighting to preserve what was healthy even if that requires us to destroy much of the infrastructure of these alien and parasitical structures that have been grafted onto our society. Live honestly and you will build trust, and you will realize the incredibly powerful truth that one decent man or woman can change everything just by refusing to go along with what is wrong. We are well educated by both indoctrination and experience to avoid the cost of divergence, but when we look over the courses of our lives, is it not those decisions that matter most?

I sleep very well at night. I wake up each day ready to resume the battles. Yes, there are days where I get frustrated and where I wish certain things would not happen, but two years into this fight, I honestly feel more sorrow than anger toward those who hate me so. In reality, they hate the image they have been taught to believe, and whether it is you or I in their sights, it's not long before you realize we deal with people who have been so brainwashed they live in a world where up is down. As such, they will never get anywhere, can never amount to anything, and always must be alone because their love is to a system rather than to their compatriots, who are only ever one change in doctrine away from being lost.

Life can be different. Each day, I get up with three goals. I want to speak truth. I want to call out lies. I want to make things better. The first two are surprisingly easy and life becomes better when you don't have to worship false idols like expediency and dishonesty. There are times that very offensive words come out of my mouth, but rarely in anger, and always with the willingness to listen, learn, and correspond. I have been corrected many times, have learned from those mistakes, and have little fear of making future errors because it is inevitable that I will.

The grace we permit ourselves allows us the opportunity of success through the inevitable realization that failure is far more common than TV would lead us to believe, and is essential to our growth. It might not be an easy life sometimes to push a revolutionary ideal, but it is an honest one where you escape the cycle of fear and disappointment because you invest in a future where you now assert free choice. Instead, the solution starts with yourself, and living the better example is how others are will be drawn to you. Not only are good ideas popular, but they build genuine friendships without deceit and the ugly self-interest which so often pops up.

You learn quickly that you can't be destroyed for speaking the truth. You can be sent into exile, you can be put into a cage, you can be beat up, and you can be bankrupted. People have suffered all of these things and more, but you never have to feel ashamed of yourself, and as the system treats you worse for your integrity, the more support you will earn for showing true courage in the face of conflict. Don't we all love the plucky underdog who stands up to the bullies?

Look at America today and ask who bullies whom? Is it the supposed threat of nationalists whose most offensive chants are cries that "they will not replace us?" Or is it these people who intervene in every aspect of our lives to criticize and control our every action? Is it the people who comb through our history with pedantic eyes to destroy all that is good because they need us to live in a world as hopeless as they do, to become the monsters they have become? I contemplate much and have little sympathy for those who are knowing destroyers, but I would never want to be so cold as to think that nothing is special, nothing is worth preserving, and everything all the same.

Imagine that world for a moment. Envision if you thought day was the same as night. Or you thought winter was just summer, but a little colder. How dull would our lives be if we reduced everything and everyone to just a basic need, like a chemistry equation made up of a million equals signs? It sounds utterly absurd when expressed so clearly, yet people fall for it each day. Some don't know any better. Others just don't want the hassle of opposing. But what you need to realize is if you let thoughts like that corrupt your mind, it's a longer road back than you might think. It's a bit like the relationship so many of us have had with someone who was wrong for us, but who kept us coming back with false promises. It's very easy to get trapped by emotions in service of a false ideal.

Well, you won't get those here. Blood, toil, tears, and sweat are the only offerings one can expect for defending our culture, our nation, and our people. Yet, they are freely given, honest, and the hearty foundation of a fresh start. So many people imagine these struggles as just the last noble stand in defense of a world gone by, but I actually don't believe it has to be that way. We can imagine new beginnings, where healthier systems are made to honor our values, enshrine our liberty, and renew our people. Despite our many failings, we are not beyond redemption and we are not without hope.

All these struggles reduce to the essential question: what do you believe, and how strongly do you believe it? So many of the books out there which talk about idealized systems and arcane philosophies are just bullshit. They are a profane distraction designed to conceal from you a far more profound truth, which is that reality is both what you make of it and what we make of it. It is an amalgam of the person you choose to be through your every thought and action, and how your interactions with others shape them into building a world common or contrary to your desire.

One of the truly incredible and inspirational things about history is understanding just how large of a difference a few people or even one person can have. The irony is you never know when that opportunity will come that might allow you to be that person, to be the hero of legend even though you were just an accountant, a teacher, a logger, a lawyer, or even a town manager. When the moment of crisis comes, you will learn who you really are. Are you what you say you are, and do you hold faith with your beliefs and your people, or do you run and hide in fear of the light?

To an honest person, the spotlight is not something to be feared, but an opportunity to spread an awakening that gives people hope and courage. The cynical saying that all publicity is good publicity conceals this deeper resonance in that anytime you can be heard, you have the opportunity to transform the world. Should you seek change, the world will obviously resist, but if you plant your flag in the sand, you just might be pleasantly surprised to learn you were never nearly as alone as you feared. I know that has been my experience, and I have brothers and sisters now whom even though we've never met, I would die to protect and defend.

In fairness, I spent much of this book trying to frighten you because what I propose is no joke. It is an uncertain step into a future we cannot know, a terrible decision save for the certain reality that what other options remain, if predictable, are going to be even worse. There are so many ways this could all go wrong, and it isn't lost upon any of us who think on these questions that the problems are so numerous as to be unpredictable, and that even in good scenarios there will still be irreparable losses. I understand the person who cannot and will not fight, because we probably share the same reasons for how we think.

But a country without a past has no future, and we see each day how the assaults against pride drive ever deeper. It will not be long before the American flag is fully branded as a hate symbol, and tearing down the statues of Washington, Jefferson, and Lincoln will become a sacred duty. We already see this happening on the college campuses, and our youngest people so often have no clue the terrible road onto which they've been misled, and it will not be long before they and all the people brought here to lead them down a path to despair decide to wreck everything in the hope that this primal scream of our civilization will finally bring absolution for guilt they feel for crimes their ancestors never committed.

It is bad news for all of us that so many feel so despondent, but the good news is that we don't have to suffer any more than our own consciences require in order to live a better life, and become who we would choose to be. Those of us who reject the idea of collective guilt must gather to one another now, if only for our own sanity as opposed to everyone else, and separate ourselves not just from political opponents, but from the people who have forgotten, and simply will not accept we can be more than this. We can choose to orient our life around such better beliefs, and if we disagree on the particulars, I bet we can talk them through and find something still much better than what we are being offered now.

Let's admit up front all this may fail terribly. Long odds, poor infrastructure, an overwhelming enemy, and not nearly enough time sound like the plot of a ridiculous motion picture. We have learned as adults that fairy tales are not real, but what we forget is that when men and women stand on principle and virtue, they inspire others through their example. Do people still remember St. Stephen today or

Nathan Hale as a secular martyr who did not merely die for a worthy cause, but who more importantly lived for it? The reality is that all of our life journeys will meet at some end, regardless of what certain insane people seek to avoid, and the question will not be how far we walked so much as if we enjoyed the view during our brief time here. Life is meant to have meaning, and whether our rewards are tremendous as I believe for the life well lived, or none at all, would that conclusion still not make it worthwhile to know that you lived honestly for a number of days righteously lived as opposed to stealing time through being less than you could have chosen?

I've thought really long and hard about this, as I did before my first book naming uncomfortable names, and even more strongly before I wrote *"The Coming Civil War"* which put me on the map and most likely put this book now in your hands. You probably bought my book because you already accept where things are heading, and you want to know what role you should play or what hope we have. This book is to tell you the scenario is harder, but that hope is not lost if we learn to work together and are unwilling to compromise who we are for the temporary benefit of security. Making myself an increasingly louder voice brings me no safety and brings my poor wife no lack of indigestion, but neither she nor I will stop because we are telling the truth as best we understand it, speaking what we believe to be good, and living our lives in service to those goals.

That's a hard thing to ask. Especially for those who have families. But I would ask you, mothers and fathers, grandmothers and grandfathers: is this world we have now that which you want to leave for those young ones? We all remember better days, and while we may indulge overly much in nostalgia to avoid the challenges of the present that seem to grow greater with each passing cycle, can we imagine our inaction now will lead to a future worthy of our posterity? The great American failure is that we forgot to ask ourselves how we leave our children a better world, and not one where they survive just as part of a hive. No parent, grandparent, uncle or aunt should be able to contemplate the world where the current course leads with any joy or satisfaction.

When I say these things, I don't really know how many people agree with me, and I suppose it doesn't matter for how I must act. If there are a hundred of us who will make the stand for liberty, then we will be as proud as Spartans and as brave as lions as we find the way forward to live those honest lives. But if my guess is right, and there are not just a hundred or a hundred thousand, but millions of our fellow citizens who still have the spark and fire needed to forge a better path, then the only question is: what are we waiting for to make it happen? The sooner we act, the sooner we can escape this circus, and aren't we all sick of this crazy ride already?

I'm ready to bet on hope, and I have a plan. We've been bringing it into action step by step up in Maine, and it doesn't require some secret plan or devious action. It just requires faith, honesty, loyalty, and commitment. Plus, some courage, because if there is one thing all our common foes hate, it's when we do something they don't expect. They can't color outside the lines, but free men can do whatever we like, especially when we work with one another for the right cause.

Chapter 26: The Tenth Amendment Plan

"The powers not delegated to the United States by the Constitution, nor prohibited by it to the States, are reserved to the States respectively, or to the people."

Our own Constitution makes explicitly clear in the above Tenth Amendment that, save for those few powers explicitly delegated to the Federal government, that the states are to take primary responsibility for the management of our daily lives with the implicit instruction being this should be done to reserve liberties and responsibilities alike to the people. An activist judiciary ignores these instructions in favor of a highly suspect and self-beneficial view of the Fourteenth Amendment, and corruption of the interstate commerce clause, to usurp authorities states should retain within their borders on the basis of the Federal obligation to facilitate trade within the country, but the actual laws are refreshingly clear when you return to the text of the Constitution.

The states are plainly meant to be the centers of power and represent an alternate source of authority to the national government which can and sometimes do contest Federal prerogatives. We certainly have seen in these past few years since President Trump came into office that states such as California regularly ignore Federal mandates on issues like immigration, a function clearly delegated to the Federal government, so one can hardly argue that asserting such autonomy is a partisan stance. If anything, the only such framing we actually see of states asserting their independence is in the predictably selective commentary by the Court, which always seems so much more reticent to use its activism against the Left. With a few recent exceptions where the Supreme Court has helped the Right in defense of troublesome Federal authority, the judiciary has not been an ally to the people. Hence, we need a revolutionary new approach that uses the law as written rather than relying upon robed men and their interpretations.

What if we defended and expanded our support for the Tenth Amendment to the same extent to which we support the First or Second Amendments? I think many people recognize that the confluence of power, corruption, and overreach from the District of Columbia is a national quagmire and represents the theft of both the wealth and autonomy from each and every state. The last hundred years have seen an unprecedented push toward centralization beginning with the passage of the Income Tax Amendment (XVI), the installation of the Federal Reserve Bank, and the creation of the Internal Revenue Service. These three implements, the authority to take our money, the ability to print limitless money, and the enforcement mechanism to punish those who do not comply are the foundation of the current welfare and warfare state. This serves as an inverted centrifuge that concentrates wealth in the Federal authority in order to deprive Americans and our various states of autonomy while it impoverishes our entire nation. It forces our diverse nations, cultures, and states into one-size-fits all solutions that inherently cannot work so well as the decentralization model which was originally enacted. Furthermore, such centralization destroys any connection to the lands where we reside, and encourages atomization at a moment when we desperately need to reconnect locally and rediscover a sense of our own homes as more than just lines printed on a map.

Let's decimate DC by defending the Tenth Amendment and encouraging each of our respective states to go their own way. Instead of allowing these the corrupt Democrat and Republican parties to split up the spoils and screw us all over in the process, we can fight government with the only weapon that has any chance of succeeding against such accumulation of power, resources, and which remains immune from the prices even the most powerful or wealthy of individuals must muster for such a contest: Government itself. Our states have many rights, and with thoughtful exploration, we can and should expand these to the fullest extent of the law to accomplish a principled and far more effective form of resistance.

Before we get into the technical detail of what the Tenth Amendment does and does not allow in light of the enumerated responsibilities in the Constitution, we should also discuss why this plan works well for those of us who are organizing. It's no secret that the different tribes of the true Right rarely agree on a pathway forward. Libertarians always want to do their own thing. Conservatives don't want to take chances. Constitutionalists are sticklers for rules. And as a nationalist at heart, it frustrates me personally to no end to see people fight to the death over abstract ideals while our homes are practically being soaked with the accelerant that will see them burn in just a few short years. Instead, we can focus upon one default to which each group seems content to return to in the Constitution, and more specifically, to the Bill of Rights, which is probably the finest expression of liberty as law ever composed in human history. If we cannot stand together in defense of this existing ground which we have all so long applauded, then those who back down now from support of these liberties are cowards unworthy of having any claim to care for this country or its people. We have reached the moment where no more bitching will help, and we must either act or submit to the will of the majority who will own us by voting.

The Tenth Amendment is already law, has a proven track record of working to our benefit, and offers a chance to break the false dialectic the two party duopoly creates. It has been abundantly clear for many years now that the accumulation of power in the capital has only served to make the Republican Party more like the Democrats, as they have actually endorsed in the last few decades amnesty, gun control, pervasive surveillance, and many other opportunities to expand government and curtail the rights of the citizenry, for which they have been richly rewarded by the same corporate donors who fund both sides of the equation. They have been fully witting accomplices to the Democrats who have used government to reach into every aspect of our personal lives including family, child rearing, education, health care, and who tirelessly seek more chances to constrain us in ever more frightful ways where the insanity of cultural Marxist programming is now starting to be enforced as law of man against the dictate of nature.

Look how California is criminalizing misuse of gender pronouns, an attack on both our freedom of speech and basic human sanity as sign pointing to where America is going, especially as the brown wave they so giddily look forward to from the Left of legal and illegal residents newly made citizens erases all the laws and standards we once held. I am not saying anything here they don't openly speak to one another, and they are counting on the Federal government to do to this American nation what California's government has already done to their people. Never mind that they exist in a rat-infested hell hole where the rich people live behind gates in their mansions as the little people rot unable to afford homes and surrounded by a mass of humanity for whom there are no resources and there is no care. The future they want looks a lot like the slums of Mexico City, and the laws they will pass will assuredly accomplish one thing first: It will become a crime to contest a government acting to promote this vision of social justice.

We can already anticipate, given the cultural control by the elites and the Left of the media, academia, the largest social media platforms, and entertainment that there will be no major platform permitted to offer outcry. The comment sections will be closed, the individual dissenters will be marginalized, and new platforms which emerge will be denied access to mobile devices as already happens with entities that support the First Amendment. The deeper you get into this, you more clearly you realize how this war of government against the people is even broader, it is truly a revolt of elites who are leveraging all their power to ensure that their separation from us is complete by creating every possible obstacle to organizing opposition to their agenda. Our efforts to find a moral path forward are constantly and deliberately disrupted, and we are offered every possible diversion of vice and hopelessness with which to satisfy our despair. This is no mere accident, but to fight the power, we need to take power back.

The failures of Trump's revolution should have amply demonstrated why the idea of taking power back at the Federal level is not currently possible. The idea was a good one and needed to be tried. Personally, based on the odds, I think it was our best shot, but the reasons why it failed run far deeper than President Trump. The entire Federal bureaucracy was willing to commit felony after felony to not comply with the wishes of the American people, and it knew in advance that the judiciary would lack either the desire or political will to prosecute any but a few token actors. Had Trump come into office firing people by the thousands, the results might have been different, but he tried to lead an evolution rather than a revolution, probably because he hoped to avoid the war such actions quite possibly may have provoked. Controversially, my last book essentially implied that such a war with Federal authority working for enforcement of the popular will might have been a better outcome than many others, but whatever might have been considered in the heady days of early 2017, it seems likely that window has now closed. We know what we will get from Trump, and we understand his many limitations render him inadequate to overcome the morass in Washington.

Ironically, unless we develop the solution included herein or some other winning strategy, what the final result of the Trump years might prove is an unprecedented opportunity for the other side to consolidate their cultural control by silencing dissent. The Left will never complain when their enemies are quieted, but what has been most disappointing is how the Right, in a fit of self-righteous nostalgia has been eerily silent about Trump's many failures and misdeeds where he needed a corrective nudge from the people rather than useless acquiescence. This administration is actively threatening the First, Second, and Fourth Amendments by supporting the idea of red flag laws, a clear violation of freedom of speech in how it makes angry dissent a crime in itself, how it allows hearsay to be used to remove a constitutional right of self-protection, and how it also circumvents the need for a warrant based on a standard of urgent need that is frankly indefensible. We should be disgusted by our government for supporting this, but it further demonstrates how the most damaging attacks will arrive against us in the future: They will offer the promise of security at the cost of directly destroying liberties. As such, we must be vigilant and defend on that basis. Shortly, we will explore precisely those red lines we need to defend, because once those fall, we will not be able to offer resistance and then people need to either contemplate exile, compliance, or revolution. The situation is that serious, and the time to have those conversations is now.

But while the Bill of Rights still stands, we should understand, as Jefferson explained in The Kentucky Resolution, that the Tenth Amendment was designed to be the protection against the tendency of centralizing power, and uniquely amongst these liberties, our actions to bolster this provision do not require us to travel into Washington where the thieves fight one another over who gets to hold the bag. Instead, we can win these battles in Augusta, in Concord, in Nashville, in Frankfort, in Boise, and in Helena. We can fight 50 battles, and if we can win just five of those, then we will have five places where liberty has a chance and a beacon will be lit to all those Americans who are not yet ready to abandon the old ways. The virtue of the Great Separation is that victory does not require a numerical majority, but a moral majority based upon will and intellect, and with the resolve only to reject any assumed obligation placed upon us beyond the law of the land which we were born into, and which we should not allow any tyranny, including that of the incoming majority, to countermand.

Before we examine what this looks like at the state level, which should be a source of hope as these methods can and do work, where I will share some details of what we are doing in Maine to build these foundations, and which can work in altered form for many others states, let's make clear just what our government does not allow us to accomplish according to the existing law. Article I – Section X of the Constitution delineates the only three exclusions state governments may not enact.

1: No State shall enter into any Treaty, Alliance, or Confederation; grant Letters of Marque and Reprisal; coin Money; emit Bills of Credit; make any Thing but gold and silver Coin a Tender in Payment of Debts; pass any Bill of Attainder, ex post facto Law, or Law impairing the Obligation of Contracts, or grant any Title of Nobility.

2: No State shall, without the Consent of the Congress, lay any Imposts or Duties on Imports or Exports, except what may be absolutely necessary for executing it's inspection Laws: and the net Produce of all Duties and Imposts, laid by any State on Imports or Exports, shall be for the Use of the Treasury of the United States; and all such Laws shall be subject to the Revision and Control of the Congress.

3: No State shall, without the Consent of Congress, lay any Duty of Tonnage, keep Troops, or Ships of War in time of Peace, enter into any Agreement or Compact with another State, or with a foreign Power, or engage in War, unless actually invaded, or in such imminent Danger as will not admit of delay.

The first section reserves the right to form currency to the United States Treasury, a right which has in practice been surrendered to the Federal Reserve Bank, a private entity.

Please note that gold and silver may be issued in payment of debts, however, which suggests that states could under this standard form their own sound financial systems, if they so choose. While we are not quite that far along, as inflation advances ever more rapidly and as the debt builds and the bond market crumbles, a state that invested in gold or silver might do very well and be ready to issue prudent safeguards against an impending economic collapse.

The second section suggests that states cannot charge duties on goods emerging from other states. Given our current economy, it would be neither helpful nor practical to oppose this as we want to encourage the flow of goods and people between states, but especially also accelerate the movement of productive talent and material from areas which will merely submit to the nationalization of all governance to areas which express rising autonomy. One reserved power of which I would remind people, and which is starting to be asserted more frequently, is that the Federal government does not have any authority to police goods and services which do not cross state borders, and as we find the need for certain materials, states would do well to remember this and enforce their prerogatives. Historically, the Federal government has used the power of the purse to compel states into compliance, as they did Montana when it asserted it did not want a speed limit and wanted gun laws for their state alone, by withholding revenue. As recent legal precedents have precluded the Federal government from withholding funds for law enforcement in sanctuary cities, the time is coming to challenge that precedent again which states should and must do as equal enforcement in their own interests.

The third section essentially argues states are not to keep a standing army or navy which again is presently beyond the desire or ability of most states. Two important exceptions are worth considering, however. States have every warrant to keep an active militia on standby, as the National Guard represents, but that entity alone does not represent a singular model for state defense. I recently learned my home state of Maine actually had a guard unit available outside that framework as late as 1972, and as the Federal law enforcement encroachment rises, it is not imprudent for states to consider creating a militia of the whole in defense of the people and their liberties. As the statute notes, if imminent danger exists, such actions are entirely justified.

Beyond these three exceptions, which in and of themselves place no prohibitions on the states against working internally to solve certain issues, it's important to discuss also the long-standing policy of dual sovereignty. Essentially, there are many state functions where the Federal government had no authority, but they created new laws so they could get involved where historically, as in most criminal acts, these powers were designed to be reserved to the states. While this has historically been used to build up Federal authority, all the various powers delegated to Washington in Article I do not exclude states from enacting their own alternatives within their respective borders so long as they do not involve either foreign powers or impinge upon other states. I would also note that it has long been practiced upon the borders between two states that entities and agreements have been brought into existence as authorities to ensure ease of commerce and work for the public benefit or safety, with no prejudice to other third parties, and ample opportunities exist here to expand state cooperation at the regional level in useful ways.

Let me ask you a question: Have you ever heard someone on the Right talk about expanding government in a way that defends liberty? I know we have not at the national level, but when you look at these questions from the state level, which you could also delve deeper into for certain issues and discuss locally as well, one finds that empowering the states to do more in a way we could support reduces the ability of the Federal government to impose its will upon us. Power, resources, and authority are drained from the swamp and returned to the hills, the valleys, and the plains where the good people of this country have been living apart from those who seek to control us. We must learn to fight fire with fire, and if we want to win this war of government against the people, the people must again have governments of the people, by the people, and for the people which we can resist.

In the Tenth Amendment, the method already exists for us to act. Now, we must take advantage of the providential planning of our Founders to stop investing our energy into trying to grab control of a broken system, but to take control at home so we can break this system so thoroughly it will never threaten our freedoms again. The best news is by doing so, we will be following the example of our forefathers and honoring the Constitution as written, a duty we have shirked for far too long.

Chapter 27: The Party is Over: The Pathway to Power

If the Right is to survive, let alone win, the Republican Party must die. We must kill this sorry excuse of an opposition party until no decent person would want to be associated with it, and whatever means this requires must be contemplated and must be executed quickly. Allow me to explain why we must act with such urgency.

We already went into exhaustive detail why the Republicans have always disappointed us and why they will always disappoint us. They represent the interests, fundamentally, of big commerce which will always choose to keep markets open over any other principle and concern, including the welfare of the people. As long as their consumers have mouths to feed and the government permits them to sell, big business has never cared what you want. In truth, as described in the problem of bigness, they would be perfectly content with a captive audience so long as it did not impinge upon their ability to maintain profits through overseas supply lines and reaching into new markets. Considering the rising global consensus toward authoritarian socialism, and that China will soon surpass us as the world's largest market, we already see how big technology and major logistics firms are harmonizing to Chinese communist expectations so we know the sellout has begun before the opportunity to vote upon such things has even come to pass domestically.

We also know the institutional leadership of the Republican Party has zero interest in discussing demographics, solving immigration, protecting liberty, or fighting a culture war. We know this because they would rather brand people who speak truth as "racists" in the small hope that their rambling about opportunity will somehow get the Latino vote over 30%, when the other side offers your food as their free lunch. They had two years to shut the border and were given a national mandate against all polling and odds to do something, and all they could manage was to talk about legalizing the dreamers and a massive corporate tax cut while well over two million legal people immigrated here, a gain of 1,400,000 prospective Democrats, and many hundreds of thousands more of illegal aliens joined them. The Republicans expand government control at every opportunity and their response to the latest criminal acts is to try to take guns away from the people based on hearsay. Why would you ever expect these people to have the gumption required to fight for anything but to keep their cushy jobs? Their sole selling point upon which we have all been held hostage for entirely too long is that they are not Democrats.

The difference is, the Democrats actually accomplish things for their base. They've managed to reach deeply into the family and make marriage into a shadow of itself. They've used the Republican accomplishment of deregulation to seize control of nearly the entire media. They've pushed student loans that the government guarantees to ensure their ideas become fixtures in young minds, and they even helped out their lender friends from Wall Street by ensuring the kids can't file bankruptcy if and when they should learn all they were taught was garbage. They have fought the long war well, funded an army of activists and militants that patrol the halls of learning and most of our cities now, with law enforcement to help them more often than not, and the lawyers guild salivating for the chance for more work in a communist future. It's almost a shame their vision is so impossible, because I wish we had people with such determination as our leaders.

Instead, we get these jokers who have an excuse for every failure. We have a national party made up of regional parts who share no common ideology except corporatism and naked self-interest. Whenever we get mad enough at what is being done to this country to return power to them, an ever more difficult proposition considering the demography they refuse to do anything about, they do less each time as they look forward to the future of a different America and just want to make sure they can be comfortable. They are sell-outs, swindlers, and the vast majority are swine. I will not endorse them, will not support them, and find no value in voting for them. They accomplish nothing but meekly nodding in acquiescence, and I care too much about this nation to see one more idiot tell me voting harder will improve a damned thing. Look at which donors pull their strings, and you'll see clearly that the American people are not the ones who run our government.

There is another way. Before the Seventeenth Amendment was enacted, which stole Senators from the states, a deliberately designed check and balance which the earliest generations of the progressive Left removed, parties were not nearly so powerful and states still worked to restrain the Federal Government. States should work to undo that Amendment through their legislatures, although that is unlikely to happen in the number required given the population dynamics, especially out west, but if we go back a little further still to the first Civil War, there was a time in America where loyalty was not given to a party, but to the people with whom one shared a home. As Robert E. Lee famously told President Lincoln, his heart would be with Virginia as were his sword and singular talents.

The answer to the singular Republican Party is not the Constitution Party, the Libertarian Party, the Conservative Party, the Nationalist Party, or any other top-level party. The answer to this idea that there will be one vision of America to which we must all adhere, and that vision must be manifested by multiple parties, nimble and dynamic, expressing themselves at the regional and state level. We must return home from DC, put down our Twitter accounts, walk away from a war that only consumes all that is good, and build in those places where we reside alternatives which make sense for our people as we actually live and want to be.

Inherently, this will be an empowering philosophy. Imagine for a moment what it would mean if in place of a centralized

Republican Party if the representatives of the opposition to the socialists who run the Democrats in Washington faced a coalition of state and regional parties who existed with but one common mandate: To protect their liberties by returning resources and authority home so the states could choose their own courses of action. Such leaders would be a far stronger bloc of representatives that would have mandates to reduce government, reduce intervention, and break the Left/Right paradigm. Even a person from Massachusetts who might support government involvement in areas a Montanan never would, could readily prefer to have their Commonwealth make the choice back home rather than acceding to some generic formula. We can recover the lost check and balance between the local and national governance, and as that conflict develops, new possibilities cannot help but arise.

More important than what it would mean in Washington, what would it mean for our home states and for popular choice to have fifty different flavors of government to consider instead of fifty stores serving just two flavors? This would be an opportunity, if boldly taken, for American renewal and for our civilization to survive in local solutions that would almost certainly reveal themselves as better suited for the needs of our respective people. While it is likely that certain states would continue making poor choices as they already do, healthy states will also emerge and serve as models for people to follow instead, ultimately drawing people away from places and systems of degradation and toward centers of health and restoration.

One thing which might surprise many people in this process is those states that will do well and those that would do poorly would not just line up neatly along Democrat/Republican lines, but it will be those states who kept a common culture and have a strong sense of their own identity that will seize this opportunity to succeed. I have faith that the states of northern New England, including far left Vermont might do quite well, because if we had environmentally friendly policies, education based upon truth, and health care for all, that might be something we could all accept and choose with a higher tax rate in exchange for a better quality of life. Such an issue has long been, but should not need to be partisan. Conversely, Wyoming might choose the opposite path and go fully libertarian, and that's a great choice for them and the people who embrace the lifestyle of greater individual autonomy with less social cohesion. There are many possibilities, and what I suspect is this would prove incredibly liberating to the people who are exhausted from a mere illusion of choice where nothing ever changes because the same donors buy the same failing policies that are killing our republic. We need to break out from these failing ways!

It's not quite launched yet, but I'm proud to say one eventual goal of the Maine for Mainers group which I help coordinate will be the development of a Maine First Party. Each state will need to develop an approach that makes sense for where they live, but what we are doing is working to return power to the people through liberty. Maine, like many other states, has a referendum process that allows people to put legislative initiatives directly before the voters, and we will be working to make that process simpler and more open so that the popular will can be expressed above the politicians who restrain it in both parties and beyond the media which up here basically is one guy declaring his cultural animus against one of the safest and most homogeneous states in our country. We don't need to ask the people to trust any of us, but rather return the right to themselves to make decisions for the future based on the ideas themselves, and we believe we will forge a much better state by taking power away from the government and returning it to the people.

For such populist thinking, I get attacked brutally by both the Left and the Right. The Left hates that I disrupt their plans to dump people in Maine to change our demographics the same way they have done elsewhere because they have nothing but scorn and contempt for our honest people who know who they are and want to honor a way of life that has served this state well going back to the 1600's. They snarl and they attack, but their every assault only makes this movement more powerful because people realize we are not the radicals, we are defending liberty and tradition. As for the Right, most people here agree with this approach and the Republicans attack us because they would rather kiss the media's backside than actually represent the people, so we are well on our way to our goal of shattering the faux opposition and getting to the conflict we want to fight: We want the people to stand up for liberty against the government that tries to impose control. Give people that choice at the ballot box, and we will win access to government with the obligation to honor your promise to defend people and the Bill of Rights.

In some ways, we are strangely fortunate where I live because we have people with high cultural coherence, a strong sense of local identity, and a weak Republican Party. Our plan makes sense for us, but in other places, the methods will necessarily be different. It may very well be in some areas that the Republican Party itself has better sense and re-brands itself in service to the rising popular will against Federal tyranny as I would expect from talking to my good friends in Texas where the opportunities are large but time is short as that state is changing quickly. I could see a Lone Star Party rising up to defend the Alamo once more and remind America that when it comes to threatening the liberty of a Texan, that they will indeed have to come and take it.

There's great power in embracing local identity, because it shifts the question of who you are away from this system battle representing a false choice between the tools of the market and the state, and toward whether you honor your home more, or want to give power to a despot far away. I think many places will find the idea of telling Washington to piss off incredibly liberating, and frankly, I think people who you could never hope to reach through the Left/Right paradigm might become very excited to return power back home. While there will certainly be partisan division even in local parties, my guess is the Left holds together under the Democrats as they are globalists, universalists, and socialists, so we can then make them constantly defend their decision in every state for their one party to take wealth and choice from the people in their homes. Make them defend their own destruction of democracy and watch the results, how we will reach young people, and how we will be the force with energy.

I know this won't matter everywhere, because there are some places that are too far gone. You're not fixing Illinois, New York, or California. But even in states like that where the great mass of people will mindlessly vote for whatever the Democrats offer, a movement like this at the state level might offer great hope for the people of Yakima, of Rochester, or Peoria to organize themselves. In truth, the Democrats will likely push harder to consolidate their control at the national level, and the states will rise in many places to resist them. The cultural civil war, instead of being the submission of those who believe in particular ideals, group by group, to the universal whole, will instead be constituted of different states, each able and eager to resist the idea that they will be told by one central regime that they must comply or else they will be punished.

Our opposition to the corrupted Federal government will then become a coalition of different regional actors. Those states which choose to act should have many allies from state governments not inclined to submit, and who stand firmly in the defense of the Bill of Rights with an unapologetic assertion of their Tenth Amendment prerogatives. Such states should prudently begin planning and preparing for the defense of their people against many different threats. They will get ready for Washington to force its will in abrogation of the Bill of Rights in order to sustain the tyranny of a majority that is unwittingly pushing the agenda of a tiny globalist minority. And these states will also be ready for economic collapse which could engulf the world, because of the reality that subpar governance could cause a national pandemic, so they need to be ready to sustain our embedded nations and our civilization in different corners of this country. Furthermore, to the extent states effectively organize themselves, they will exert a gravitational effect on the saner people who share their concerns and repulse those who will find it easier to retreat to those places where the new religion of egalitarian humanism holds force of law. We will solve the conundrum of having organization to defend ourselves, and then we will have options we cannot imagine at present.

Even at this late hour, where we probably have no more than ten, more likely four or five, and perhaps as few as two years to bring this plan into fruition, localism remains a hopeful vision which at least presents a possibility by which America can save itself. In a large and uncertain world, where other countries are largely being led in the opposite direction of liberty, even those of us who mistrust the government and might otherwise prefer complete separation need to consider the value of common defense just as those who sat down in 1787 did between Dixie and New England, two nations I both love which have very different ways of viewing the world and do not make the most natural of companions, to which 1861 does most thoroughly attest. But whatever our differences, they are slight compared to a rising communist China, a falling socialist Europe, the pressures of international migration, and the reality that even a free America consisting ultimately of one nation or of many will face the same forces of international finance, elites and their bankers, and the mass of humanity working toward one authoritarian goal.

It would be useful to save America against those threats, but not if we are going to be a mockery of ourselves, which is all the Republicans have offered us. So, despite the many risks involved, we have to empower the states as the final reminder that America can pick a different path before we have to seriously contemplate going our separate ways. As I said, this solution combines the best elements of decentralization, separation, and secession, allowing for the process to move down a path which honors our existing law, seeks to establish peace, works to protect all people from the risks that are external to our union as well as internal, but ultimately refuses to contemplate that the surrender of our liberties in exchange for security is an option in any form.

The reality is we do not know how popular such a program would prove because it has never been tried. But if we work hard in our respective states, and we see victories start in just one or two, there is no greater inspiration to bring others along than success in one place it is tried. I know we are already on the path up here in Maine, and New Hampshire is hot on our trail. We have the advantage that it is easier to change things in those states with low population density and smaller numbers, something to consider as other efforts begin, but despite having entirely too many naïve progressives, it might surprise you to know that we still take defense of our liberty seriously up here also, and we remember that we led a revolution once from these cold hard lands that accomplished something great. Do you feel up to trying something like that again?

I choose to be optimistic because life is short and it's painful to be miserable. Besides, people need hope, and I want to share how we are pushing liberty to be even stronger than ever before, and remind everyone that we all benefit when we citizens defend our own choices against any idea or ideology which demands that we must all be the same. Only in death is that possible, and our movement, whatever challenges it encounters, must be one of life that claims not only honor for our past, but a claim we have waited far too long to make on our future. Should we choose to be different, we can find victory in being ourselves, wonderfully distinctive and unique, not what we are told our states must be.

Chapter 28: How It Could Work: The Legitimate Marriage of Liberty and Authority

The challenge of taking the hopeful and optimistic vision we are starting to build here and making it into reality is not to be underestimated. Leaving aside the reality that the entire system will work to defend its own privileges and prerogatives, there are many challenges to us putting together a new vision of what the future will look like beyond mere organization. We have questions we need to answer if the people will put their faith in an alternate model instead of just taking their chances with the status quo, and this chapter offers some concrete examples from what we are doing up in New England – not to present a final solution, but rather as a model from which to begin your own exploration in imagining what works for your people in your area.

The first commandment of the new order is that all solutions must be local. What differentiates us from the people we oppose at the fundamental level is while they are each presenting a defense of an existing order which must be imposed upon the people through force or subterfuge, our movements should take advantage of the nimble and localized nature we are adopting to defend and build upon existing traditions and expectations. America has long been a country divided between many different nations, as our climate and geography, as well as centuries of variant habit, have shaped where we live in widely divergent fashions.

Where the old Republican plan required us to subsume our regionality, the approach of using local parties embraces our differences as a source of strength.

This solves one of the biggest problems that has haunted the Right for years, which is developing a common identity that actually works to our benefit in this age of identity politics. I understand many people may not like identity politics, but you must realize in turn that as it is working for the Left and as the underlying patterns will likely pay increasing dividends for them moving forward, they have no logical reason to abandon these attacks. Attacks on those of the fading majoritarian status, whether of ethnicity, religion, or habit will only increase and as they come closer to the tipping point, the rhetoric is likely to become more heated and cruel as those near the top jockey for position to serve as the cutting edge of the coalition of resentment. We don't have to like reality, but we should not expect to succeed if we refuse to acknowledge these things and act intelligently in self-defense for response.

What we are offering is a way to redefine identity away from the division of ideology, and away from the identitarian contest of race which has been mostly rejected, and instead build this battle of blood and soil from families fighting for their home territory. If we are still unwilling and unable to rouse ourselves to defense of our liberty on that most fundamental basis, then all is already lost. I would be remiss to not admit that I share that fear along with many others, yet while there is still time, while we still have energy and options, our states now represent battlefields where we can win. If we succeed in ten states, five states, or even just one state, then how much better served will we be than how we are now?

We face a philosophy of culturally inculcated sickness and state sponsored violence which spreads itself like a dark and parasitic religion. What we know beyond any question from history is such thinking eventually exhausts itself after it consumes all that is there, and after a long period of death and deterioration, eventually the system collapses to the realm of the theoretical just as the Soviet Union did. What this means is as we separate ourselves from this contagion, if we simply have the will to exist apart from those who choose differently and refuse to offer them support for the consequences of their choices, those states that exercise legitimate authority in defense of liberty and their unique identity will survive and be there to regain all that was lost and then some. But this comes down essentially to a test of wills, where our enemies count on our better nature to see us sustain them in their failure and to subjugate what we have to them, sustaining their system via the uniquely evil way in which it corrupts the best of intentions to serve nefarious ends.

In the same way, so too was the Bill of Rights corrupted because we began to see liberty as licentiousness, and we abandoned the idea that responsibilities are the integral balance to the privileges that have been protected in our nation. Liberty without responsibility is anarchy, and contrary to the idealistic notions of some free market libertarian types, it looks much more like Somalia than Utopia, where the law of the jungle prevails, and the market of violence overwhelms the market of exchange which relies upon trust, a cultural artifact which only can ever emerge in a society with a deliberate cultural order based upon universally agreed upon and practiced truths.

While your region may define those truths slightly differently, especially in terms of flavor and identity, the core values of truth and development through reason to find truth, acceptance and balance with nature, and courage and confidence through grace served America well, unites us still, and can represent a starting point for the conversation as the least common denominator of what the Right has historically supported, and perhaps the last alliance which we can form now given the shortness of time, differences of opinion, and our functional inability to articulate alternatives given the rising censorship and oppression. They are more than good enough, and simplicity is an asset to a revolution rather than a detriment, especially as the government makes so many rules and ideas mandatory for us, the idea of keeping things basic should have great appeal.

Allow me to share with some pride what our modest group of 400 people are working on up here in Maine as a possible model. We built Maine for Mainers upon the idea that the basic responsibility of government was popular sovereignty, that the government exists to conduct the will of the people rather than to impose the interests of donors upon us, whether they be the commercial interests of the Right, or the progressive money from California that primarily funds our Left. We agreed that we who live here, work here, and serve as the tax base to the government should have the primary say, and upon the election of a truly odious socialist as governor, who manages to both be an ideologue in terms of the policies she signs, and also corrupt in how her family manages to benefit from all her donors, we had the perfect opportunity to demonstrate to the citizens of our state, new to the culture war in so many ways, how they are being screwed.

Predictably, a "spontaneous" opposition group appeared, whose leader was a young woman without much political experience, but whose mother had long been a fixture of the scene and represented a coalition of well-funded progressive organizations who had deep roots, including several marriages into the established media. Give the Left credit – they play this game like champions where the Right has long been a joke by comparison. In opposition to populism, which is a funny word to brand as dirty since it literally means giving the people what they want, they have attacked us unrelentingly including many cases of libel against yours truly for which, if I ever find the right attorney, I may file the suit to ensure my retirement is comfortable. However, we did something different. They called us racists, sexists, bigots, and all the usual Trotskyite garbage, but what we did was simple: we did not back down. We stood on reason, defended our facts, honored traditional identity including defending Christians, Whites, and married folk, and reached out to the other groups they targeted. The media hit us harder, the Republicans ran, and our group kept growing bigger. It turns out, even though many people are scared to be publicly affiliated with the truth, we're still pretty good at spotting lies and I am certain it would grieve the people at the deceptively named Maine for Everyone group to know just how many of the ordinary citizens in our state love that someone finally speaks up for them against these bullies and brats.

I know the other side hates this as they mock the good people of this state as closet racists, inbred hicks, and fools who don't deserve a say in their own future. We read what they write publicly to know this, and I can only imagine how much more scathing their contempt must be in private. This is what happens when your ideology requires you to fit people to a system, as theirs does, and the way we are beating them is we are building our system to fit the people, always flexible, open and honest in our agreements and disagreements, and as we learn to crawl we are building our character as moral actors, a legitimate alternative to the failure of elected government because they put the need to win elections with the money required far above their obligations to the people to govern wisely, a common occurrence in most states with all parties.

We continue to grow, existing within the bounds of good decorum, and unless the real possibility happens where we are censored – not for what we say, but merely for what we represent which is likely the next escalation especially as we slide toward 2020 – we are growing deeper roots between our supporters, and building the elements of a new people powered movement that makes sense for the people of Maine, open to working with anyone who shares these concerns. It would shock the people who hate us so much to hear that we have minorities among our members, we have people who came from the Left, and we all get along just fine because we stumbled onto the answer that was there all along: Liberty.

I share these anecdotes to give you a taste of the challenges ahead, and to let you know that while there is opposition, they often will give you the best ability to grow because they cannot change their stripes. They are true believers, and you can count on them to bring torches and gasoline rather than a bucket brigade to the fire because that's all they know. This last week has seen the tolerant progressive group of Maine attack a 40-year LGBTQ advocate for not issuing an ideological test to customers entering her restaurant. Their attack was so ill-advised even the media had to call them out on it claiming they were almost as bad as our group which they defame daily. If the media goes that far, how much further will sane and reasonable people go in acknowledging who is radical and who is sane?

We build on our successes locally by mostly ignoring our opposition and their many foolish provocations. We stopped reacting, and we've learned to act in our own interest which is why our current project has been to build our own list of rights and responsibilities that we believe will work well not just for Maine, but some of our neighbor states in New England, with our own activists now connecting what we are doing to some of the talent from the old Free State Project next door in New Hampshire. Always remember for all the resources others have, the human network matters most and the capital we require are talented and motivated people, so we are closing in on the final draft of a simple list of twelve rights and twelve responsibilities which we have agreed will serve as our mandate and motivation.

Allow me to share what we are thinking in a little more depth here since these discussions have been most fruitful and optimistic in encouraging us to think about the future we want, and begin looking to ourselves as the means to create this without having to rely on faithless middlemen. Below, I've included a summary of what items we seek to redress, which include both the core liberties already enshrined within our Constitution, other liberties we might benefit from in this new technological age, and corresponding responsibilities lest corrupt figures, activist judges, or just the procession of ignorance against time allow people to forget our reasoning.

Right	#	Responsibility
Freedom of speech, assembly, worship, and association	I	Defend the traditional nuclear and extended family, honoring men and women as

		valued and interdependent partners
Arms, self-defense, militias	II	Preserve all enumerated liberties within and seek to protect future liberties
Equal opportunity, merit-based consideration only	III	Put people above systems or ideologies
Protection against search and seizure, privacy, warrants	IV	To honor our history, heritage, and homeland
Against self-incrimination	V	To serve as refuge for fellow citizens of majority status or belief who are now persecuted as such
Require human accuser/witness for criminality	VI	To ensure a better future for our children and that our homeland is theirs to inherit
Trial by jury to settle civil or criminal cases	VII	Seek public consensus in defense of one common culture to unite us
Parental sovereignty – to raise your kids how you choose	VIII	Discover truth through the use of reason
Health Choice – body sovereignty, life, and freedom from forced care	IX	Exercise responsible stewardship over nature
School Choice – end state monopoly on	X	Provide for the public health, safety, and wellness

schooling to permit parental choice		
No Wage Tax – keep what you earn	**XI**	Avoid needless conflict, entanglements, and debt usury
No Property Tax for Homes – own where you live, not rent from government	**XII**	Keep secure the homeland

The final language is something we're still working out even as I write this book, but thus far we've found broad agreement on the goals and the obligations we agree to share, and our people are excited about the idea that we don't have to live in a world where the only choices we have are those which others make for us, but where we instead exercise sovereignty again over our own fate.

We added some new rights that made sense in response to attacks we have faced up here which I am certain have been shared by those of you who live elsewhere. We rebuked the accusation our group was racist by putting into code the truth that men should be judged merely by merit and the common standards – no free advantages, no assumed bias. In an age of technological surveillance, we inserted humanity back into the equation beyond our tools by adding a requirement for human involvement if a charge will be made, erring wisely on the side of protecting our people and privacy. We wanted to strengthen the family, so we gave parents back the power to decide how their kids will be brought up against the state. Furthermore, the school your child goes to should be your choice, not just a trap into which they walk blindly, and we pay willingly. Health matters, and we felt it was worth protecting, but not in forcing you to be poked, prodded, or chipped. Your body is your own, including for the not yet born. Lastly, we know the government has made us renters and debtors in our own land, so we decided to change that by erasing the mistake that was the 16th Amendment in what we suggest and destroying both the wage tax and the land tax. Now, you keep what you earn, and the home where you live, so the government will get money from business income, tariffs, and sales taxes instead, which creates a more fair system that is less subject to abuse.

I know we can't implement these rules today, but Jefferson could not force the Declaration of Independence to be adhered to either, so we begin planning today for a future where we build upon what we did right, and just as importantly, learn from what we did wrong. The responsibilities should mostly be self-explanatory, but I have always believed we need to honor our past, care for our present, and provide for the future. We want to find a common culture that works to mutual benefit, and we have set out suggestions of how we get there, and a simple but basic definition of what we mutually agree to be good and useful, as we also acknowledge how many issues exist outside those boundaries where people need to rightly find their own way, including faith. The one point we talked about most thoroughly is Responsibility V, whereby we opened up our movement to people not from here but who want to preserve what we have and have become targets because they are of the majority as Christians and Whites, amongst others will be. The future will be decided by people, just as the past, and we realized that in order to defend our homes, we would do well to seek out new allies and friends from the other states in our region and neighborhood which very likely will take the opposite path from the one which we contemplate.

From here, we will move forward to adopt new symbols, develop our own honest media, and we will use high technology when we can but invest just as much energy into traditional and reliable solutions. We don't look to build lobbies to work the system, which would only serve as target for destruction by lawfare but work instead as a collaborative effort of our best citizens in self-defense and mutual loyalty. Some of us weren't born in Maine. Many more were. But it's a positive experience, and I can say every attack against us has only brought us closer to one another. This is our home – we have nowhere else to go, so we will organize, we will fight if we must, and we will eventually win.

As I've hinted elsewhere, we will work to get our ideas on the ballot. Many times, as we see in Washington, and for which Augusta is no different, we expect that commonsense measures most people will support without a second thought will be opposed by both parties. Such deceit does not matter, because the choice will return to the people, and as these parties reveal themselves and their disconnect from the people, then we will organize further with our new allies and friends to offer a genuine choice not just of ideas, but of leaders as well. My hope is we will get there within the next three years, where the primary idea is to go our own way. And it starts with a dream and a book, to which I have to thank the eponymous Thomas Hobbes and the brilliant *Victoria* novel for inspiration. We can choose a different way, and up here, we are trying. It's a long road, but at least we know the challenges ahead and understand our purpose and take responsibility for our vision and actions.

Events may overtake our efforts just as they may do to you, but each day we spend organizing and connecting gives us better odds no matter what situation prevails going forward. Most importantly, it removes people from the learned hopelessness and helplessness with which we are so often surrounded, and reminds everyone that we have choices. I encourage you to gather with others where you live and talk honestly about what you want, and do not let what is possible prevent you from achieving what must be necessary. Faith moves mountains and it's time we start breaking ground on the new America, whatever final form it ends up taking.

Chapter 29: Red Lines and the Bottom Line

We can talk about what we want to do and present an optimistic vision for the future. We can, given enough time, turn at least a few states of ours into something resembling the America we once knew and loved again. But what we need to talk about before the end is the harder question of what we will do when the rubber hits the road and our plans run into contact with the hostile Federal regime, oppressive culture of subjugation, and the economic sanctions we must realize to be inevitable. These choices will inherently be different for each individual and each family, but it's important we talk about two interrelated questions: Red lines and the bottom line.

It's easy to say control of the future is at stake, but we need to really understand what that means. I spent six painful chapters in *Loyal Revolutionary* imagining precisely what clown world fully realized would mean for the rest of us, and with the daily sequence of events showing just how much further we have to dive into insanity before the thirst of our leaders is fully satiated, we'll just sneak the slightest glimpse into what the future of submission would mean for all Americans if our course is not corrected.

We know we will have far fewer meaningful choices. Look to what is being promised today, and it is a government with taxation rates that would take the vast majority of your earnings from any job you could get, and that will offer cradle to grave guidance on how we should live. We may be permitted certain indulgences of fantasy and vice, or those too may be restricted once the illusion of choice disappears, but we know we can count on a state prone to violence and overreach with an ideological majority that likes to punish those who disagree.

Expect the future to have a social credit score where the government and big technology companies work in conjunction to police thought patterns, with those who offer dissent or even abnormal patterns branded as potential terrorists. The promise of greater security, which will be interrupted periodically by patriots arriving too late who launch attacks rooted more in desperation than any hope of success, will serve as justification for criminalization of self-defense at multiple levels. We already see this happening after El Paso even though an equally grizzly slaughter in Philadelphia just one week later wasn't even mentioned because the shooter was a Black Muslim who had done time before. Expect the selective enforcement to continue, media censorship to worsen, and the government to eventually take control of how you can access the Internet.

If you want to live outside the system, you're going to find it very difficult. Even if you have built a bunker or sustain yourself independently from the land, the newly empowered FBI is going to look at Ruby Ridge as a how-to-guide for how to treat citizens who claim sovereignty. Isolated and living apart, it would not surprise me if economic deterioration turns hoarding into a crime whereby preparations are punished save for those who are on the correct side of ideology. For the elite within the dictatorship of the cultural proletariat, life will be comfortable as ever.

The media will serve as willing collaborators in branding the public as the number one threat and an atmosphere of fear will persuade the government into abandoning their last vestiges of the Bill of Rights in favor of the promise of security. Most will reckon the fantasies they have to indulge in a world of 50 genders and 500 pronouns a worth surrendering their liberty to achieve, and children will grow up accepting the new normal. In time, it would not surprise me to see the cultural conquest complete as the Christian church will become a perversion of itself, Whites to be branded as second class citizens with social justice taxation, and marriage itself as well as child rearing to be branded as obsolete as the state becomes directly responsible for the raising of all children as a chance to equalize outcomes while also liberating men and women from the costs and dangers of parenthood. We're not far from that being a possibility, and nearly every authoritarian regime in history has loved the idea of owning those young minds to control the future.

Without parents to protect the children, technology will become the monitor of all, and the age of the human drones will arrive. All will be equal, all will succeed, and the all-American child might just look exactly like everyone else. Free thought will seem obsolete, and we might just see our ability to compete with the Chinese ascend as we become carefully calibrated clones in flesh. We will become a hive without ever choosing it, with families gone and the dream of communism realized in the destruction of the very truth of what it means to be human. This is actually the happy vision of what the promised authoritarianism will enact.

If they go poorly, then violence will be the key. Gangs will own the streets. Some will wear blue, some will wear black, some will enforce laws, and some will resist them. People will scrimp out a living as best they can and use their identity to survive and their connections to continue. America will collapse in that scenario and be just like so many other tinpot dictatorships from the Third World. A few rich people will live well, and a lot of poor people will be lucky to survive.

I don't know the future, but what I cannot imagine for the life of me is any reality which these people can create which will be happy for those of us who only want to live and to be left alone, and that's the bottom line which I want to share with you. You can choose not to fight these people, to say these aren't your problems, but if that is your final choice, then you are giving power to them to enact their fantasies over all of us. Before you accept that, take some time to read what the transhumanists imagine, or what the cultural Marxists propose, and ask yourself if you are fine with either of those outcomes, because that's what you are signing up for if you think we can just continue our free ride and that voting alone will be enough. Money or resources won't save you either.

The alternative is harder, and it begins when we start making red lines of our own. We have already surrendered far too much as the predominant symbol for the Right in this culture war has most often been the white flag of surrender. For decades now, we have always traded very real and important rights and responsibilities away in exchange for temporary and illusory peace, believing the useful lie that tolerance was all that was being sought. We cannot give another inch, or the system will collapse. Worse still, we cannot simply defend the status quo, or we will lose. I will share with you what lines must be set to give us any chance at all of survival at the national level.

The first is we must not compromise any further on the Bill of Rights. We must, in fact, do the opposite and work to strengthen these protections at every level. We need to attack those who seek to restrict our free speech and rights of association and protest, oppose any effort at gun control and see the proliferation of new weapons to ensure the citizens have a fighting chance, constrain the Deep State from its unwarranted surveillance upon us, and as I emphasize here, make the reserved powers of the states a linchpin onto which we hold desperately as we fight the Federal overreach. We will struggle because whole generations are coming into this country both from our broken school system and through the corrupt immigration pipeline who will largely look just to be taken care of by the state and who will see security as liberty, an inversion caught up in fear, inexperience, and poverty.

Such knowledge suggests the second and third propositions for which we must fight. We need to shut down immigration. We need to shut down illegal immigration, remove those people who do not belong here, and hold to account those who facilitate the entry of illegals and their survival here in the United States. We also need to close legal immigration for the demographic and voting reasons made throughout this book as we can no longer afford to gift those who want to enact socialism voters by the millions every few years. It is insane, has destroyed several states politically and culturally, and will destroy the entire nation if unstopped.

After we halt immigration, the next battles we must fight are ugly cultural battles to bring balance back to the debate. There are a hundred different ways in which our tax dollars fund what the Left teaches to our students, puts onto our screens, and collects through the nonprofits. We must aggressively disrupt, defund, and delegitimize all of these. The easiest beginning point is to end subsidy to so many programs in education, media, and entertainment which are clearly biased. We must begin articulating new alternatives that emphasize cultural cohesion and allow us the chance, locally more likely than nationally, to integrate whomever we have in place to a common ethic and recruit others to join us in those places where such efforts can prove fruitful.

What we must not do is accept excuses or compromises. We know they are coming, and it isn't hard to predict some of the worst ideas that our Republican friends will tell us we have to accept. When they say we must agree to red flag laws that make dissent a crime and home invasions a reality, we should tell them to go to hell. When they tell us that we have to make people who came here illegally citizens because they want to ignore their own laws and pander to win a few minority votes, we must tell them where they can stick their heads. When they say that we have to remain silent so we can all get along, allowing technology companies to enforce "reasonable standards" which will be written, as ever, by the other side, we can tell them they can all go jump together off the same bridge because the American people do not choose this path.

I am fully aware this will bring government screeching to a halt and upset the stock market. It does not matter. Money, as we established earlier, is just a fiction used to control us, and if it is so prevalent, then it will prove itself even more illusory the moment this conflict begins and all the dollar bills in the world are not worth more than kindling for the flames the financial malfeasance has wrought upon us. In a culture war, one does not win by surrendering one's beliefs, and so we should stand on those values we know to be correct and true without apology and push aside those collaborators who only argue for why we must submit. We know from the unending string of broken promises given by our opposition that they will not honor their agreements, so we will only compromise moving forward when we move inch by inch back toward sanity. This is especially true at the Federal level where we must aggressively reverse the trend of over a hundred years of stealing power from the people, ignoring the highest law, and creating a country that is a mockery of all America once believed.

We should also be wary of the one tactic most commonly used to persuade us to rally around the flag: an external threat. I am aware we live in a dangerous world with many enemies, and America has earned the enmity of so many others because of our willingness to play not just world's policeman, but also world's mercenary against our own interest. Apologizing for such stupidity is useless, but to learn from it is profitable as we have to remember that as things get more dangerous here at home, the government will naturally think the best way to destroy resistance to their impending tyranny will be to send those young men most vital to our future out of harm's way by putting them into some Middle Eastern flavored meat grinder like Iran, or perhaps even in a civilization destroying conflict against the Chinese. Maybe even both.

Remember who the true enemy is: elites who see borders as just lines on a chess board and who would willingly even sacrifice a true queen like America if that is what it takes to keep the game playing a little longer. We are the pieces constantly being moved around as a new world order is clearly coming into being where the revolt of the elites requires the sacrifice of every pawn who won't be fitted with collars for the future they intend. Where America was once the grand dame who was valued for our wealth, our ingenuity, and our unfortunate willingness to serve as the foot soldiers of their regime, we've shown one too many nationalist impulses lately and the people who think themselves our betters have no love for liberty for those outside their ranks. Do not delude yourself into thinking we would ever be considered beyond expendable because of past services or glories. These people are far too vain for that.

As an identitarian who has been at this struggle for a little while, it might hearten you to know the battle we are fighting here in America is not a solitary one. Throughout many lands we have friends and allies in a similar boat, each striking out against governments that deny the people their prerogatives, who seek to force the new religion and its shimmering pronouns upon us as the bankers look to exploit those final markets and displace the native people of many different countries from their homes. The contours shift slightly depending upon the place, but in the same way we are fighting a global system, the desire for liberty is universal and we in America, as ever, are looked upon to take the lead.

As cynical as those demonstrations may yet prove, look to the events this August in Hong Kong where people not only flew American flags to protest China, but a few wiser souls amongst them chanted they wanted the Second Amendment. You don't hear that on the news, but people around the world are learning the scam to disarm nationalists and patriots is an effort to force us all into quiet submission and subjugation, two mistakes we cannot afford to make. It is not enough to simply refuse to comply with these laws, but we must also punish those who push them forward in both major parties, and we must take back our ability to resist and advance it to the next level.

The people cannot be a paper tiger, or the government will simply reduce us to cogs, drones, and then erase our legacy, command our present, and make miserable the future. I can only speculate what that victory looks like because there's no way I would be permitted to see it myself given all the ideas that I've shared with you here. But even these brief glimpses, I hope, will prove sufficiently compelling to remind you that lines in the sand once drawn must be defended to the last man if they are to have meaning.

The Bill of Rights is at stake. Our honor and our survival depend upon demonstrating insight and courage now in common defense. We have a plan to make it there peacefully that our people could follow, and we should start there. We are righteous because we honor liberty, choose to live in grace, and have declared openly under what terms we can live, separate, and co-exist. One cannot concede any more than that and still retain dignity, and if our opposition demands their tyranny be given complete control, then we must admit that they are not people with whom we could ever live and let those consequences play out as they will.

As Patrick Henry righteously remarked of such a question before his Virginian colleagues, "Is life so dear, or peace so sweet, as to be purchased at the price of chains and slavery?

Forbid it, Almighty God! I know not what course others may take; but as for me, give me liberty or give me death!"

Chapter 30: Si Vis Pacem, Para Bellum

Over fifteen centuries ago, the Roman strategist Vegetius uttered these famous words which translate roughly as "Let he who would have peace prepare for war." Our Founders warned us that the cost of liberty was eternal vigilance and Jefferson advised a time would come when the tree liberty upon which our foundation rests would require watering with the blood of tyrants lest it wither, because what liberty cannot abide is any form of tyranny, arbitrariness, or capricious control. Dear reader, I submit to you we are already in such a war, and whether it goes hot or not, we are quickly reaching a point where our choices are victory or defeat with no second chances to be had if the contest goes poorly.

We imagine that we must live in a more civilized time than our ancestors because we eschew the direct approach of arms and assault for the more indirect form of backbiting warfare using accusations and embargoes. This strange beginning to the fight where we can destroy people's reputations, their livelihoods, their property, and see combatants sent to jail on petty misdemeanors will not continue indefinitely if both sides refuse to reduce their provocations. I can say with absolute certainty that we will not see any such cessation from the Left as they advance, because as the zealots they are, they cannot help but to destroy and attack those last healthy institutions in America and to demonize the few brave men and women who arise in their defense. As they remove other options for peaceably resolving this conflict, as censorship grows and the impoverishment of whole groups of people based on their thought or identity becomes commonplace, violence is inevitable. The other side knows this, and they seek to provoke the fight because they trust the system to protect them, which is why we are goaded relentlessly and held to account as a whole for the rash actions of a few who strike prematurely in frustration or folly.

I do not love the fight ahead, and no sane man looks upon these crazy days with anything but uncertainty, but I know myself and what I believe. In this book, I tried to share that with you to inspire courage and vision to rise to these challenges and build a better tomorrow. As ever, I try to find the course we can chart to get past this war being forced upon us, knowing that our enemies today will be our shared commiserates tomorrow once the full depth of the plan is revealed, yet little has historically been accomplished by telling the deluded they are wrong. I expect little success in dialogue, which is why it is incumbent upon each of us to now draw near to those who understand the dangers ahead and to build the largest circle of trust which we can manage.

Whether you agree with my argument that we do better to plan for the fight and build the means for self-defense or whether you choose to live in delusion hoping to be the last criminal apprehended for free thought, this advice is equally applicable in that you need to make very shrewd decisions now. Far be it from me to tell anyone to leave their home, but if you live in the cities, you cannot expect life to continue as you know it if and when disruptions occur. Survival is not a given if the worst of all scenarios should play out. In the countryside, you have a fighting chance and broadly speaking, people who are better prepared for the return of nature against the fantasy world which our cosmopolitans have fabricated for our distraction, but it is not without perils either.

An important point I want to make as I advocate preparing for this conflict to go hot, is that the most probable path to honorable peace is to seek one another out in separation based upon local action, to arm ourselves to the teeth in defense of the liberties protected in our Bill of Rights, and make clear that we cannot be tread upon without offering resistance in those places where our numbers allow such a stand. We cannot let them simply replace us, so we must separate ourselves now from our countrymen who have gone astray, and hold dear enough those freedoms we have long enjoyed to make clear we will not surrender them at any cost.

I take faith, despite the uncertainties involved, that the men and women of this country who wore and still wear the uniform swore an oath not to the government and the people who happen to occupy those offices for but a season, but to the ideals of the Constitution and against those enemies foreign and domestic which might arise to destroy our Bill of Rights. There remain patriots in the republic, and so long as they remain true to the cause, we have more than a fighting chance as providence will bring allies to our cause from both within and without. If you were to have these conversations often enough, as I have since writing that first book, you would start to realize we, in fact, might even be the majority. I have no doubt we are the more capable faction, but we are trapped within a system that given the time will suffocate us for lack of options and we are by no means obliged to submit to such a trap.

We might be fighting for Maine, for Montana, for Missouri, and for Mississippi, but where the last civil war was fought for regional concerns against the whole, our cause is different and better. We are ultimately fighting for survival, for liberty, and for the right to choose our own identity in every state against a tyranny that would turn us into people not of our choosing, but enslave us through force and coercion. It is an ugly, arrogant, and haughty coalition we face with disdain enough to make George III look charitable by comparison and all the pompous parliamentarians seem like kindly gentlemen compared to these people. I use that last term loosely because in truth, these fools would willingly discard their humanity to be something else, and so our fight is for our race, our human race where we are all different, all worthwhile, and to advance past this war of pitting A against B forever to break all that is good.

When this all works out, it might be that people go separate ways in some places. We might stay together in others. Each state and each group will have to make their own choices, and I have zero doubt that the choices of these next few years will highly color the results, but this is one of those unique times in human history when we have to make decisions which will really matter. Rarely has a generation been less suited or less prepared than we who face these challenges, and our many toys and technologies make us the most unlikely lot to defend liberty, yet I still have hope because the values for which we are ultimately, in the final outcome, being forced to organize around are that good. They are an eternal imperative which elevate us morally, physically, and spiritually.

Even still, I think we have to admit this might just all end up a mess where no one wins and nothing survives. Lord knows that is an outcome I hate to envision yet if conflict results, it is impossible to accurately predict what chaos will ensue in our various regions as well as beyond our borders. An American Civil War will inevitably end up some sort of a global conflict as the earlier book predicted with our absence leading to the release of many other conflicts which have been held in check. Some wise people caution against any contemplation of rash action on that basis, whose concern I share, and why I have tried so hard in this effort to forge an ethical path toward liberation that avoids those pitfalls. What I simply cannot stomach is the idea that the only way to survive is to submit, and even if it proves selfish in the end, I will not accept that.

Let us imagine things go that badly, and we enter a new dark age. If, we do not destroy ourselves completely in the process, what occurs to me is that, if nothing else, we will have a long period during which to finally ask the questions we have so long avoided about what is good and how we preserve our humanity instead of corrupting it. The cruel rule of nature is at least fair, and we will be quickly denuded of this insanity which is such an evil and corrupting blight upon our minds. Just as the Great Flood wiped away all the iniquities of ancient antiquity, perhaps we now face a cleansing fire if the lamps of our intellect prove too dim to solve these problems. I hate to think that necessary, but as a scholar on the Soviet Union and communism, I can tell you that what is planned for us is still worse.

My value as a writer is in my willingness to say what others won't, and to use my mean insights to glimpse a little further into the future so that you may survive and prepare for perilous days. As mentioned earlier, you really should take the time to read a book like *The Gulag Archipelago* by Aleksandr Solzhenitsyn to understand why this book is not just an exercise in alarmism. Civilizations make the mistake of allowing false idealism to consume them time and again, and then you end up in a place such as where the Chinese did in the Cultural Revolution, where people were reduced to eating one another to survive and children were attacking and beating their parents. Man is a cruel beast when his survival is dependent upon it, and do not underestimate how quickly we in America who would survive at least could descend to those depths.

If even a few of us escape this fate through foresight and providential planning, then we would become the nucleus from which a new core emerges. That's what I think about in all I do up here in Maine, how to build the proverbial ark for our civilization as America self-destructs. There are other places thinking the same way, like the good men in Tennessee, Idaho, Wisconsin, and other places I know that you wouldn't think of as the centers of our civilization, but where the old ways are honored by those who have long resided there and so many of the new arrivals like myself are working to learn quickly. You will be worth what skills you have in the near future, not your ability as an influencer or your passion for whatever doctrine you hold dear.

I do not believe America will survive if this is forced to a fight. It may actually be wiser to contemplate separation before that happens through several different means. The sanest way to avoid this conflict would be to take each region, see them separate into contingent parts based on the way people wish to live, and divide rationally. It's too bad we are too mixed up and too driven by hate for that to seem preferable to a winner-take-all struggle. But absent that, states serve as decent proxies, and once you understand the lines of where cultures intersect, it's not so hard to predict where the different nations of America could emerge. Even as there is a pang of sadness if that is what proves necessary for our mother country, perhaps that might be the only way we finally plug the vacuum that DC has become, and with more modest goals, we might finally ask better questions and seek to live in concord in a few wiser places. It will make me no friends there, but I'm pretty convinced

California is screwed no matter what as some other places also are, but there is a justice in making people live the consequences of their own beliefs as they should, as well as separating ourselves away from those who are clearly going to self-destruct.

As we draw near to the close, and we have explored across two books the actors and the institutions of America in decay, decadence, and conflict, we see the emerging sides and the visions they posit for our future. We see the elites and their eternal technocracy which would remake America as their playground. Their minions on the Left believe they can usurp the power by promising social justice by equalizing outcomes and remaking man through brute force and intimidation into the long promised communal man, their own separate religion. On the Right, our faith is older, deeper, and timeless as we honor the old ways and believe liberty to be a gift from our Creator and that we live in freedom to discover truth and, uniquely, we know the world is bigger than man and we call upon that insight to free us from the bonds with which others would see us forever bound. If the elites love control, and the Left loves coercion, we love creation and for that reason we deserve to survive, are obliged to fight, and should be able to win.

For years, we have been propagandized that we owe our allegiance to democracy, a system which was never favored by any of our Founders, which has been the least successful historically, which is always riddled with corruption as our Congress and Deep State both indubitably demonstrate, and is a deliberate corruption of the republic. We have seen over forty million people imported into our country so only a few people could benefit from a limitless pool of cheap labor and avoid most taxes through schemes while the rest of us pay more to earn less and sustain a welfare state of people brought in here who are taught with our money to despise those of us kind enough to permit them entry. Then, we are told the reward for our generosity is to hand over our future and our lands to them without dispute because we have been bad, we who gave everything and received so little from our country for years of service and support. My friends, we have been betrayed by our government for too many years, and the time is coming where must hold them to account.

Our politicians beg, our media proclaims, and our academics sneer as they state that we must honor the will of this most illegitimate majority they have cultivated to make this country different than the one envisioned for us, the one sustained for nearly two hundred years before this insanity fully took root, all because they breed more. We, who tried to responsibly have and sustain our own families, are now outnumbered by those who in many cases did not follow such rules and are being rewarded by the promise they will have the power to force their control over us. They hate our ways, hate our traditions, hate our symbols, and in many cases, hate our very being. Read what the Left writes about us and see if you can avoid the dripping contempt.

Furthermore, they believe the case is already won because the current rules of the game are one voice, one vote.

They might be right, except they forgot one thing. People may vote how they like, and they may vote foolishly to destroy themselves. But the tyranny of the majority is still tyranny, and if sixty people sanction the destruction of forty others, that does not make their cause just. It creates instead precisely the situation for which our Founders prepared us where the liberties and rights we have retained reveal their brilliance as we in the moral minority now must strike back as men in defense of our rights, of which we can permit no force on this Earth to ever deprive us.

The answer to democracy can only be liberty, because the tyranny of the majority can only be undone by the bravery of a minority driven by justice, the desire to defend tradition, family, morality, and home. We who have not sought these fights, who have spent decades doing all we can to avoid them, are not the agitators of this conflict, but instead we are those who, having been pushed too far can find no options but to fight or to surrender. Even here at the last, we offer a book like this as our Olive Branch Petition to separate in amity before events force us to take the field in enmity.

Let us be clear, that such a wise option deserves success, and we approach it in good faith, but for people so corrupted as those who are driving this country into the ground, they probably won't even understand that we are offering them one last chance against their own destruction. Yet, having said our piece, we must now stand our ground as patriots and make clear that our Bill of Rights is sacred, and we will honor it with any sacrifice necessary, including the blood which beats in our still American hearts.

I love my nation. I will fight for her, whether Maine or America. If necessary, I will die for her. But the fight I pick is not against those petty despots overseas, but instead the wicked leaders who have so corrupted us here at home. To those wicked leaders I say this: You will not be exempt from these battles ahead, and the people are awakening to your malice. Enough people still remember that liberty has meaning, and we have strength enough to ensure you will not dominate us, you will not control us, and if you are determined to see this through to conclusion, we shall not disappoint.

People ask me where the coming civil war leads and all roads end with this one decision: Do you choose to submit to democracy, or will you find a way to fight for liberty? I cannot guarantee we will win or live if we pick that battle, but I can assure only death and despair come if we follow the path of weakness and without will. We must find a way to survive, and hopefully this book impresses upon you the urgency of that quest and the possibilities available. Time is not our friend, so I hope to see you in the field as I have long been out there getting ready for those days to come. God Bless America and her many patriots who deserve to live forever more in liberty.

Aftermath: Personal Reflections upon a Most Impossible Subject

Honestly, this is a book I did not want to write on so many different levels. Firstly, despite my profound disappointment, I wanted to see a national solution emerge and succeed but the failure of the Trumpian pause as it might eventually now be known has left us all in a bad spot. Secondly, even writing a book as honest as this draws immense attention from people with whom I would rather not have to contend any more than I already do. Thirdly, no sane man wishes to essentially make the case for war, but I believe in this volume I've identified the last possible peaceful exit before our choice reduces to surrender or fight. Sadly, I've written that book in my head already and I pray this work and the immense gravity of the subject which so many more are now realizing and talking about opens up other opportunities than that tragic result.

I get asked so often how much time we have, and my somewhat pithy answer is until the next Democrat takes the White House or until the economy collapses. As I write in December of 2019, the latter looks far more possible on a quicker time frame than I would have previously assumed, and this recurring problem of time speeding up is unsettling. Our entire range of possibilities is literally changing year by year, and it seems like whatever happens in the end, we will not be able to escape being caught up in the maelstrom. But as partisan as my answer sounds, it really isn't. If you've been able to watch any of the debates on the Left, they're promising 90% taxes, gun confiscation, and banning combustion. Do not make the mistake of not believing what they say – history has shown they might be insane, but they're sincere in pursuing their absurdity.

In the three months that elapsed between when I finished the first draft of this document, and when my editor returned a far more polished manuscript to me, many new developments have arisen. Impeachment has been perverted into political theater, active threats of confiscation have led to sanctuary counties in Virginia and throughout the land, with some places forming acting militias, and red-flag law standoffs have seen the risk of another Lexington and Concord, a future reality that is coming much more clearly into focus.

There are many structural reasons why Trump should be very vulnerable in 2020, but the ineptitude of the opposition makes his re-election a probability should the economy be permitted to continue along successful with QE inflation. The problem is the price of four more years of Trump is the destruction of all who follow him being able to offer meaningful resistance at the national level.

While he has been playing footsie with the media and bringing in every swamp dweller into his administration, the cultural civil war has been a real struggle. Much of the effective Right flank has been decapitated and is already collapsing so much so that now even Christians who support traditional marriage are being targeted and censored for their offenses. Just like in a military battle, the Left has swept from both sides and are now working their way back to the center. Our craven leaders are just pushing away from the people they supposedly care about, so they are the last to be taken, and if I speak with contempt for the Republican Party, it is because I am well familiar with just how two-faced they are for what they think and what they promote. Love me or hate me, I give it to you straight which is more than they can handle but not than what you deserve. The problem is Trump's bubble believes those lies and he has lost the faith of many once true believers and he is instead now relying upon the center which is always unfaithful.

The media will push through censorship as necessary for security, big government will complete their marriage to big technology in mutual financial interest, and the odd man out will be the idea that people should be able to disrupt these cozy arrangements. Socialists, who only ever care about people in the abstract, are the perfect foils for this system and will be encouraged toward power while the nationalists are hunted down in disrepute and infamy. Efforts to change the demography will be accelerated, and the electoral map will be reworked however necessary between moving people with nonprofit dollars, the importation of all sorts of immigrants, and good old-fashioned fraud to ensure a repeat of 2016 never happens. Silenced or subsumed, the alternative media cannot access platforms the way it once did, and that leaves us with the unhappy conclusion that the state will give itself over to the Left who will enact their vengeance upon the people who gave them Trump. And whatever campaign promises are made or media conciliation to the contrary, it will be ugly for the rest of us.

Since *"The Coming Civil War"*, I have said that will be the moment of decision where America will have to decide what we are about. I very much hope it is delayed until 2024 or later so we have more time to push back, and I'm not above praying for the miraculous, but we need to prepare now for things which were once unthinkable. They are coming upon us very quickly and we do not have the luxury of trusting to hope and avoiding action. Sadly, I think people who we desperately need will devote too much energy to the charade that is the election, and not enough to realizing that game has already failed us once.

It's funny how so many people don't believe me about this, but my wife and I didn't move to a rural town of less than a thousand people in an obscure part of Maine because we sought to draw attention to ourselves or make waves. What few people know about me is my full-time job for which I am paid with nothing but the love and satisfaction of a wife whom I cherish is when I am not writing, and even between chapters, is that I now work as a full-time caregiver for Dana whose health sadly but steadily continues to decline. If I can write about death and destruction with a little more familiarity than others, then perhaps it is because I've learned to live in overcoming the reality that she who is most dear to me might not awaken some morning.

When I say she has Lyme Disease, people often have no clue what that means, but for those families who have been impacted as ours has by this terrible affliction which has devastated so many throughout the country and beyond, they understand the reality which is fighting an enemy that never kills you, but just maims and mocks you until your body cannot defend itself. I lift her up when she falls, catch her when she trembles, hold her when she seizes, and now push her into seeing the doctors so they can display their ignorance anew at considerable expense. These books help keep her alive, so you have my thanks and I always ask for your prayers and kindly thoughts for her recovery.

I share this glimpse into my world because people might think I write glibly about these events as someone with nothing to lose. While it is very true my good name has been tarnished, I've been on a hell of a redemption arc lately as my truth telling puts me in good stead compared to the deceit of the local media. It is equally true they stole my job from me for acting in the interests of the people I was honored to serve, and I accept that my charge did not end when the paychecks stopped coming. As you will no doubt see if you check out these reviews, the efforts to silence me never end and they look to economically destroy both me and my wife for good by denying you even the opportunity to read my words. Eventually, they will succeed, and that's why I'm taking on new challenges by taking these important messages to the public at large. But beyond what they can do to me in the interim, what they are forcing us into is a world where my wife and I very likely cannot survive. My odds are better than hers, but despite all my preparations, we don't have the resources to make it with her needs unless we find a better way. Others we love are in the same boat and so we keep trying to seek a solution even as more doors close each day.

Despite my loathing for these people who are so self-destructive, survival is why I work so hard to forge a path for peace. They attack and slander me despite these efforts, and I cannot understand for the life of me how people who have so much and usually have it so good are so full of bile and vitriol. I can only imagine a deeper evil possesses them, and when I look at their pride, envy, and wrath, it almost feels like the hand of the demonic is behind what is being enacted. As I sometimes hint, I only write about the edges of the conflict, and what we all see on the surface seems to me only the slightest edge of what is really happening.

In other places, I will be talking more about these beliefs for those who are interested, because I believe that goodness is not some arbitrary designation, but essential to victory and to having a future worth shaping. I am a man of faith, blessed to be saved, and born again without hesitation in proclaiming my love for and service to Jesus Christ. Many hard nights, He has been my only hope and friend, and as we go into more challenging times, I encourage others to look past the many failures of the church to consider building a deeper foundation to understand this world. I know how lonely so many of us have been, and finding God helps.

But since I started writing these books, my life has been interesting. I've been genuinely shocked to learn some of the people who read my works, and how influential certain ideas have been. They trust me to tell things as they are, not merely as I wish them to be, and count on me to see our survival through. I am grateful for all the correspondence, the friendships, and the trust you have placed in me as I complete this sixth non-fiction book and eighth work in total. My hope is that my analysis is fruitful, and if this is a different style of book than what I have written before, it is because we face a far different challenge that requires more hope, creativity, and passion from each of us than just hoping another might rescue us. Just as I warned we are our own worst enemy, we also remain our singular best hope for a workable solution.

I have a good friend who especially helped me gain a better understanding of the military and law enforcement between these books who flatters me by telling me I write like the next Jefferson. Such an honor is above any man, and my writing is certainly unworthy of such acclaim, but I felt like at least someone should be making the case for why we should not just surrender our future and let this catastrophe just happen. By no means am I the ideal person to articulate this case, but the case is there to be made and perhaps my encouragement will serve to inspire the person who can more effectively draw upon these thoughts to offer a transcendent explanation that inspires more people to action, and if done well enough, perhaps a new unity I cannot imagine.

As I shared before, writing this book took its toll upon me and I hope to take a break from non-fiction for a little while and focus on other areas of my life. The project we are putting together in Maine is bearing real fruit and I am both excited for what we are achieving, even if it is a modest beginning, and for the quality of ideas we are developing. The men and women, patriots all, with whom I interact are taking their lives into their own hands and refuse to be intimidated. Some have lost their jobs just for associating with us as these intolerant bastards try to punish us for opposing their rancid hypocrisy, but we have stood together and built a brotherhood and sisterhood. As much as I have played with politics, being a candidate and speaker from time to time, I have never found the answer in trying to be the one voice for the people. Instead, I've found happiness in leading from within and helping others work together to realize their goals and to identify the common goals between us. My hope is the list of rights and responsibilities we share does become a foundation for more, and to that project I must now devote what energy I have left beyond my wife.

However, writing remains a love and for years now, I've longed to write the book of what I imagine could happen to show you just how we might hope to see our future play out. I'm not sure if I will write my book on the relationship between God and the state first, because frankly I don't expect many people will buy it as essential as this is, but before too long, you'll be hearing about novels based on the question of constitutional secession. One thing I rarely have had the chance to share in this rewarding, but difficult journey is my sense of humor, my desire to be happy, and that I too want to hope that a better future awaits. As dark as the topic will make such books, there are things that must be said that are perhaps said in voices other than my own far more effectively.

This book is disturbing and difficult, as is much of my writing. People get paid to write books which give you answers not which leave you with questions. I apologize that my writing cannot solve an impossible quandary, but at least I hope to have genuinely conveyed the stakes, the hope for victory, and the cost of failure. What has long worried me is how many people believe the status quo can maintain itself indefinitely, and what I'm telling you is thanks to the demographic shift and the cultural blockade, the America we are living in now is already dead. We just don't know it yet, and because everyone prefers to maintain the lie rather than acknowledge the ugly consequences of admitting this truth, we continue to indulge fantasy to delay the inescapable.

Any nationalist worth their salt can tell you a thousand examples of how history proves a nation is its people, and when America stopped being American – people born, raised, and bathed in our traditions and love of country, we were lost. Immigration has not helped, but if we're being frank, the majority of children who are now coming to their majority who were born here might be even more delusional. We can blame them if we like, but the reality is we should blame ourselves for enabling this outcome, giving our children over to the state for generations, and refusing to stand up. If the cost is too high to pay now, it's because we delayed paying the interest until it became so onerous.

One other misconception I want to clear up about me is because I speak so forcefully against immigration is that I hate all sorts of people. That's not it at all. I love our people so much that I do not want to see us damaged by foolishly trying to help others beyond our capacity to reach. I also get attacked constantly for defending White people, but I do so because it seems like no one else is willing to do so, and it remains utterly astounding to me that the group of people who make up two hundred million Americans today and who represent the vast majority of a history that we coming from the Right at least, claim to love, are allowed to be set up as the comic villains in this story with no one to defend us or our story. That pisses me off each and every day, especially as it is yet another false wedge used to divide us, and so I speak to many young men and women especially of European extraction who need hope, to know they have a place in the future, and to feel confidence in themselves in a world which has nothing but scorn to offer.

We can't be great if we hate ourselves, and the reality is we do. The Democrats hate everything because they can't bear distinction without having a panic attack. There's no cure for them. But the Republicans should know better, although our representatives are secretly ashamed and contemptuous of us because they want to be better also. Everyone wants to be the new elite, and everyone has a new system to fix the people, but no one cares about the people. Least of all those who move the pieces on the board and watch us dance mindlessly.

With that in mind, I write these books so you have a choice and you have a chance. Even you who hate me, if you actually read what I write, maybe you'll understand I'm even trying to save your dumb asses because my faith calls me to do so, and my poor sick wife cries for you even as you assault her. We're not the bad guys in this story, but I hope we live to see the day of our redemption when the truth fully reveals itself and we reclaim those values of reason, nature, and grace which we so desperately need.

For those who are kindlier of disposition, forgive my occasional outburst and my acerbic humor. If this book is hard for you to read, imagine how much more so it must have been for me during these many hours I sat here in front of a screen and ignored the fading days of a beautiful summer to share with you some things I thought you needed to know. I hope that peace finds us, but whatever happens, do not fear to choose liberty over democracy. History is on your side, divine right follows, and you will like who you become so much better. Be brave and win back our country. God bless you and your families.

Acknowledgments

My wife Dana made me promise to give her all the credit she deserves for sharing me with you for the many hours this book took to complete as this was a much deeper and harder effort than the thought pieces I often prefer to write. I am glad to return the compliment as my poor, brave, empathetic wife has born the slings of anger and envy with both courage and grace. Unlike myself who can usually overlook these things, she felt every hurt and yet she keeps fighting for the cause of righteousness with the heart of a woman who would be mother to a new future for us all, and she is truly my humanity, my conscience, and my inspiration.

We need to thank our families. My brother James, wife Renee, and their four children have always been supportive. Dana's parents have stepped in to serve as family to us both since mine have both passed, and we are grateful for them, as well as for her sister and brother. It is a difficult business to do this when everyone you love is targeted, but they have all stood with integrity and honor to keep us going through hard times.

I have so many friends and allies I want to thank, but to include them all would only make them targets, so I will thank my friends in Boston, in Tennessee, in the PNW, and in Wisconsin. You know who you are, and we will continue working toward our liberation together until we achieve victory. We have no other choice, but you give me confidence, hope, and I am grateful for your friendship and support.

The Maine for Mainers crew are patriots of the highest caliber and without them, this book doesn't exist. I want to especially thank Dave and Camille for standing on the front line with me, Kenaz for bringing himself into the fight, and those people like Brittney, Josh, Sean, Quinn, Joe, Arin, and the other men and women who are making a better way possible. I am proud of you all and honored to be your compatriot.

I need to offer special thanks to John Young, my editor who takes these scribbles and turns them into the readable work you are now enjoying. Considering the depth of the topic, I brought several peer readers aboard this time to offer additional insights, so I have to also thank Mitch, Nick, and Quinn, gentlemen of talent, experience, and honor whose perceptiveness and insights greatly enhanced this text.

We need to thank the crew at home with Murray leading the way along with Arthur, Emmett, Simon, Quincy, and BB. We know you are always there for us, and always will be. One can ask for no better friends.

On Mondays, Wednesdays, and Friday I have been popping onto Facebook under my own name at 9 pm Eastern where we talk about anything and everything for an hour or more. If they haven't banned me yet, join us if you like, and if you have any questions, send them to me at tom@nationalright.us.

Lastly, allow me to thank the Good Lord himself for keeping us safe, leading us on the narrow path between justice and mercy, and asking forgiveness for the many missteps we will make in these uncertain days. Remembering what He suffered for us gives us the strength to bear the unbearable.

I pray you and your family may find such comfort, true friends, and genuine compatriots and safety in these uncertain times as we thank you for your support. Check out my other books if you like, and any gestures of support, commentary, or other words of encouragement are most welcome. Reach me at:

Tom Kawczynski
PO Box 35
Greenville Junction, ME 04442

Until the next one, keep safe and never give up. We live in an age where heroes are needed. All you have to do to be one is not back down from the obligations we all share to our future.

Lastly, hope is on the way. If America won't fix itself, then perhaps my ideas about a new home in New Albion might prove of interest. I am already in the field working, and hope to meet you out there, fellow patriot.

Yours,
Tom

Made in the USA
San Bernardino, CA
31 March 2020